806 NAVAL AIR SQUADRON

THE FAA's TOP-SCORING FIGHTER SQUADRON
OF THE SECOND WORLD WAR

Sursum in Pugnam

Up! and into the Fight

806 NAVAL AIR SQUADRON

THE FAA'S TOP-SCORING FIGHTER SQUADRON OF THE SECOND WORLD WAR

Brian Cull and Frederick Galea

FONTHILL

Norway—Dunkirk—Mediterranean—Malta—Crete—
Western Desert—Ceylon—Madagascar—Pedestal Convoy

Roc—Skua—Fulmar—Hurricane—Martlet

HMS *Illustrious*—HMS *Formidable*—HMS *Indomitable*

Fonthill Media Limited
Stroud House
Russell Street
Stroud GL5 3AN

Fonthill Media LLC
12 Sires Street
Charleston SC 29403

www.fonthillmedia.com
office@fonthillmedia.com

First published in the United Kingdom
and the United States of America 2019

British Library Cataloguing in Publication Data:
A catalogue record for this book is available from the British Library

ISBN 978-1-78155-750-1

Typeset in Minion Pro 10pt on 13pt
Printed and bound in England

Authors' Note and Introduction

As will be immediately apparent, the authors owe much to the literary efforts of two former members of 806 Squadron whose accounts are recorded by way of personal journals and memoirs. Therefore, our utmost thanks are directed to these two fine gentlemen, now sailing and flying in a better world, whose previously-unpublished words have enabled us to reconstruct this account. Three cheers for:

Captain Desmond Vincent-Jones RN DSC*
and
Lt(A) Graham Angus Hogg RNVR DSC*

Tragically, Graham Hogg was killed as a passenger in an aircraft accident in 1943, while Captain Vincent-Jones passed away in 1992.

It will also be noted and hopefully appreciated, that this account contains a number of references to 803 Squadron aircrew experiences, particularly when operating from the aircraft carrier HMS *Formidable* in 1941. Since many are first-hand accounts of piloting a Fulmar or observing from the rear seat, it was considered expedient to use these historical gems, since the crews of 806 Squadron would have experienced similar adventures.

Acknowledgements

First and foremost, Brian and Frederick thank their long-suffering better halves, Val and Val. What would we do without them?

Dennis Hogg, the younger brother of the late Lt(A) Graham *Gus* Hogg DSC+, generously made available the latter's hand-written journal, without which this comprehensive account of 806 Squadron's early operations would not have been feasible. Dennis also kindly loaned Gus's photograph album, from which many of the images within emanate.

Many of the 806 Squadron veterans were contacted several years ago when researching earlier publications and their valuable and atmospheric contributions have again been brought to life. They may have passed to a better place but their words have survived. Prominent amongst these gallant gentlemen was the late Captain Desmond Vincent-Jones DSC*, who provided copious notes of his time with 806 Squadron; while other contributors included Cdr Stan Orr DSC**, Cdr Robert Henley DSC, Lt-Cdr Robert MacDonald-Hall, Lt-Cdr Henry Allingham, Cdr John Sykes, Lt-Cdr Michael Hordern, Lt-Cdr Harry Phillips, TAG Dennis Tribe. All now flying high.

Also to be thanked is Hans Houterman (j.n.Houterman@wxs.nl) for the use of photographs from his collection. Similarly, Ben Dunnell, the editor of *Aeroplane Monthly* for permitting extracts from his article *The Showmen of 806* to be used. Gratitude is extended to Barbara Gilbert and Catherine Cooper of the Fleet Air Arm Museum Archives, thanks are extended to Tinus le Roux (reference the Heinz Migeod interview), to Bruce Dennis for making time to search specific archives at the National War Museum, to John Riddett for the photograph of Lt Pat Massy DSC and to Major Shuan Chalker for the picture of his Grandfather Lt-Cdr Colin Hearnshaw DSM. Greg Page-Turner of *Artware Fineart* is thanked for permission to use a copy the portrait of Vice-Admiral

Charles Evans (greg@artwarefineart.com) and Raymond Dominic Agius for the paintings on the dustjacket back cover. It should be noted that Chapter VII relies heavily upon Christopher Shores' masterly account of Madagascar operations in our co-authored *Bloody Shambles Volume Two* (Grub Street 1993). And we thank Alan Sutton and his team at Fonthill Media for their continued support.

Contents

I

In the Beginning

Four months or so into the war the Fleet Air Arm possessed just six fighter squadrons—all stationed at Hatston in the Orkneys, four of them—800, 801, 803 and 806—equipped with Skuas and a few Rocs, the latter suited only to local patrols due to its lack of endurance. The other two squadrons—802 and 804—were flying Sea Gladiators, which were suitable only for local defence.

806 Squadron was formed at RNAS Eastleigh on 15 February 1940, with eight Skuas and six Rocs[1] and was to provide the fighter component of the soon-to-be-operational new aircraft carrier HMS *Illustrious*. The Squadron's newly appointed Senior Observer, Lt Desmond Vincent-Jones:

> The two types were similar in design and had the same engine but the Roc was fitted with a Boulton-Paul turret in place of the normal Skua back seat, with a Vickers K machine-gun. To compensate, the Roc was required to sacrifice a long-range tank, thus halving its range to less than 200 nautical miles. Both types were fitted for a dive-bombing role and the Skua also had four Browning front-mounted machine-guns. The Skua was comparable to the Ju87 Stuka in performance and bomb load and was reputed to provide a steadier bomb-platform than the German aircraft.

The new Squadron was commanded by Lt-Cdr Charles Evans, who had been flying with Skua-equipped 803 Squadron and had shared in shooting down the first German aircraft of the war (a Do18 on 26 September 1939). The Squadron was composed entirely of regulars, as recalled by Lt Vincent-Jones:

> The Commanding Officer was Lt-Cdr Charles Evans, also known as *Crash* Evans[2] or the *Flying Christ*—and possibly one of the greatest FAA characters of all time,

with his flaming red hair and pointed beard and piercing blue eyes. The remaining pilots were reportedly hand-picked from the best that the FAA could produce at the time—the section leaders being Lt Roger Nicolls, Senior Pilot and Lts Colin Campbell-Horsfall and Bill Barnes. The remainder were sub-lieutenants, a Royal Marine and a few Rating Pilots [including newly qualified PO(A) Arthur Jopling]. The whole Squadron were regular RN entries. As Senior Observer, I flew in the CO's back seat. The three rating observers, the senior being PO(A) George Muskett, flew with the section leaders and the remaining seats were occupied by TAGs. The ground personnel were a mixture of RN and RAF ratings with RAF flight sergeants predominating in the senior ranks. At the time the training of naval ratings as maintenance personnel was in its infancy.

806 moved to West Freugh near Stranraer, one of the RAF's Armament Training Camps. After two weeks of firing at drogue and ground targets, dive-bombing on the ranges offshore and other usual flying practices, the aircrew began to become reasonably proficient in the handling of their aircraft and the use of their weapons; only to be expected when taking into consideration the experience of the pilots concerned. At least the CO began to look fairly pleased and talk about the makings of a good squadron.

I remember well the wet afternoon, when no flying could take place, the CO sent for me to the draughty Nissen hut that served as the squadron office. He was standing beside the coke brazier, which provided the only means of heating and gazing with horror at a message he was holding up to the light, as if he couldn't believe his eyes. He handed the offending message to me, saying: 'I've got news for you, my boy!' The gist of the Admiralty signal was that all the Squadron aircrew except the four section leaders and their observers were to leave the following day and would be distributed amongst other squadrons then being formed, where they would be appointed for training duties. Their replacements would arrive two days later and consisted of three RNVR sub-lieutenants and five RNVR midshipmen, all of whom were coming directly from Flying Schools, together with eight Reservist Air Gunners, who had completed on a few months ab-initio training. At least I was happy to know that we would be retaining my excellent Petty Officer Observers to help get the other back-seat boys into shape.

I went with Charles Evans to Stranraer station to meet the new recruits and seldom can a more motley or dejected collection of individuals had been decanted onto a wet and windy platform. Their uniforms were obviously new, their caps were worn at odd angles and they barely knew how to salute! The look on the CO's face was unforgettable and horrific but first impressions can often be deceptive. Little did we imagine what destruction this strange group would achieve in the months ahead. At least two of them hadn't started shaving!

806 Squadron now comprised:

Lt-Cdr C. L. G. Evans RN

Pilots	Observers
Lt O. J. R. Nicolls RN (Senior Pilot)	Lt D. Vincent-Jones (Senior Observer)
Lt W. L. LeC. Barnes RN	PO(A) G. A. Muskett
Sub-Lt(A) I. L. F. Lowe RNVR	PO(A) L. G. Clare
Sub-Lt(A) S. G. Orr RNVR	PO(A) S. H. Gould
Sub-Lt(A) E. Buttle RNVR	**TAGs**
Midshpmn(A) A. L. Ayres RNVR	L/Air N. E. Tallack
Midshpmn(A) A. G. Day RNVR	L/Air C. Hearnshaw
Midshpmn(A) G. A. Hogg RNVR	N/Air K. Jones
Midshpmn(A) R. M. S. Martin RNVR	N/Air D. Pulsford
Midshpmn(A) J. Marshall RNVR	N/Air C. H. Thompson
PO(A) A. Jopling RN	N/Air J. B. Burton
	N/Air P. Bolton
	N/Air H. Newton

The newly-fledged, would-be fighter pilots had completed their training aboard the old aircraft carrier *Argus*, stationed off the French Mediterranean coast at Toulon, where they had practised take-offs and landings in Sea Gladiators. 18-year-old Edinburgh-born Midshipman(A) Graham Angus Hogg, known as Gus, was one of the new arrivals. Prior to this posting, waiting for an operational unit, he had been told:

> 'You'll like Gladiators but a cow could fly those. But, Hell, Skuas, it's no use trying to fly them, you'll just have to pray. They stall at 100 miles per hour and spin if you turn with the flaps down. They killed one third of our course.'
>
> I thought, at the time that they must be clever pilots still to be alive but, later, at fighter school, I came to think that they and their dead friends must have been ham-fisted elephants. Nevertheless, there was a Skua in a hangar at Lee and the first time I saw it, I nearly deserted. The Hart had looked big after the Tiger Moth; this looked an impossible size. With its high undercarriage and cockpit windscreen it resembled some kind of bird, a crane perhaps. I sat in the cockpit and gaped at thousands of levers and dials, wondering how one possibly remembers the position and use of them all.

On joining 806 Squadron, Gus Hogg confided his first impressions to his journal:

> The CO expressed himself satisfied that we would not disgrace the squadron completely. As for ourselves, we felt that we had landed in as fine a crowd of fellows as could be found anywhere. There were twelve of us: the CO; Nick [Lt

> Nicolls], senior flight commander; Bill [Lt Barnes], second flight commander, V-J. [Lt Vincent-Jones] senior observer, Ivan [Sub-Lt Lowe] the adjutant, who had not long left Fighter School and the seven of us, Stanley [Orr], Eric [Buttle], *Lew*[Ayres],[3] *Daisy* [Day],[4] Jack [Marshall], Dick [Martin] and myself.

Shortly thereafter, Gus added:

> The CO, himself, took us up in pairs to test our ability at formation flying and I have always flattered myself that we impressed him considerably. The orders were to come in close to the leader only when we were certain that there would be no collision. Having just finished 24 hours Skua formation flying, our wingtips could have been tied together—almost. We commenced our aerodrome dummy deck landing, taking it in turns to fly the Gladiators, Skuas and Rocs. The whole essence of deck landing is to come in slowly with plenty of engine and doing this in a Skua scared the daylights out of me—and a few others. Should one come in too slowly accidents are likely to happen, as *Daisy* found out—to his cost.
>
> He came in very neatly and, oh, so very, very slowly. At twenty feet he closed his throttle and came down like a brick, landing, or perhaps I should say arriving, with an almighty crash. The undercarriage gave way, the airscrew chewed grass, the engine came off and rolled onto the starboard wing. The tail and undercarriage oleo legs were left sticking vertically out of the muddy ground, completely separated from the aircraft. *Daisy* stepped out: 'She just came away in me 'ands', said he. That evening he was taken into Southampton and filled up with liquor in celebration of his first crash. On completion of our practice dive-bombing, during which we managed to score a direct hit on the married quarters, killing several chickens, we were ready for our real deck-landings.

Senior Observer Lt Vincent-Jones wrote:

> The Admiralty graciously allowed us a further two weeks of armament training and every moment that the aircraft could fly was spent airborne, training the new boys how to use their weapons. After a few days of perilous manoeuvres and practice bombs falling anywhere but, on the ranges, a very noticeable improvement became apparent and by the end of the fortnight several of these young pilots were achieving results in every way comparable with their more senior predecessors. Trying to teach them how to behave on ground was harder!

Gus Hogg's journal confirmed the successful training period:

> During our fortnight at West Freugh we continually practised dive-bombing and air firing. The CO warned us not to expect too many hits on the air-firing drogue:

'It's a very small target and the best score yet is eight points.' *Lew* [Ayres] and Dick [Martin] took-off and returned with a score of twenty-four points apiece—they had proved their worth as pilots. All were doing their best to become smart and efficient, so that when the squadron went into action and it was coming soon, we should be ready for anything.

806 Squadron was put on alert, on 26 March, causing Gus to write:

The Squadron was in a terrific flap. It was to fly north to the Orkneys as soon as possible to join [aircraft carrier HMS] *Glorious*. No one thought much of the idea; we were obviously going to assist in the Norwegian campaign, which probably meant landing on a frozen lake or something equally frightening. It was impossible to get near a telephone for officers saying good-bye to their wives and families. I bid my farewells lying on a stretcher in the sick bay, using the doctor's telephone. On all sides of the wardroom, pilots and observers were writing last letters and composing heart-rending telegrams. The ground crews and equipment were sent off that night by special train, the aircraft having been left ready for a hurried take-off. We 'stood by'.

Scottish weather, however, ordained that we should not take-off until two days later [28 March]. When we did, the clouds were only at about 1,500 feet, which is not a great height when aviating in the North of Scotland. We took-off singly and joined up on the CO as he became airborne. I was flying a heavily loaded Roc on the left of the leader, which was about the best position I could have been considering the flight that followed. We flew up the west coast, finding it extremely bumpy, until we reached the Caledonian Canal, up which we headed. The clouds were down on the mountainsides and we were flying up a natural tunnel. The Squadron went into sections, in line astern stepped up, the leading section being fairly low. The air was full of pockets and sometimes we would rise or fall 300 or 400 feet, stopping at the denser air with a body-shaking crash. If the cloud had come down to sea level there would have been no turning back, the mountain enclosed us on both sides. The last sections spent a large part of the trip in the clouds. Everyone was extremely thankful when we emerged from the mountains and saw Inverness ahead. A short trip over some small hills and we were at Evanton, where the CO had decided to land for the night. The sections broke up and came in to land independently.

Being heavily loaded, my Roc had to be brought in fairly fast. I was rather worried, since Evanton is comparatively small and we were landing from the side which is surrounded by trees. Missing the trees by about ten feet, I cut my throttle and went into a steep dive to keep sufficient speed. I happened to look over the right-hand side and saw that I was about to land on the wing of a Harrow [an RAF transport]. I gave sufficient throttle to clear this and once again dived to the

> ground. I touched down with considerable force in the mud, tipped forward till I was practically on my nose, then slowly sank back and ran for about a hundred yards. When I parked and climbed out, I discovered that the fairings were stripped from the undercarriage—I must have sunk at least a foot in the mud. If it had not been for the extra weight in the back, I should certainly have finished my landing on the nose. That night an extremely shaken man went early to bed.

The Rocs were giving the Squadron lots of problems, PO(A) Arthur Jopling for example experiencing electrical fires in the gun turrets of both L3102 and L3105. On the first occasion, the fire broke out when five miles from base and although he managed to land safely, his TAG N/Air Pat Bolton was recovered from the turret almost unconscious. The same pair escaped injury four days later during another training flight.

At this time a former senior pilot returned to the Squadron, Lt Colin Campbell-Horsfall, who had been flying with 801 Squadron in Norway; at the same time Midshipman(A) Dick Martin departed for pastures anew (he later joined 808 Squadron flying Fulmars aboard *Ark Royal* and was killed in action). Gus Hogg, who found himself detailed to fly with Lt Campbell-Horsfall, wrote:

> C.H. had just arrived from a sister squadron which had been badly mauled in Norway. The tales he had to tell cooled our ardour slightly but we were still madly keen to have a swipe ourselves.

Of this uncertain period, Lt Vincent-Jones recalled:

> 806 Squadron were assigned the particularly unpleasant task of attacking enemy installations in Bergen. These targets were situated at the extreme limits of the Skua's range and the return flight to Hatston was the most hazardous part of the journey. The Rocs, having only half the endurance of a Skua, did not participate.

Another pilot wrote:

> Because the Skuas were not fast, even without bombs, we soon latched onto one of the fundamentals, which have since formed basic requirements for naval air attack. The first of these was that, if aircraft were successfully to penetrate well-defended targets, for whatever purpose, then the first requirement to be achieved was surprise. This meant, whenever possible, a low-level, approach, below the enemy warning system. The main problem about this technique was that the final climb for the attack for the under-powered old Skua. The Skuas dive-brakes were really in the wrong position and they had the effect of pushing you forward and over your target.[5]

At 16:30 on **9 May**, 806 Squadron finally went to war. Eight Skuas, each armed with a single 500 lb SAP (Semi-Armoured Piercing) bomb and led by Lt-Cdr Evans, accompanied by six Blenheim IVFs of 254 Squadron as fighter escort, departed Hatston to attack Bergen, where the German gunnery training ship *Bremse*[6] was reported at Doksjeir Jetty. This was not, in fact, the case. The Skua crews were:

Blue Section

L3011	Lt-Cdr C. L. G. Evans/Lt D. Vincent-Jones
L2878	Lt W. L. LeC. Barnes/PO(A) S. H. Gould
L2939	Sub-Lt(A) S. G. Orr/N/Air C. H. Thompson

Red Section

L3013	Lt O. J. R. Nicolls/PO(A) G. A. Muskett
L2935	Sub-Lt(A) I. L. F. Lowe/L/Air N. E. Tallack
L3014	PO(A) A. Jopling/N/Air K. Jones

White Section

L3016	Lt C.P. Campbell-Horsfall/PO(A) L. G. Clare
L3018	Mid(A) G. A. Hogg/N/Air D. Pulsford

The defences at Bergen were taken by complete surprise and when the Skuas emerged from cloud, two ships were seen alongside the jetty. The pilots all later reported that on coming down through the clouds they were already practically in a dive and had insufficient time to select the best target. Between three and five hits were claimed on the ships. Two other Skuas attacked a merchant/auxiliary vessel alongside Skoltegrund Mole, gaining a near miss. An escort vessel in Byfjord was machine-gunned as were five or six MTBs and their depot ship at the entrance to Puddefjord. To complete this successful sortie, the CO strafed fuel tanks at Breivikin but without visible effect. As a result of this attack the 500-ton minesweeper M.134 was sunk, with three dead and eight wounded, although the latter was later salvaged and restored to service as patrol boat *Jngingen*. Of his first operational sortie (flying with N/Air Doug Pulsford), Gus Hogg wrote in his journal:

> At 4 o'clock we received our orders and instructions and were airborne by 4:30. It was a lovely evening with light, wispy clouds and 200 miles of North Sea stretching in front of us. What lay on the other side? As I flew, I looked at my body—my hands on the control column and my legs and feet on the rudder bar. Would they be slashed and torn by flying steel? Could I stand the awful agony?
>
> For just under two hours we flew over the grey menacing North Sea, with anxious eyes on our engine gauges. A line loomed up on the horizon—the coast of Norway. Crossing over it a few minutes later, we went into line astern. My heart

was thudding like a steam hammer and I had a funny feeling in the pit of my stomach. We swept round the back of Bergen and came in at 5,000 feet, through a thick black cloud. The bay lay below us; it was filled with shipping. I picked my target, two large ships anchored alongside one another and dived down with my diving brakes lowered. At 2,000 feet I released my bomb and pulled up my flaps, continuing in a shallower dive to keep up a good speed. As I screamed down the fjord I espied a German sloop escorted by three MTBs. I immediately made towards them and machine-gunned the decks of the largest ship. To get away I had to cross over the MTBs and climb to avoid a hill. Slowly! Oh, so slowly, I left them behind. Tracers were flying past my right wing. Would I ever get over that hill? That mass of earth became indelibly printed on my mind—I can see it now.

At last I was over and, finding some more of our aircraft, flew back with them to Sumburgh, in the Shetlands, where I successfully landed. I saw Stanley [Orr] make a doubtful touch-down and noticed that his aircraft [L2939] was covered in oil. As soon as I could get hold of him, I asked him how he had fared.

'Well', he said, 'when we went through that cloud over Bergen, instead of flying by my instruments I tried to follow the man in front. I lost sight of him and while peering round, the aircraft stalled and I fell 4,000 feet on my back. I turned the right way up at 1,000 feet to find myself a few miles from Bergen. I climbed up slowly and dived from no great height. Ack-Ack was bursting all round and I heard one or two nasty clangs. Crossing the enemy coast on the way back I was somewhat disturbed to find that the engine would only run with the throttle in the take-off position—imagine the amount of petrol it was using! I was practically growing grey hairs all the way across the North Sea. As I was circling the aerodrome here, the engine coughed and stopped. I put the nose down to land in the sea and the motion must have pumped the last drop of petrol into the carburettor. The engine lasted long enough for me to land—my prop stopped as I finished my landing run. There seems to be a hole in the air intake and a few other places.'

As Stan finished talking, two Shetland girls asked us for our autographs. We flew back to Hatston in the failing light and landed in semi-darkness, using lights. I landed and was very proud to discover that the man before me [Jopling] had pranged. I had not. The whole squadron was waiting to welcome us and I am sorry to say that some of the officers had become inebriated to celebrate our safe return, or mourn our loss. I went to bed a thankful man.

L3014 was the crash-landed Skua but there were no injuries to PO(A) Jopling nor his TAG. He annotated his logbook thus:

Direct hit on German light cruiser *Bremse* (believed sunk). Attacked and machine-gunned destroyer and six MTBs (damage unknown). Received shrapnel in undercarriage. Night landing.

The other six Skuas landed at Hatston, where one tipped onto its nose and was considerably damaged though the crew was unhurt. Meanwhile, the Blenheims attacked various targets with 20 lb bombs, also machine-gunning as they swept over. One was hit by AA fire and crashed into the harbour at Bergen, in which the crew were lost including the FAA observer. Captain Howe, OC RNAS Hatston, sent a message to Vice-Admiral Commanding, Orkneys and Shetlands, praising 806 Squadron's effort:

> I have the honour to report in accordance with your instructions. Eight Skuas and six Blenheims carried out an attack on Bergen at 18:20 on 9 May. Three hits were obtained on a ship alongside the jetty. Some doubt exists as to the identity of this ship. Pilots all reported that on coming down through the clouds they were already practically in the dive and had insufficient time to select the best target.
>
> No.806 Squadron had not attacked before and was composed largely of young and inexperienced pilots. The difficulty of selecting a target without previous reconnaissance and the choice of targets given, resulted in insufficient bombs being retained for the fuel tanks [at Breivikin]. These will, however, be the target for our next attack. Lt-Cdr Charles Evans led his squadron in a most able manner and achieved complete surprise. In this he was assisted by Lt Desmond Vincent-Jones whose navigation was excellent. PO(A) George Muskett and PO(A) Leslie Clare deserve mention for the part they played in the operation.

Early next day (**11 May**), six Skuas led by Lt-Cdr Evans departed Hatston escorted by three Blenheims of 254 Squadron to repeat the attack on fuel dumps at Asko Island near Bergen. Cloud covered the target but the Skuas managed to dive-bomb seven oil tanks at Florvaag on the island of Strusshamn from 8,000 feet, claiming to have set two of these on fire. The Blenheims then added their incendiaries to the conflagration and strafed the area generally. In fact, all seven tanks were destroyed, burning for nearly a week. It proved impossible to extinguish the blaze and 19,000 litres of oil and petrol were lost. Captain Howe, OC RNAS Hatston sent a further report to Vice-Admiral Commanding, Orkneys and Shetlands, again praising 806 Squadron's effort:

> I have the honour to report that six Skuas of No.806 Squadron, supported by three Blenheims of No.254 Squadron, attacked oil fuel tanks at Bergen at 7:00 on 11 May. The target was two petrol tanks at Strudshavn. On arrival the aircraft found these to be very small and closely surrounded by cottages. The eight tanks at Florvaagspynt were therefore attacked instead. The Squadron delivered a skilful attack in rapid succession. Complete surprise was achieved and the Skuas' part was over in about one and a half minutes. Two large tanks at once burst into fire, which gave off an orange flame and dense black smoke but the others appeared to have been unhit

> [*sic*]. The fire was spreading to the undergrowth when last seen and it is hoped engulfed the whole place. Aircraft returning could see the smoke for 30 miles.
>
> The attack was facilitated by the full knowledge of the position and appearance of the target and the valuable experience gained on 9 May. The whole affair went from start to finish precisely as planned. Another group of [oil] tanks had been located at Kvarven (two miles north-west of Bergen) and these appear to be a profitable target for further attack.
>
> I have the honour to bring to your notice the names of the following:
>
> Midshipman (A) Graham Angus Hogg RNVR, who has showed commendable skill in working with a first-line squadron, which he has only just joined.
>
> Leading Airman [Petty Officer(A)] Samuel Howard Gould, who as senior air-gunner took every care to ensure that the air-gunners understood every detail of the duties required of them.
>
> Lt William Lawrence Le Cocq Barnes RN, Squadron Armament Officer, who took the place of the Station Armament Officer in preparing for the attack.
>
> Corporal Cyril Hyslop [RAF], who showed care and devotion to duty in arming up the aircraft and personally testing through the night before they left.

Of the action, Gus Hogg later wrote in his journal:

> Strangely enough, I slept like a top but did not feel so good creeping around in the half-light at 4 o'clock in the morning. We repeated the same manoeuvres as before and successfully fired some oil tanks without damage to any of us. It was a goodly blaze. I certainly enjoyed my breakfast at 9 o'clock.

He added:

> Photographs that came in that morning showed that in our first raid [9 May] we had sunk a training cruiser [*sic*]. She had received three direct hits—one forward, one amidships and one astern. My bomb looked uncommonly like the splash plume in the middle of the harbour. Two Norwegians, who had just rowed across from Bergen, said that the last bomb in the first raid had been an unqualified success. It must have been Stanley's. German Officers of occupation had been entertaining some local Quislings to a big party in a hotel on the dockside. Just as the President rose to propose a toast, a large and beautiful bomb spoilt the whole proceedings by landing smack in the middle of the room. The majority of the revellers are now, undoubtedly, toasting in Hell.[7]

On **15 May**, nine Skuas and three Blenheims set out from Hatston to raid Bergen but were forced to return owing to fog. Next day (**16 May**), nine Skuas again attempted to raid Bergen during the midday period, on this occasion claiming six oil tanks bombed and destroyed at Kaarven, Florgasaaspynt and Strudshavn. All aircraft returned safely. PO(A) Jopling flying L3004, noted: 'Attacked oil tanks—several left burning—own bomb unobserved.' A merchant ship was also targeted. Of this sortie, Gus Hogg wrote:

> We set off to attack shipping in the mouth of the fjord and discovered a medium-sized merchant ship steaming towards Bergen, escorted by two MTBs. Taking full advantage of a suitable cloud formation, we swept down one after the other. As soon as they saw us coming, the two MTBs scuttled off as fast as they could go and away from the steamer. I was last to dive and, to my alarm, saw that all the other bombs had dropped about 50 yards astern. It was all up to me. I dived down, taking extremely careful aim and released the bomb at 1,500 feet. I would like to say that the ship heeled over, blew up and sank! She did no such thing. I missed by a good 100 yards and the enemy vessel carried onto Bergen!

Probably for the benefit of his family, especially his young brother Dennis, Gus recorded in his journal:

> I take the opportunity, here, of noting how one feels before any action. Prior to take-off, I, personally, have a horrid sensation in the pit of my stomach, which soon goes away until the lead starts to fly. Then it comes back again but I am like a man possessed and completely ignore it. To my knowledge, very few people are unfrightened [*sic*] in action but the majority hide or overcome it extremely well. I know one or two pilots who are impervious to fear but I consider that they are the exceptions.

This proved to be 806's final raid of the Norwegian adventure and all were ordered to return to Worthy Down. Lt Vincent-Jones summed up the Squadron's brief involvement in the campaign:

> A measure of success was achieved in dive-bombing our targets. A complex of oil tanks was destroyed and a small German gunboat was sunk alongside the Bergen waterfront, as well as inflicting damage on other shipping in the harbour. To sight the targets, it was necessary to dive through the cloud, which always seemed to cover the town at this time of the year. This cloud also covered the surrounding mountains and any misjudgement in position at the top of the dive would mean missing the fjord and running into the top of one of the adjacent peaks.
>
> On one memorable occasion Stan Orr started to spin while plunging through the cloud, an easy thing to happen in a Skua, and in correcting his altitude was

> forced to release his 500 lb bomb over the centre of Bergen. A month or so later the Norwegian underground sent over news that Stan's bomb went through the roof of a hotel, which the Wehrmacht had commandeered as its local headquarters, killing some twenty senior German officers taking part a conference. The report also stated that the Germans were astonished at the exactitude of our intelligence, which they attributed to the Norwegians, and even more astonished that our confidence in our pilots was so great that only one aircraft was allocated for this mission![8]

For his leadership Lt-Cdr Evans received the DSC as did Lt Vincent-Jones, while DSMs were awarded to PO(A)s George Muskett and Leslie Clare for their navigational skills. Gus Hogg received a Mention in Despatches. At about this time the squadron received a new pilot when Midshipman John Roberts reported for duty. Lt Vincent-Jones continued:

> With no regret and with our Squadron fully intact, we returned to Worthy Down on **24 May.** Knowing that we were due for a week's rest, the squadron held a celebration party in *Scullards* Restaurant in Southampton. Having consumed most of the local stock of wine, the party was reaching a climax at about one in the morning. At this point the Duty Officer from Worthy Down made an appearance and informed the CO that we were due to take-off at 05:00 for Detling in Kent and he had transport available to take us back to the airfield forthwith. Feeling much the worse for wear, the squadron was airborne at first light and landed half-an-hour later at 05:30 (**28 May**), to be told that the Army was being evacuated from Dunkirk and that every available aircraft was needed for air cover. This time we would be operating in the fighter role and our responsibility would be to protect the small ships on their way from the beaches to the coast of Kent.

Gus and some friends were at a party in Winchester when the alarm went up:

> Reporting to the CO, we were told to stand-by at four a.m. to fly to an unknown destination. As it now midnight, we went to bed to get what sleep we could. It was not very much and I taxied out in my Skua feeling cold and miserable. No breakfast had lowered my morale. As the first streak of dawn lightened the Eastern sky, the first machine thundered into the air. Apart from the CO no one knew where we were going, or why but our guns were loaded for action. After a short flight, we landed at a small aerodrome in the south-west and discovered it to be Detling. We assumed we were going to dive-bomb bridges in Belgium in order to help stop the German advance. The idea did not appeal to us.

Eight Skuas, four Rocs and their crews were therefore ready, if not entirely sober, for what the next few hours would bring. Lt Campbell-Horsfall (L2878/

L6B) was to lead the first patrol, which included Gus Hogg in another Skua (L2896) and Midshipman Jack Marshall in a Roc:

> Two of us took-off and waited for Jack to start. We watched him from the air. He tried one machine but it would not start. Climbing into a second, he waited for the engine to warm and took-off in coarse pitch towards some trees. Jack hadn't a chance—he flew straight into the wood. CH and I set course for the Channel alone.

Marshall and his gunner N/Air Ken Jones were extracted from the wreckage and taken away for treatment, though neither was badly hurt. Gus continued:

> I was flying in open formation, just off the French coast, when it happened. CH suddenly turned over on his side and dived for the sea, closely followed by myself—some twelve fighters were attacking us. As I screamed down, I felt bullets striking the aircraft and I could see tracers entering the belly of the leader's machine. My gunner [N/Air Jack Burton] fired a few bursts and then stopped. I called to him on the inter-communication but received no reply. We pulled out of the dive at 8,000 feet with the fighters still close behind. A hole appeared in the side of my cockpit; metal dust and splinters fell onto my head as a bullet whistled through the top of the back seat. We dived again and I saw tracer crashing through the leader's fuselage. Our general direction had been towards the British shore and as we pulled out of this second dive the fighters left us. CH held up a bloody hand to wave me away, signalling that he was going to land in the drink. I followed him down until certain that he would be picked up by some destroyers steaming just below us and then having watched him land, set off towards Margate.

Indeed, both Lt Campbell-Horsfall and his observer, PO(A) Les Clare, were plucked out of the sea, both having suffered bullet wounds. Meanwhile, Gus Hogg continued:

> My intention was to land as quickly as possible. The aircraft was riddled and I could get no reply from the air-gunner; he would doubtless require medical aid. I crossed safely over the coast and started looking for an aerodrome. I attempted to land at Margate but this was impossible, as it was disused and covered by old cars, etc. Worried stiff, in case my air gunner was bleeding to death, I set course for Manston and arrived there within five minutes. Having circled once, I prepared to land. Only one undercarriage leg would come down! I should have to come in fairly fast, with my wing down, the wing, which had a leg down. The speed would keep my legless wing in the air until I had run some distance and lost flying speed when the wingtip would dip to the ground and the aircraft slowly slew round. I carried out the fast approach and touched the ground at 80 knots.

> She immediately stood on her nose, the airscrew shattered, the leg gave way and I skidded to a standstill on the aircraft's belly. Later, I discovered that both my tyres had been deflated by bullets, causing the remaining wheel to act as a brake, thus bringing about the accident. Throwing off my straps, I leapt out and looked in the back cockpit. I was very nearly sick. The air-gunner was huddled in a corner, obviously stone dead; the whole cockpit was drenched in blood. The fire engine arrived, I climbed aboard and was taken to the Duty Pilot who sent an ambulance out to the crash.

A witness at Manston to the carnage inflicted on the returning Skua was trainee RAF fighter pilot 18-year-old Sgt Jerry Parker:

> I spent a lot of time at the airfield hanging around the Hurricane squadron based there and was very thrilled at being given chores such as polishing windscreens and even more envious of the young pilots. However, Dunkirk was on and crippled aircraft from the battles over France were flopping in. Only once did I see a weary pilot return from action. He was in a Skua, which had been mistaken by a French Bloch fighter [*sic*] for a Ju87 and attacked by cannon fire. The pilot was unharmed and got out, very excited and relieved and waited for his navigator who didn't move. Somebody went to unstrap his helmet but his neck had been shot through and his head came off as well, sickening both the pilot and me.

None of this drama was known to the others at the time, as noted by Lt Vincent-Jones:

> At 06:00, our first section with Lt Colin Campbell-Horsfall took-off from Detling—consisted of two Skuas and one Roc [the latter crashed on take-off]. Within 20 minutes were told that this section had been shot down and we were to replace it immediately. Another section was airborne by 06:30 and within another 20 minutes a message was passed through to us, followed by the news that the second section had found themselves sharing a patrol with a squadron of Me109s [although they apparently evaded and returned safely]. Our next patrol was advised to hold offshore further to the northward. Feeling as if we were living through some frightful nightmare—and still suffering from intense hangovers—the CO and myself took-off, accompanied by another Skua and a Roc, deciding after what had gone before that discretion was the better part of valour, we accepted the advice to patrol further from the shore and to take advantage of available cloud—and survived.

Both Campbell-Horsfall and Hogg had unknowingly only just escaped an earlier such fate during their patrol, as Flg Off Gordon Olive, an Australian Spitfire pilot serving with 65 Squadron, recalled:[9]

> As we crossed the coast, one of the few rays of sun penetrating the scene lit up a pair of grey-coloured aeroplanes down near the docks of Dunkirk. They were heading in the opposite direction. Cookie [Sqn Ldr Desmond Cook] was wing leader. His voice came over the radio: 'Hullo Red Leader. Investigate two bogies below at eight o'clock.' After acknowledging I rolled out of formation and spiralled down with [Sgt] MacPherson on one side and [Sgt] Phillips on the other. We positioned ourselves for an attack from the rear. Square wingtips, they looked like Me109s. I turned on the gun button to 'fire' and waited for the wingtips of the leader to fill the range finder's gap. The leaden tiredness evaporated as I tensed up with anticipation. As soon as I fired, the fight would be on. Anything could happen. Now! No! At the last minute I held fire—there were blue and red roundels on the wings—British! I flew past my target—a Royal Navy Skua, a lumbering two-seater, single-engined Navy fighter. He should not be in this area unless he wanted to die. He was lucky I had not fired at him. The Navy was like that, undaunted by its vulnerability. We waggled our wings in greeting and left to return to our wing.

Flg Off Olive later found himself at Manston, his Spitfire having been shot up during a subsequent encounter:

> Near the first hangar was a Skua identical to the two I had checked just before the dogfight. It had clearly been in a scrap as it was even more full of holes than my Spitfire. I climbed up and looked inside, then was violently sick—the rear cockpit had obviously been badly hit and blood and human fragments were everywhere. It brought home to me how close had been my escape—yet the pilot must have survived long enough to get back to Manston. The rear cockpit is the air gunner's so maybe the pilot had escaped serious injury—not so the poor gunner. There was no sign of the other Skua—probably down at the bottom of the Channel.

It seems likely that the two Skuas were victims of Hurricanes rather than Spitfires, two 'Messerschmitts' being claimed by Flt Lt *Widge* Wight and Plt Off Bill Sizer of 213 Squadron at about that time, a third being claimed probably destroyed by Flt Lt Don Miller of 242 Squadron, which was flying top cover. On his return, Wight reported experiencing cannon fire from a backwards-firing gun on the Bf109 [*sic*]—obviously the Skua's TAG was desperately trying to defend his aircraft. Wight's subsequent combat report was unwittingly damning:

> Saw six 109s. Selected one and gave him a burst. He dived and I followed him down. I then noticed cannon fire coming from port wing, directed at myself, the cannon pointing aft. I gave him a long burst and he caught fire at the tail and then broke up; the pilot did not escape.

Gus Hogg continued:

> When I had fully recovered from the shock, I had lunch and went to the sick-bay to find out about my dead air-gunner. He never knew what hit him. I believe he was hit in six different places. To this day, I cannot understand how I escaped unscathed.

Meanwhile, other 806 Squadron Skuas carried out patrols over the Channel throughout the day, attempting to provide protection for the evacuation, PO(A) Arthur Jopling/N/Air Les Stevens in L2935 flying a two-hour patrol without incident. While his colleagues were fighting for their lives in the skies above, Gus Hogg was having adventures of his own.[10]

Next day (**29 May**), 806 Squadron was back in the action and despatched a section comprising two Skuas flown by Lt Bill Barnes (L3016/L6C) and Sub-Lt(A) *Lew* Ayres (L6Q) and a Roc (L6M) crewed by Mid(A) *Daisy* Day and N/Air Harry Newton. At 16:30 the patrol came across a small formation identified as Ju88s (probably He111s of 1./KG1) north-east of Ostend, as noted in the official report:

> Yellow Section consisting of two Skuas and one Roc was patrolling from 16:00 to 18:00 and at approximately 16:30 made contact with five Ju88s in the vicinity of Ostend at a height of 1,000 feet. The Junkers were in the process of attacking a convoy and did not realise the presence of the Section. The two Skuas immediately attacked the leading aircraft from astern as it was in the middle of its dive. The Roc followed the Skuas down and as the Junkers commenced avoiding action, succeeded in getting in a long burst from close range, while the Skuas at the same time continued their attack from astern. One enemy machine was observed to crash into the sea out of control, while another fell away from the rest of the formation and when last seen, was staggering towards the shore losing height rapidly. The remainder of the enemy aircraft had meanwhile headed for home and the Section finished the patrol without further incident.

Of the success, Lt Vincent-Jones wrote:

> A section surprised a Heinkel lurking over the line of ships. The Skuas attacked from above, attracting the attention of the German aircrew, while the Roc piloted by Midshipman Day flew directly under the Heinkel and, as described by one of the Skua pilots, 'literally sawed it in half with the four guns in its turret firing upwards.'

While Gus Hogg wrote in his journal:

> Bill, *Lew* and *Daisy* were not far from Dunkirk when they discovered five Ju88s about to bomb some troop-filled barges. Our boys at once went in to attack with the result that two of the bombers made off. Bill and *Lew*, in the Skuas, went up astern of the remainder while *Daisy*, in his Roc, positioned himself underneath the air gunner [Harry Newton], firing his four guns into the belly of the 88s. The Skuas opened fire and the bomber crashed into the sea. Before breaking-off the engagement they managed to damage one other aircraft. The Germans had been too cocksure to provide themselves with a fighter escort and our three returned safely.

Their victim may have been the aircraft flown by Uffz Walter Johann, which was abandoned in flames by its crew south of St-Omer, though the gunner Flgr Siegfried Cimander was killed.

Next day (**30 May**), Yellow Section again encountered an enemy aircraft while on patrol, on this occasion a single Heinkel. Clouds were low and visibility poor and, on being attacked, the Heinkel immediately jettisoned its bombs and made good its escape into the clouds. Lt Vincent-Jones, from the back seat of the CO's Skua, had time to survey the surreal scene that unfolded below:

> One abiding memory when patrolling at 10,000 feet off Dover, was looking down over Kent and seeing white figures playing cricket on village greens, others on tennis courts and around swimming pools—and by turning one's head 180° you could just as easily see the bombs exploding on the beaches; smoke and flames everywhere along the Belgian coastline and the long stream of small ships plying between the holocaust of Dunkirk and the safety of the Thames Estuary.

Of this period of intensive fighting on land, sea and in the air, Gus Hogg noted in his journal:

> The patrols continued for a few more days without incident though a sister Skua squadron [801] had a rough time while dive-bombing in France. They successfully completed their attack but were set on by a squadron of 109s while making their get-away. The fighters concentrated on a section, which had dropped behind and shot down two, one in flames. The third piloted by Dick [Martin] who used to be with us, battled grimly on towards the safety of home. Then came his chance. One of the Messerschmitts overshot, passed underneath Dick and pulled up in front of him. Wasting no time, Dick pressed the gun button and the enemy fighter fell out of the sky. The Skua landed at our base, riddled like a sieve and both the crew wounded but victorious.

Next day (**2 June**), an 806 Squadron patrol (three sections) over the returning ships of the Dunkirk evacuation encountered a Ju88 head-on, which Lt-Cdr

Evans in L2989 (with L/Air Colin Hearnshaw as TAG) promptly attacked. In his report the CO wrote:

> At approximately 11:15, a Ju88 was observed to commence a dive-bombing attack on a large cruiser, believed to be the *Coventry*. [I] was the leading aircraft and attacked the Junkers head-on and the enemy machine was seen to disappear into the clouds in a slow spiral. Shortly afterwards, Yellow Section [Barnes, Ayres and Day] attacked another Ju88 which dived away into the clouds. An Anson patrol later reported having seen a Ju88 endeavouring to return to Dunkirk from the seaward shortly after this time. The port engine of this aircraft was observed to be on fire.

Since no Ju88s were reported lost or damaged in the Dunkirk area, these aircraft may have been He111s of KG54, the *Gruppe* losing six of its aircraft in the area. Gus Hogg was also on patrol:

> The day after my return from leave, I was up on patrol again, casting worried glances round the sky and waiting for that horrible metallic noise as bullets bit into my wings and fuselage. At the end of two hours, we [including Stan Orr] spotted a 'Flying Pencil' [Do17] some six thousand feet above and made a hopeless attempt to catch him. As we climbed up, I happened to look down to see a flock of Ju88s diving through the cloud below. We gave chase but lost them in the cloud so returned to our base feeling extremely disgusted at having missed such a wonderful opportunity.

Lt-Cdr Evans led the last patrol from Detling, as Lt Vincent-Jones vividly remembered:

> The cloud and mist came down reducing visibility to about half-a-mile. I knew we were at one stage just north of Dunkirk, so we flew to the north-east. After we lost our bearings over the Belgian coast, I thought the best thing to do was fly due west, then fly up the estuary of the Thames. As soon as I saw something, I turned south and hit the north Kent coast. What we had not realised, was that there had been a strong wind to the eastward. We flew what I thought was well up the Thames and then turned south. Charles asked me where we were. I said I think we are coming into Whitstable or Hearne Bay—and he said: 'I don't see any oyster beds!' We were actually flying straight into Calais harbour, which was held by the Germans and, within seconds, every gun on the foreshore opened up. They must have thought we were mad, because the recognition signal was to fly low with our wheels down, which is what we were doing, to establish our recognition with what we thought was the English coastline. Anyway, the CO

> made the sharpest turn he'd ever made in his life and nearly bent the throttle forward trying to get us out of it, pursued by endless bursts of AA fire. We had two young midshipmen flying behind us, who thought it was great fun. I apologised to them afterwards but they thought it was the CO teasing the Germans, until I explained what had happened. Luckily, we got away with it and I had never been so relieved to see the white cliffs of Dover up ahead.

The next day 806 Squadron returned to Worthy Down, there to await its next call. Although Lt-Cdr Evans knew what to expect, his pilots were pleasantly surprised to learn that they were to re-equip with the Navy's new reconnaissance fighter, the two-seat Fulmar and to prepare for carrier operations aboard the brand-new HMS *Illustrious.* With her three-inch armoured deck, the carrier was 740 feet in length and weighed in at 23,369 tons. The main armament consisted of sixteen quick-firing dual-purpose guns in eight twin-gun turrets four in sponsons on each side of the hull. The roofs of the gun turrets protruded above the level of the flight deck to allow them to fire across the deck at high elevations. Her light anti-aircraft defences included six octuple mounts for pom-poms, two each fore and aft of the island and two in sponsons on the port side of the hull. The completion of *Illustrious* was delayed two months to fit her with a Type 79Z early-warning radar; she was the first aircraft carrier in the world to be fitted with radar before completion. Her complement was approximately 1,300 officers and enlisted men upon completion and would be home not only to 806 Squadron for the next six months but also for two squadrons of Swordfish. In command of *Illustrious* was Captain Denis Boyd, of whom Lt Vincent-Jones wrote:

> Although a torpedo specialist himself, Captain Boyd was one of the few more senior officers who had come to appreciate the full possibilities of air power applied from ships as opposed to land bases. He saw to it that his ship existed primarily to provide the maximum service for her air squadrons in the execution of their allotted roles. As a result, she became a byword as an efficient and happy ship. Even at this early stage we knew she had been earmarked to be the first modern carrier to enter the Mediterranean Fleet where she was to be wear the flag of Admiral Aircraft Carriers (Mediterranean), Rear Admiral Lumley-Lister.

Newly promoted Sub-Lt(A) Gus Hogg wrote in his journal:

> Our Squadron settled down at Worthy Down to prepare for carrier work—and to master the flying of Fulmars, of which we now had three for training purposes. After the high cockpit of the Skua, the Fulmar made one feel that one was sitting on the ground but they were delightful to handle and comparatively fast. The first

> time that I flew one, things happened so quickly that I became quite confused: the ground flashed past at an incredible rate, or so I thought at the time. At the end of a fortnight it became fairly obvious that something was in the wind—the CO had that certain look on his face. Only too true: The troops were sent on board *Illustrious* and the pilots snatched a last two days leave before taking off from Worthy Down for the last time.

Thus, on **11 June**, three sections of Skuas led the way with an upper guard consisting of the section of Fulmars. Lt Vincent-Jones recalled:

> We found *Illustrious* steaming majestically down channel off Portland Bill. Charles Evans and the Senior Pilot Roger Nicolls landed safely aboard as expected but then came the turn of the novices who were getting a first sighting of an aircraft carrier's deck and in two cases of an aircraft carrier.

Gus Hogg added

> We were to meet the carrier at sea and land-on as quickly as possible. We saluted Dartmouth Naval College en route, with a passably good shoot-up and carried on over the sea until we could see *Illustrious* taking on the Swordfish. We waited until these were on board and then started to come on ourselves. It was the first time that the squadron had landed on a carrier and the first time that the carrier had taken aboard a complete fighter squadron, with the natural result that it was a somewhat lengthy procedure. One by one we arrived safely and it came to my turn. I was following Ivan [Lowe] up the wake of the ship, flying about two hundred feet above and behind him. He seemed to be getting rather low and suddenly, to my surprise, he landed [L2965] in the sea! I carried on and made a successful landing. It turned out later that his engine had stopped some two hundred yards astern of the ship and he had had no option but to do what he did. His air gunner [N/Air Paul Douet] got out the dinghy and they filled this with the luggage that they had in the back seat; they swam around, pushing the dinghy until picked up by a destroyer.

However, Lt Vincent-Jones recalled a second sea landing with a dash of humour:

> Stan Orr, having more hours flying than most, made an immaculate landing, catching the first wire but unfortunately raising the wrath of Captain Boyd by climbing out of his cockpit and combing his hair in full view of the bridge! The next landing was spectacular in the extreme. Sub-Lieutenant Buttle being unfamiliar with aircraft carriers, mistook the bow for the stern and with the ship steaming at 20 knots made his approach from ahead of the ship at a closing speed of some 120

> knots. Nothing could distract him, so everyone ducked and after bouncing one on the flight deck the aircraft nose-dived into the wake of the ship. I remember Charles Evans' only remark, 'Oh my God, there goes the family silver!' Buttle had the squadron's personal baggage in his rear seat. He was however safely retrieved by the attendant destroyer, who found him floating amongst the suitcases.
>
> The remaining young pilots each made a number of attempts to land on the deck but without success. Eventually, as fuel began to run short, they were ordered to go and land onshore. Three of them landed in fields in various parts of Devonshire. Jackie Sewell decided that the road across Slapton Sands would make an ideal landing strip and finished up by having an encounter with a traction engine, thereby considerably startling the driver.

Illustrious returned to port where she remained for a few days while receiving replacement aircraft for those lost and retrieving all aircrew, making ready for her working-up trip. During this time the pilots practised dive-bombing and mock fighter combat, as noted by N/Air James Beach from the back seat of Gus Hogg's aircraft: 'Skua L2902/K—dive-bombing; Skua L—fighter attack with Lt Henley.' Gus continued:

> The whole of the ship's company was making guesses as to where we should go, the favourite bets being West Africa and Bermuda. I was certain that it was the latter as I had found a piece of paper on the chart board showing distances and times to Bermuda. I kept my mouth shut and, later, found it to be a good deduction. Fighter patrol overhead, *Illustrious* proudly steamed out on her maiden voyage, escorted by a screen of destroyers. We headed west—it was to be Bermuda.

II

Caribbean Cruise

Of the voyage to Bermuda, Lt Vincent-Jones wrote:

> The passage to Bermuda was uneventful apart from a few days of heavy seas, which provided a good test for the ship but also dislodged the degaussing gear (anti-magnetic mine-detecting equipment) from the side of the ship.

But, as Gus Hogg confided to his journal:

> The cruise was far from being a rest for us. We had to practise fighter interceptions and attacks, dive-bombing and snappy deck landings. It was during dive-bombing practice that three of us nearly ended our short service career. Ivan [Lowe], Stanley [Orr] and I set off in stormy weather to drop some practice bombs on smoke floats, five miles astern of the ship. Ivan dropped the smoke float and we dived to unload our first bomb. As we pulled out, we looked around to ascertain the carrier's position, it was nowhere to be seen! Dark, menacing rain clouds had descended to sea level, reducing the visibility to less than a mile. The observer had not brought his navigating instruments with him, we had no R/T and the ship had to maintain wireless silence because of lurking U-boats. We were completely lost in mid-Atlantic!
>
> Getting into formation, we set off on a search through the storm clouds, hoping to catch a glimpse of the fleet through the squalls. The longer we searched, the more hopelessly lost we became. During the first hour I felt fairly certain that we should soon find our whereabouts; as the second hour crept past, without any sign of the ships, I sank into dark despair. When my clock showed that three hours had passed, I nearly went mad at the thought of a slow, horrible death in a dinghy in the cold Atlantic but this feeling slowly changed to one of resignation—I

was finished.

Suddenly, an answer was received to the repeated wireless messages, which we had been hopefully transmitting. Thank God! The ship had broken strict wireless silence to save our damn-fool necks. They sent us our bearing from the fleet and it was passed to me as a course, which I promptly steered, taking us even further away than we were already. Twenty minutes later, the Captain realised that we were complete fools and sent us a course to steer, which was corrected at ten-minute intervals. We had some hundred and fifty miles to go. Would the petrol last? The gauges sank lower and lower. Oh, God, please. It's another of those damned mirages. I won't be fooled this time. I wonder if it is? No! Don't give way to your imagination. But I tell you it is the fleet this time. It is, it is! I burst into hysterical laughter. We landed, having been in the air for five hours, with a few drops of petrol in our tanks. Stanley was so relieved to find that his time had not yet come that he crashed into the island structure, fortunately without hurt to himself. The CO gave us a strafing for losing ourselves but we did not mind: better a strafing than death.

The next three days produced nothing more thrilling for those aboard the carrier than the sight of sharks but soon Bermuda came into sight. *Illustrious* flew off a dummy strike force that carried out mock dive-bombing and strafing of the island, flying over the villages and towns at nought feet. It turned out that the populace had had no idea that an aircraft carrier was in the vicinity and when they saw landplanes diving on them, they thought that the Germans had arrived. Many of the natives had seen nothing but flying boats and seaplanes and gazed in wonder at these small, feetless aeroplanes. Several of the local bucks were busily engaged in their annual cricket match when the engines of the 'devil' machines were heard above. As they started to dive, the players and spectators hurriedly dispersed and, soon, all that could be seen of the gallant array were several pairs of black feet projecting from nearby bushes and huts! Later in the day, the game was resumed and wickets fell rapidly, due to the nervous disability of the batsmen.

Lt Vincent-Jones added:

We were sad to read in the following day's *Bermudian* newspaper that one of the senior residents had become over-depressed by the rapid advance of the German forces in Europe. He assumed on seeing the descent of the Skuas, that the Luftwaffe was now converging on Bermuda, so decided to put an end to himself on the spot.

The morning after the display, the carrier anchored in the roads, to await the opportunity of steaming into a more sheltered anchorage. That evening, liberty boats were full to the gunwales. *Illustrious* was unable to leave her anchorage during the first week as repairs had to be carried out to the degaussing gear and hull. The Swordfish, with their low landing speeds, were able to take-off and land in the calm, which prevailed for six days. The Skuas had to remain in the hangars waiting for a stiff breeze, sufficient to enable them to land.

The aircrews were able to explore the many attractions ashore and get to know the inhabitants, who were found to be very friendly and hospitable. At dawn on the seventh day a stiff breeze sprung up and the crews of 806 Squadron had to be rounded up from the fleshpots and brought back to get airborne.

Gus Hogg again takes up the story:

> Five Skuas and two Fulmars took-off to carry out interception exercises; the Skuas were to dive-bomb the harbour and the Fulmars were to try and stop them with mock fighter attacks. When we set off there was a fairly good wind-speed but it died away while we were in the air, leaving no wind-speed over the deck. The result was that when landing, the relative speed of approach was higher, putting a great strain on the aircraft deck landing hooks.
>
> Finishing the exercise, I prepared to land and, coming up astern, noticed an aircraft hanging over the side from the starboard cradle. This was not entirely unusual and I paid no attention, pulling off a fast and uneventful landing. I went down to the hangar with my Fulmar but arrived on deck again in time to see Eric [Buttle] land. He touched the flight deck and slowly trickled over the bows. There was a concerted rush and I got there just as Eric climbed out of his still floating Skua. The deck was made ready again for Nick [Lt Nicolls] to land and the ship's company lined the sides to watch the fun. He also landed successfully but tore his hook out; taking no chances, he opened his throttle and took-off—minus a hook. It was now impossible for him to land on the ship, so he flew off to have a look at the prospects of landing on the golf course, as there was no land aerodrome on Bermuda at that time. He flew low along one of the fairways to make sure that there were no bunkers and was so intent on his task that he flew straight into a wood and crashed. He and his observer climbed out badly shaken and set off to the clubhouse. On the way there they were waylaid by an American who asked, in a nasal twang, if they were naval aviators. Nicolls replied: 'We were—until a few minutes ago.'

The Skua (L2904) had landed on the 16th fairway of the *Mid-Ocean Golf Club*. The engine allegedly finished on the 17th green. The remains were later salvaged and returned to the carrier. Gus continued:

> The Skua I had seen hanging from the crane was the CO's. His hook had also broken off, the aircraft had swung towards the side and the undercarriage was sliced off by a small obstruction. He and VJ [Lt Vincent-Jones] sat there for a minute until, suddenly, the same thought struck them simultaneously—fire! They shot out of their cockpits like startled rabbits. Robert [Henley], new to

> the Squadron, had a narrow escape, his aircraft finishing its landing with its tail hanging over the port side. Both Fulmars landed safely due to the fact that their hooks were new and strong.

Of the CO's crash, his observer Lt Vincent-Jones added:

> We hit the deck with a crunch, the hook caught the first wire but was pulled out of the aircraft. By a brilliant piece of manoeuvring, Charles by hitting a gun mounting with his wingtip and then scraping what was left of the wing alongside of the island (the superstructure on the starboard side of the flight deck) brought us safely to rest in the middle of the deck. The first and only time I knew the CO to justify his nickname of *Crash!* After dismounting and seeing the wreckage cleared away, we joined the spectators on the bridge.
>
> Surprisingly, no one was hurt in this series of incidents though one or two were understandingly shaken. Within a few days, repairs carried out, *Illustrious* departed for the trip back to troubled waters. The dangers of flying, especially over the sea, were never far away from carrier aircrew, however and the squadron suffered another loss on the way home.
>
> Death had seemed chary of visiting us in Bermuda and I do not wonder, since it is an earthly paradise but as soon as we were one day out, he knocked. Peter [Dean] was a fairly new arrival who had replaced Jack [Marshall], when that worthy went to hospital after his crash. He was flying round the ship when he saw a Swordfish below him and decided to do a dummy attack on it. It was fairly-low on the water and Peter went right up behind, until he must have hit the slipstream, stalled and spun into the sea. A destroyer raced to the rescue and found—nothing. As I stood watching from the flight deck I happened to look down, to see a shark stalking us. Poor Peter.

With Lt Peter Dean in L2941 died his TAG, N/Air Ken Jones. The Swordfish, an aircraft of 815 Squadron, was being flown by Lt Charles Lamb, who later wrote.[1]

> I was sent off one afternoon, in company with a Skua pilot, to work out the best defence for Swordfish from fighter attack in daylight. We climbed to 10,000 feet and then the Skua pilot flew off into the sun to begin his first attack. He was friend of mine whose wife had just had their first baby. When he dived out of the sun on my port quarter, I did what I had always planned to do if I was caught by an enemy fighter. I wrenched the aircraft into a violent stall turn towards him and stood the aircraft on its tail. When his target suddenly stood still, he tried hard to keep me in his sights but spun over on his back in the attempt, temporarily out of control. As he was heading for the sea in an inverted loop, I was relieved to see him roll out and climb safely away for his next attack.

> We were only about 50 feet above the sea when the fighter pilot began his second attack, from two or three thousand feet. In all the excitement of the chase I can only image that the pilot of the Skua omitted to glance at his altimeter and had no idea that I was sown at sea level. To my horror he did another dive attack and instead of breaking away at a safe height he kept coming, trying to keep the Swordfish in his sights and when he spun over onto his back there was no room to recover and he plunged into the sea upside down. There was no chance of his survival after entering the water in an inverted dive but in the hope of a miracle, we flew around the spot for quite some time. The only thing to come to the surface was the Skua's tail wheel.

Illustrious returned to the Clyde on **28 July** for some minor modifications. Gus Hogg's final entry in his journal for the Caribbean cruise revealed a minor landing mishap:

> My last landing in a Skua was when we arrived at Donibristle and it was rather hectic. The aerodrome there is not very large and I landed about halfway down it. At the end was a gap in the fence, leading into the dispersal fields and there stood a quantity of gold braid, directing us to our various parking places. I could not possibly stop in time and as I went whistling through the gap, braid went flying in all directions. I ran to the end of the field and stopped right on my picketing position. The whole thing was quite a 'la Comic Opera', although the gold braid did not seem to think so!

806 Squadron stayed at Donibristle for the next month, fully re-equipping with Fulmars.[2] The pilots knew they were to go abroad, and six new pilots were drafted in to give the squadron nineteen aircraft and crews.[3] The new pilots were straight out of fighter school.

> Very few of them had flown a Fulmar before and not one had seen an aircraft carrier, so we were kept pretty busy giving them flying practice and dummy deck landings. Fortunately, all were good pilots and the task of getting them ready for operations was not as difficult as it might have been. One of them [Sub-Lt(A) Henry Isherwood] did not stay with us very long. He slow-rolled his Fulmar [N1880] at a thousand feet and did not pull out of the dive which ensued. He disappeared behind a hill; there was a crump and the nasty crackling caused by exploding cartridges. His funeral was two days later.

The Fulmar spun into the ground near Whitehill, Aberdour.

> After a few false alarms, we finally set off to join the ship in Scapa Flow. We had bid very sad farewells—we might be away for years and some would not come

> back—ever. Nineteen of us took the air that day. In addition to the older members including Jack [Marshall], who had just returned following his crash, there were Bill [Clisby], Jackie [Sewell], *Pappy* [Leslie Hill], 'P' [Geoff Pudney], 'G' [George Golden] and 'I. P.' [Ingram Paul Godfrey]. We were a gallant array.

The next day the pilots circled Hatston before setting off to embark on *Illustrious*, which was steaming outside Scapa Flow but was one aircraft short, Jackie Sewell having suffered engine failure while flying over Kirkwall. He managed to force-land the Fulmar in a field and escape injury, with only minor damage to his aircraft. Gus continued:

> The carrier was soon found and the first sections commenced to land. All went well until it came to *Pappy's* turn. He approached as he had been taught at Donibristle but in attempting to keep the deck in sight, he drifted to the port side. His hook caught B wire but, being well off centre, it pulled the aircraft round—over the side. If he had been lucky the hook would have stayed on the wire and held the Fulmar suspended over the sea but the lucky charm must have dropped out of his pocket for the hook broke and *Pappy* plunged into the drink. He extricated himself but was furious at the loss of a valuable cine-camera, which he had put in the back seat. The only other accident was Billy who did exactly the same thing except that in his case the hook held. His Fulmar perched itself perpendicularly on the brink of the flight; William could have spat into the sea!
>
> Considering the fact that out of nineteen pilots, six had never seen an aircraft carrier, it is remarkable that there were only two casualties. The other four new people did extremely good landings, even better than some of the old hands. All aircraft embarked, the ship returned to Scapa to await last-minute stores and replacements for the crashed Fulmars. When we once again had our full complement of nineteen, three had to be picketed on the flight deck due to the lack of hangar space and, in the ensuing voyage, they were a curse to the Squadron Duty Officer who had to inspect them throughout the night watches.
>
> We left Scapa in a gale and the ship was rising and falling with a slow, steady motion which brought pangs to many a stomach. Spray was lashing over the Fulmars on the flight deck and soaking the deck party to the skin. Down in the hangar, the smell of petrol and oil, combined with the steady pitching, was too much for some of the fitters who had to go below to their hammocks. Old England was giving us a typical send-off. Only the 'high-ups' knew where we were going but the general buzz was Alexandria and this idea was borne out by our course. We went around the top of Ireland and then to the middle of the Atlantic, until opposite Gibraltar, when we turned east.

Fighter patrols were constantly in the air, more for practice than for defence and it was during one of these that there occurred a disaster:

> On this particular day [**24 August**] they went up with the CO and, having completed their patrol, returned to the ship to land-on. I have never discovered why but for some reason *Lew* dived straight into *Daisy* whose machine immediately fell to pieces, *Lew* went into a flat spin from a thousand feet and hit the sea without baling out. *Daisy*'s body was never found but *Lew* was picked up—quite dead. During the five months that I had been in 806 Squadron, *Lew* and *Daisy* had been two of my best friends; I always felt lost if they were not somewhere around. That night, the beds on either side of me were empty. The next morning the fleet slowed down, a short burial service was held and *Lew*'s body slipped to its last resting place in the cold Atlantic. I spent the afternoon packing their kit and trying to realise that I should never see them again. I was still mourning the loss of my friends when *Ark Royal* hove into sight and escorted us into Gibraltar, where we remained for a day or two.

Killed with Sub-Lt Arthur *Daisy* Day in N1887 was his TAG N/Air Harry Newton, while lost with Sub-Lt Albert Lew Ayres in N1885 was his observer PO(A) Sam Gould.

III

806 Wins Its Spurs

Illustrious arrived there [Gibraltar] ready and anxious to show her paces. Flying had now reached a high standard and the new radar interception technique showed great promise. Under Captain Boyd's inspired leadership, a happy ship's company had been created whose high spirits mounted all the time. The young pilots were fanatically keen, longing to show their strength. At times they were overzealous … a careless youngster sitting happily in his Fulmar down below, pressed the firing button and sprayed the hangar with the contents of eight Browning machine-guns.[1]

On **31 August**, *Illustrious* entered the Mediterranean joined by the battleship *Valiant* from Force H, she was to become part of Admiral Cunningham's Mediterranean Fleet. These two mighty vessels brought this fleet an added precious advantage beyond the strength of their presence, both were equipped with RDF (radar), a luxury previously denied to Force H. Although the small carrier *Eagle* had been doing valiant work, she carried only a flight of Sea Gladiators to protect her two squadrons of Swordfish. In addition to the Fulmars of 806 Squadron, *Illustrious* also carried aboard two Swordfish squadrons (815 and 819). Amongst the passengers taken aboard was 815 Squadron's former CO Cdr Robin Kilroy, who was on his way to Egypt to take command of the Royal Naval Air Station at Dekheila, just outside Alexandria.

It was intended that the two ships should be escorted as far as the Sicilian Narrows by Force H and there would be met by the Mediterranean Fleet. Force H, which included the carrier *Ark Royal*, was already at sea and her Skuas [800 and 803 Squadrons] had already notched up several victories against Italian reconnaissance aircraft, mainly Z.501 and Z.501 seaplanes. L/Air Denis Tribe explained:

> Our normal duties were to give fighter protection for the Eastern Med Fleet when it moved out of Alex harbour in its various missions as far as Malta. Normally there was a sub-flight of three Fulmars in the air with another at readiness on the flight deck. With the latest radar installed in *Illustrious* we were directed onto the shadowing enemy aircraft and attack them before they located our fleet. This was usually 90% effective.
>
> When we were working nearer land it was usually high-level bombers [SM79s] and sometimes with fighter escort [CR42s] and our second sub-flight would join us or take over until the first sub-flight had to return to refuel and rearm. In a sub-flight it was difficult to register a kill as the enemy plane might only be damaged by the first to attack and the second plane brought it down. In fairness, one must understand that some of our pilots opened fire at a greater distance and it was less effective than those who opened fire at much closer range. Sometimes it made a claim doubtful.

As *Illustrious* and her escort approached the Sicilian Narrows constant fighter patrols were maintained and during the early evening of the first day of the new month [**1 September**], patrolling Skuas from *Ark Royal* were vectored onto an unidentified aircraft approaching from the south-east, some 18 miles distant. As the Skua leader closed in he recognised the intruder as a Hudson and the two pilots exchanged friendly signals when, without warning, three Fulmars led by Cdr Kilroy, who had volunteered to fly patrols with 806 Squadron while on board, appeared from below. Gus Hogg was flying No.2 position with L/Air Paul Douet in the backseat:

> Our Section was on patrol when we saw three Skuas chasing a twin-engined bomber. Keen to show how superior our new Fulmars were to Skuas, we set off in pursuit and cut out the other three. Diving down underneath the bomber the leader pulled up, firing into the target's belly and Stanley and I, who were following, saw chunks fly off the port engine. The leader broke away and, being in the right position, I opened fire. As I pressed the gun button recognition lights started shooting out of the aircraft in my sights and I ceased fire, drawing close to have better look. It was an RAF Hudson! Feeling asses, we landed on and discovered that Blue Section was chasing something.

Cdr Kilroy had opened fire on the unsuspecting Hudson, believing it to be a Ju88, only breaking off its attack when recognition flares were fired from both Hudson and Skua (800 Squadron from *Ark Royal*), Kilroy at the same time spotting the roundel on the Hudson's fuselage. The Hudson, N7342 out from Malta, was badly damaged and the pilot Flg Off Vincent Davies made for nearest land, the Cap Bon Peninsula (Tunisia) where he crash-landed on El

Aouina airfield at Tunis. Two of the crew, Flt Sgt Burnett and Sgt Wright were injured and removed to hospital, while Davies and co-pilot Flt Lt L.F. Cooper were interned at Le Kef.[2]

That night, Swordfish from *Ark Royal* were engaged in a diversionary strike against Cagliari airfield (Sardinia) to cover the passage of *Illustrious* through the Narrows, codenamed Operation *Smash*, to be repeated the following night as Operation *Grab*. The first raid was considered a success and by the morning of **2 September,** *Illustrious* and *Valiant* were making progress eastwards for the rendezvous with the Mediterranean Fleet to the south of Malta but 'shadowers' were about and the carrier was spotted by a searching Z.501 when still 35 miles to the west of Malta. Fortunately, Blue Section of 806 Squadron was already patrolling the ships and was directed onto the seaplane by somewhat primitive Morse code radio transmissions at 11:20. Lt-Cdr Evans was leading Lt-Cdr Kilroy and Sub-Lt Lowe (flying with N/Air Kensett), the three Fulmars attacking from astern, 500 feet above the sea and shot it down in flames, as recorded by the CO:

> Led quarter to astern attack and enemy aircraft dived to 10 feet above the water. Fired from 350 yards to 150 yards and enemy aircraft went down in flames.

Lt Vincent-Jones, observing the event from the rear seat of the CO's Fulmar, later wrote:

> We soon found a Cant Z.501. These flying boats had a single engine fitted in a nacelle in the centre of the big wing. At the rear of the nacelle a turret was mounted, containing a single cannon, the only form of armament provided. The Italian air gunner spent most of his time in the main hull but on the approach of an enemy aircraft could be seen climbing up a ladder from the hull to man his turret, fully exposed to the elements. Once inside his turret he became the central point of aim for an attacking fighter; a less attractive occupation could hardly be imagined. Charles, who always kept me fully informed of enemy movements, used to describe the manoeuvre as, 'The king sucker is on his way up to his pulpit'.

He added:

> The dying cries of the Cant usually brought on the bombers in the form of SM79s. They were quite fast and not easy to catch, they kept good formation and had good gun discipline, making them unpleasant to approach from directly astern. For a time, a SM79 only had to sight a Fulmar before jettisoning his bombs and racing for home but as time went on they got used to us and became quite tough to shoot down.

Although not involved in this action, Gus Hogg wrote in his diary:

> They had found a Cant flying boat, low on the water and had promptly opened fire. They went into the attack, one after the other and, after absorbing a considerable amount of lead, the Cant crashed into the sea and broke up. This was the first *Illustrious* fighter success and Ivan [Lowe] was credited with having been the one to fire the fatal shots.

This was an aircraft from 182ª *Squadriglia RM* flown by *Sottotenente* Ottavio De Martis, who was reported missing with his crew. Even C-in-C Admiral Cunningham, aboard *Warspite*, wrote glowingly of *Illustrious*' first success:

> The *Illustrious*' Fulmar fighters came into action at once. The Fleet, of course, was being shadowed as usual when it started its passage east and when [Vice-Admiral] Jack Tovey brought his squadron in from the north where he had been patrolling during the night, he also brought his little Italian friend with him. The Fulmars quickly tumbled [him] into the sea to the loud cheers of the ships' companies, who had had just about as much as they could stand of being bombed without retaliation. The tremendous effect of this incident upon everyone in the Fleet was indescribable. From that moment, whenever an armoured carrier was in company, we had command of the air over the Fleet. I do not mean that bombing attacks ceased. Far from it but we felt that we now had a weapon which enabled us to give back as good as we were getting and also gave us vastly increased freedom of movement.

However, the Z.501 had managed to get off a sighting report before its own demise. Ten SM79s of 60° *Gruppo* led by *Tenente Colonello* D'Ippolito, followed by nine from the 59° *Gruppo* led by *Tenente Colonello* Draghelli, were sent out. The former found nothing but at 14:50, the latter aircraft discovered *Illustrious* and headed towards her. Fulmars were already up on patrol—Lt Bill Barnes with Yellow Section, as Gus noted:

> Wasting no time, Bill headed straight towards them, getting into line astern as they went. Turning in astern of the starboard tail-most SM79, Bill opened fire. The bomber burst into flames and Bill transferred his aim to the next one. Closing in to 50 yards, he broke away and Jackie opened fire on the same target, which was rapidly dropping behind. It, too, went down and, before breaking off the engagement, Jackie shot down another. As he swung away, there was a nasty 'ping' and a hole appeared in his windscreen. Before long the engine started to pack up and, seeing Malta below him, he wasted no time in executing a snappy forced-landing on one of the local aerodromes.

Lt Jackie Sewell's TAG, L/Air Denis Tribe recalled:

> We claimed two shot down but, in the action, caught up with fire from the enemy (turret and single machine-guns). From the rear seat it was difficult to see except for tracers coming at us—a row of holes in my perspex cover; the glycol coolant pouring into my cockpit. Also, the intercom was damaged and out of action. I thought I was badly hit as whenever I moved, I could see blood. I was greatly relieved to find it was coming from a flesh wound under my right forearm. Although Jackie Sewell had armour-plated glass in front of him, I thought he must have been hit because the plane seemed out of control. I could not communicate owing to the damage and I could not open my sliding cover. Fortunately, he regained control and with damaged engine we made quite a good landing at Hal Far, guided by Lt Barnes who also landed at Hal Far. I had first aid locally and in the early evening we were picked up by one of our Swordfish from *Illustrious.*

An hour later, Lt Nicolls (N1879) and Red Section spotted two SM79s flying at 9,000 feet, probably stragglers from 60° *Gruppo.* The pilots carried out a stern attack from below but were on this occasion unable to overtake the bombers.

At 19:15, when only a few miles off Malta, six more SM79s attempted to bomb *Illustrious* but two Fulmars of Yellow Section were up—Lt Barnes and Sub-Lt George Golden, with L/Air Harry Phillips in the back seat of N1874, claimed three of the SM79s shot down. Barnes reported shooting down one from 250 yards and then attacked a second which was finished off by *Illustrious'* guns, while Golden also claimed one and a damaged. One SM79 of 235[a] *Squadriglia* was indeed shot down and a second badly damaged, while in a third one member of the crew had been mortally wounded. Gus Hogg noted:

> Towards the end of the patrol we found a Cant Red Cross seaplane, probably come to pick up survivors of the bombers that Yellow Section pranged and, as it was fast approaching the Fleet, we had to set on it. We chased it for nearly sixty miles, firing as often as we got the chance but it got away.

With fuel running low, the Fulmars returned to the Fleet only to find that *Illustrious* was not currently with the main battlefleet. Espying *Eagle* in a suitable position, Lt-Cdr Kilroy led the three Fulmars down for a landing, as Gus wrote:

> As I approached the stern there was a funny noise and a fountain of water sprang up in front of me—we were being bombed! Not waiting to see what was happening, I hastily removed myself from the area till things cooled off a bit. The action finished in about ten minutes and I landed-on, over the leading machine's wing which had been left unfolded with the aircraft parked on the round-down (stern).

> Stanley followed me but, in his determination to catch a wire, dropped from twenty feet and burst a tyre. We were given a royal welcome by the wardroom whose officers were pleased to see us, their reliefs.

The Fulmar Section would be stranded on *Eagle* until next morning, when a Swordfish flew over from *Illustrious*, some 90 miles away, with a replacement tyre for Orr's aircraft.

The attack on *Eagle* and *Illustrious*, was carried out by two flights of Italian Ju87s, each of four aircraft, which were out hunting for the Fleet. One quartet, escorted by MC200s, attacked and *Tenente* Brezzi claimed to have hit the bows of a cruiser, while the other four attacked a carrier and another large vessel, claiming hits on both—although the bomb that hit *Illustrious* did not explode. Naval AA gunners were highly optimistic as to the success they had gained, obviously assuming that many of the bombers' dives were terminal; they claimed five shot down although only *Tenente* Antonio Cumbat's aircraft was damaged.

The greatly-strengthened Mediterranean Fleet now headed eastwards to launch an unescorted dawn air strike with aircraft from both carriers against airfields on the Italian-occupied Aegean island of Rhodes. As dawn broke on **4 September**, Swordfish from *Illustrious* attacked the airfield at Calato. However, *Eagle's* Swordfish squadrons had been delayed in take-off and the 13 aircraft arrived over Maritza to find the defences alerted. The defending CR32s and CR42s shot down four of the Swordfish for the loss of one fighter. Of the twelve naval aircrew lost, four were killed and the remainder taken prisoner.

At 10:05, Lt-Cdr Kilroy took-off with Sub-Lts Orr and Hogg and were vectored onto an aircraft which they identified as a Caproni Ca.133 bomber-transport (in fact an SM81 of 223ª *Squadriglia* flown by *Sottotenente* Filippo Tedesco) as it was going into land at Rhodes. Gus Hogg wrote:

> While we were on patrol, we sighted an old Caproni and dived to intercept. Pulling up underneath, my leader opened fire and then broke off to give me a crack. I closed in, right underneath, took a sight and pressed the firing button—nothing happened, my gun bottle was empty! Furious, I broke away from this lumbering old crate.
>
> 'He's coming down on our tail' shouted my air gunner. 'What?' 'The bomber is on our tail'. 'I thought you said he's on our tail'. 'He is'. 'Strewth!' Pulling back on the stick, I climbed like a monkey and soon shook him off. What a nerve!
>
> As soon as I was out of the way Stanley [with L/Air Douet in N1884] closed in and I watched his bullets going straight through the Wop. Suddenly there was an explosion, clouds of smoke and Stanley disappeared into what had once been an Italian bomber. A moment later, two parachutes arrived out of the bottom of the smoke cloud and I thought it was Stanley but it was two of the Wop crew and

the Fulmar soon popped out of the other side. I felt rather sorry for the two 'Itis', saving their skins by parachute, only to perish miserably in the sea.

When I landed, my armourer found himself rather unpopular. It was the first real chance that I had and I was very annoyed that it should be wasted by such carelessness.

Formations of SM79s from 34° and 92° *Gruppi BT* took-off from Gadurra (Rhodes) in order to attack the warships. The crews reported being attacked by carrier-based Hurricanes. Off the island the patrolling Fulmars enjoyed some success. At 10:30, Lts Bill Barnes and Jackie Sewell of Yellow Section engaged four SM79s, these escaping after each pilot had inflicted damage on them. The same pair met two more of these aircraft at 11:05, attacking *Tenente* Nicola Dall'Olio's 201ª *Squadriglia* aircraft[3] and shooting it down in flames, before damaging the other machine. Meanwhile, Yellow 3, Sub-Lt Paul Godfrey with L/Air Harry Phillips in N1871, attacked two more:

Godfrey got a burst at a 79 and put rear-gunner out of action. Trail of smoke from port engine and another which fell out of formation.

92° *Gruppo* reported damage to three of its aircraft during these attacks, two of them severely and these aircraft landed with two dead and five wounded on board.[4]

During the early afternoon, at 13:45, Red Section met two SM79s at 7,000 feet some 50 miles south of Castello Point. Senior pilot Lt Roger Nicolls/PO(A) George Muskett in N1879, leading the patrol, closed to 100 yards and saw pieces fly off the starboard engine of the aircraft he attacked but the bombers escaped serious damage. Red 2, Sub-Lt Eric Buttle (with L/Air Stevens in N1876) also claimed a probable, probably the same aircraft.

By midday on **5 September**, *Illustrious* had entered the breakwater at Alexandria, as Gus Hogg noted with a certain humour:

Everyone was on the flight deck to see what could be seen. The harbour was packed with all kinds of warships, merchant ships, Greek schooners, Arab dhows and RAF Sunderland flying boats. Needless to say, the dhows were all round us trying to cadge a fare to shore but we were not quite ready for that. Shore-going rig [clothes] had to be donned and all our English money changed into Egyptian piastres. Even when we were ready to go ashore, the Arabs were still disappointed, as we went in a service liberty boat.

Picking the least infectious-looking taxi with the least villainous-looking driver, we asked to be taken to the European part of the town. The driver got two of his pals to swing her over, while he pulled a disused-looking wire which caused the

> engine to make horrific noises. This performance carried on for a few moments until there was a bang, a crash, a blast on the horn—and we were off. Travelling at a good 25 miles-per-hour, we turned right into a narrow street of the native quarter. All down the street the Arab tradesmen had parked their small handcarts, which were full of different kinds of food and most of the local inhabitants had collected to buy their Sunday dinner.
>
> We tore down the street, paying no attention to pedestrians crossing over from one side to the other. We thought this rather dangerous but our driver knows the Egyptian mentality. When an Arab wants to cross a road, he casually sets off without looking, until he hears a honk right behind him, when he turns to have a look. He then carries on, paying no attention, until he is in danger of losing his life, at that moment, he nimbly sidesteps and proceeds to harangue the murderer who tried to kill him! Should he run out of suitable language, the passers-by are only too willing to provide him with some more vocabulary. If the taxi driver stays to listen to all this, his occupants are in danger of being mobbed. Our driver knew this and went down that street as though the devil was after him, sending Arabs flying in all directions and paying no attention to what they shouted regarding our ancestry. At the bottom of the street we whizzed across some tram lines, missed a tram by inches, bumped over a heap of rubble and arrived on the Corniche, which is the boulevard running between Alexandria and the sea. Things were slightly more peaceful here and, a few minutes later, we drew up at the Cecil Hotel.

Having survived the hair-raising experience, Gus and his companions probably concurred that flying was a safer occupation. Fed and watered, the officers attended a cabaret or two before making their way back to the carrier that evening. *Illustrious* remained in harbour for the next few days before she put to sea in order to disperse her aircraft. The Swordfish flew off to Aboukir, while the Fulmars headed for Dekheila. Also flown to Dekheila were four redundant Skuas that had been embarked for dispersal to second-line units in the Delta area. The journal of Gus Hogg revealed:

> We spent the next five days under canvas, resting and eating in the wooden mess, which was divided into two rooms; one for eating and the other for a mess. The Squadron started its first night flying in Fulmars but the concrete runways wore out tyres after three landings and the idea had to be postponed. I managed to complete two landings without difficulty.
>
> **Sunday 15th**: When I got up this morning, I was surprised to hear we were re-embarking. I went down to the hangar and loaded up the lorries. This took about an hour and then I went for a swim. After lunch I fell asleep and at four, we took-off. I had a lot of trouble with the machine but got on [landed] alright.

Monday 16th: I found that [Lt] Nicolls has gone sick now, with a temperature. [Jack] Marshall has also gone to bed with tummy ache—my own isn't so good.

While the sick Lt Nicolls and Jack Marshall were thus temporarily indisposed, as was Eric Buttle, the squadron now found itself further depleted when Sub-Lt *Pappy* Hill joined the ever-growing sick list. Gus continued:

Orr led White Section today and we did a fighter patrol. I don't think I have ever been so bored. The Swordfish raid Benghazi tonight—I wish them luck. They reckon four hundred bombers will be after us tomorrow, so I hope we all come through.

The Swordfish attack was very successful. A destroyer was sunk, a steamer left ablaze and a second steamer and a torpedo-boat were damaged, as were a tug and a pontoon crane. A second destroyer was sunk when she hit one of the mines laid in the harbour. All aircraft returned safely.

Tuesday 17th: We are running away from Benghazi today as fast as we can go. No bombers arrived but we (Orr and I) shot down a Cant flying boat. We knew that he was around and searched all over without sighting a thing. Giving up in disgust, we started to climb up to patrol height. As we did, we saw, simultaneously, a flying boat about 3,000 feet above us. We gave chase and it was a race to see who got there first.

I was talking nineteen to the dozen to myself—give her everything she's got! Throttle open, twenty-eight hundred revolutions, pull the boost cut-out. Come on, don't let the others get there first. There's Stanley opening fire; he's closing too fast; he's broken away. Now, in you go. Gun button on? Sight on? Flying level? OK, let's go! Now he's in range, press the button. Look at those tracers—lovely but wide. Bring 'em onto the engine. Close to 50 yards—strewth, he's going into a diving turn. Break away and give Billy [Lt Barnes] a chance.

The Cant was diving steeply in a turn, almost spinning. Billy and then Stanley again went in and filled him with lead. Then it was my turn and I got behind him and stayed there, blazing away. Down he went, my eyes glued to the target, which still seemed unharmed. Suddenly, to my surprise, the flying boat turned into a big splash. I nearly turned into one, too! I pulled out and skiffed the sea, slowly realising that the Cant had crashed—the first victim in which I had had a share. Whoopee!

Sub-Lt Orr (N1879) described the colourful paintwork on its top-wing: '… orange and red stripes like a … rising sun.' This was an aircraft from 143ª *Squadriglia RM* (MM35348) flown by *Sottotenente* Renato Balestrero, he and his crew being rescued from the sea by one of the British warships.

> **Wednesday 18th**: We all thought we were going back to Alexandria but I woke to find us 30 miles from Libya. *Kent* had been torpedoed while shelling troop concentrations and could only make six knots. We turned back to help her out. We expected to be bombed to blazes but never saw a single enemy plane. I did one fighter patrol.

The heavy cruiser *Kent* had been struck by one of two torpedoes launched by two SM79s of 278ª *Squadriglia AS*, flown by *Tenente* Carlo Buscaglia and *Tenente* Guido Robone. In the dim moonlight the crews were unable to ascertain who had hit the cruiser. The effect was an abandonment of the proposed bombardment of Bardia. *Illustrious* arrived back at Alexandria next day (**19 September**), her aircraft flying off to RNAS *Grebe* (Dekheila). The aircrew were able to relax at the Sporting Club, where those who wished could swim or play indoor sports:

> **Sunday 22nd**: We [Gus was accompanied by Jack Marshall] went by taxi to the Anglo-Swiss hospital where Buttle is laid up with a jimmy arm. We stayed talking to him for an hour or so. We went down to the Hotel Cecil where we met some English [*sic*] nurses, one of whom comes from Edinburgh.

> **Monday 23rd**: We went along to the Cecil and a party of us took these English nurses to the Sporting Club. They enjoyed this very much. We gave them tea there. After supper we chatted with them for a while and took them to the Carlton. We came back on the eleven o'clock boat, which is forbidden but nobody said anything.

> **Tuesday 24th**: This morning I was Officer i/c Sabotage Patrol round the Sunderlands [228 Squadron] anchored off Ras-el-Tin. We started at one and I drove the boat around till three-thirty, when I turned in. I got up at nine, went up on deck for quarter of an hour and turned in again.

> **Wednesday 25th**: I was in the unlucky position of being second officer of the watch. I inspected the liberty men and went the rounds of the sentries; one sentry had turned the hose on a suspicious-looking felucca.

Gus Hogg had seemingly drawn the short straw while *Illustrious* was in port but most of the junior officers would have been similarly occupied:

> **Thursday 26th**: I am Squadron Duty Officer today. I range all the planes on the flight deck and started cleaning them [authorising others to clean them]. I was so bored with nothing to do that I started myself to clean my kite. In the afternoon a pasha, or somebody, came visiting with a party. I struck down the aircraft at half-past seven. What a day!

> **Saturday 28th**: Marshall and I went ashore at one fifteen and took a taxi to see [Sub-Lt] Buttle at the Anglo-Swiss hospital. He doesn't look any better and he doesn't look any worse. We went to the Sporting Club where we had a bathe. We had tea there, too, we went to see 'Three Smart Girls Grow Up'. Quite good. We returned to the ship to find we are putting to sea tonight.

On **29 September**, with *Illustrious* again at sea, her Fulmars patrolled and gained further successes against the unfortunate Italian shadowers unlucky enough to be intercepted. At 11:24, Blue Section intercepted a Z.501 at 8,000 feet and was shot down by Lt-Cdr Evans. The seaplane was also attacked by Sub-Lt Ivan Lowe (flying N1877 with N/Air Bob Kensett) but his aircraft was hit by return fire and forced to ditch five miles astern of escorting destroyer HMAS *Stuart*; both were soon plucked from the sea and taken to Aboukir. To add to 806's problems, two Fulmars flown by Sub-Lts Paul Godfrey (N1866) and Jack Marshall (N1893) became lost after chasing an SM79, which was claimed probably destroyed and were obliged to land in Crete. Both crews, which included TAGs L/Air Les Stevens and N/Air Alf Rush, were interned, causing Gus Hogg to write:

> Marshall and Godfrey force-landed in Greece when they got lost and I suppose will be interned for the rest of the war. Now we have ten aircraft and nine pilots, so I have gone to Blue Section since Lowe was shot down. Orr and Clisby to Red.

However, the two crews were only briefly interned and were released later when Greece entered the war. Three hours later White Section was vectored onto another shadower, with Sub-Lt Stan Orr/PO(A) Hyde in N1879 leading Gus Hogg:

> White Section attacked a Cant but Orr shot it down before I even got there!

The two Z.501s (MM35473 and MM35504) shot down by the Fulmars were both aircraft of 143ª *Squadriglia RM* and the crews of *Maggiore* Nicola Covacovich, believed to have been the base commander at Ghibli and *Sottotenente* Ugo Leardi, were all lost.

After a short rest and recovery following his ditching, Sub-Lt Ivan Lowe flew back to *Illustrious* with Fulmar N1871 with 815 Squadron's Lt Julian Sparke in the back seat. The experienced and decorated Swordfish pilot had requested a transfer to fighters. Meanwhile, at 11:15 on **1 October**, Blue Section Fulmars intercepted yet another shadower, flying at 4,000 feet and this was shot down into the sea. Gus Hogg wrote:

> I went on patrol with Blue Section again this morning, CO leading as usual. We went after a shadower and after an hour's search we discovered a Cant Z.506B floatplane. We dived [from] 6,000 feet. Roberts attacked first, me second. After three attacks he fell in the sea, smashed up, with two chaps standing on the wings.

A few days later the body of an Italian airman, simply identified as A. Girandola, was picked up from the sea by the destroyer HMS *Coral*. It was believed that he was one of the crew from the downed aircraft. Gus Hogg wrote in his journal:

> The Italian system is to send out flying boats and seaplanes to locate the Fleet and then shadow it, giving directions to the approaching bombers. Our job is to prevent these bombers from reaching the vitals of the naval force, the battleships and the carrier and the best way of doing this was to push down the shadower before he could wireless the Fleet's position. In fact, if a section did find a shadower and failed to remove it, there would be trouble brewing on the bridge. Just one well-aimed bullet is all that might be necessary to save a battleship. It was quite a responsibility on us fighters. If we shot down the target, we have done our duty; if we fail, we could conceivably affect the whole course of the war.

Meantime, *Illustrious* returned once again to Alexandria and the Fulmars flew to Aboukir. Another quite but restless period followed, while rumours abounded that the carrier's services would soon again be called upon, as Gus noted:

> **Monday 7th**: There have been a lot of rumours about the ship going to sea and today, about twelve, orders were received to have our troops aboard by five tonight. As Duty Officer I had to wait in the mess in the evening for the signal for the aircraft to embark but it didn't come.

> **Tuesday 8th**: We sat around in the mess all day until about three, when we walked down to the kites and set off for the ship. We got to the ship and landed on quite safely and settled down for our stay. We are taking a convoy to Malta and bringing another one back.

> **Wednesday 9th**: We started the usual fighter patrols today with two-and-a-half hours of absolutely nothing. The Admiral is hoping to run across the Italian Fleet and give it a pasting.

The journal continues:

> **Thursday 10th**: Fighter patrol again today but still the Italians refuse to come out and play. We reach Malta tomorrow and will hang about till tomorrow night,

> when we set of home again. We hung about all day today but saw nothing at all. However, at night *Ajax* met two or three enemy destroyers. She sank two outright; the other staggered off.

On this date, L/Air Harry Phillips, who was officially on the strength of *Illustrious*' 819 Squadron, found himself in the back seat of a Swordfish flown by Lt Morford:

> We depth-charged a surfaced Italian submarine. It sailed through the middle of the charges, neither of which went off. My radio was damaged by their machine-gun fire.

The convoy bound for Alexandria finally brought out the Italian bombers in force on **12 October**, units from Sicily launching 84 bomber sorties and 38 escorting fighter sorties. 806's Fulmars were soon in action, Lts Barnes and Sewell (Yellow Section) catching a shadowing Z.501 at 11:45, chasing it down from 3,000 feet to sea level, where it ditched. They strafed it but saw no signs of life. At 12:30, Red Section led by Lt Nicolls with PO(A) Muskett in N1876, sighted a dozen SM79s at 14,000 feet, the leader carrying out a beam attack on the second section of three and then a stern attack on a lone aircraft. He saw white smoke pour from its starboard engine and pieces flying off and it was considered unlikely that it would have got home. Gus Hogg was involved but …

> Nicolls led us in badly and we had to clear out early without shooting any down because of Fleet gunfire.

Blue Section met five more SM79s flying at 16,000 feet at 13:50, Lt-Cdr Evans leading the attack, with Sub-Lts Lowe and Roberts, reporting one shot down in flames and a second that was seen to ditch. The Italian bombers again suffered quite heavily in these actions. The first attack by 34° *Stormo* escaped interception but the following formation from 36° *Stormo* was savaged by the Fulmars; two SM79s flown by *Tenente* Alberto Soldati (257-4) and *Tenente* Francesco Tempra (259-2) were shot down, while a third, 257-7 flown by *Tenente* Casadio, returned badly damaged with one dead (*1°Av.Arm.* Ignazio Zanini, who had continued returning fire after being wounded and was subsequently killed during a further attack) and two wounded on board. A fourth bomber (258-7), possibly also badly damaged, flew into a mountainside on its return to Sicily, killing *Tenente* Giorgio Peiri and his crew.

In addition to these bomber losses, a civil SM73 airliner which had strayed into the battle zone, landed at Catania damaged by both AA fire and fighter attack. The aircraft, I-SAMO belonging to *Ala Littoria* but now militarised and serving with 605[a] *Squadriglia*, 148° *Gruppo*, had departed from Benghazi to fly to Catania with 24 passengers including women and children. *Capitano* Valentino Valentini, the pilot, had not been warned that he would be flying into a war zone and consequently overflew the British Fleet. Having been fired at by the warships, the SM73 was then attacked by a single fighter; one woman passenger was killed, two other women, a soldier and *Capitano* Valentini were wounded, the latter died three days later.

And finally, on this black day for the Italians, a third raid against the ships by seven SM79s of 34° *Stormo*, culminated in an attack on Italian warships by mistake. Meantime, *Illustrious* continued her patrol but no further attack was forthcoming, although her Swordfish carried out a night attack on the Italian-occupied island of Leros, as Gus recorded:

> **Monday 14th**: During the night the Swordfish boys raided Leros. Apparently, they made a pretty big mess, splattering things in all directions. The Fleet stayed just off Crete the whole time and we had continuous fighter patrols. *Liverpool* was hit by a torpedo and set on fire. Petrol exploded and blew her bows off. She is making nine knots, so we won't get to Alex until tomorrow night.
>
> **Tuesday 15th:** We had fighter patrols over *Liverpool* but saw no enemy aircraft. About three [pm], the CO said I was to fly off with him and go to Aboukir. We took-off at four [pm] and got there just after five.

Illustrious arrived safely in port and her Fulmars again flew off to Aboukir, where the aircraft were serviced and the aircrews were able to relax though some soon became bored and again craved for action. Gus was one of the latter:

> We had the usual type of day today, except for one thing—the CO was in a bad temper. What a temper! He was raving at everybody, even Lt V-J. I got one or two tick-offs.
>
> **Tuesday 22nd**: I have been getting up before the others lately, so having nothing else to do I strolled down to flights for an early start. I found that during an air raid last night, the hangar next to ours had been hit, slightly damaging a Fulmar. A bomb dropped beside another Fulmar and filled it with holes.

Gus Hogg now joined the army of the sick, going down with sandfly fever and several others were also beginning to feel unwell including observer Sub-Lt Norman Cullen. Both were sent to hospital.

Illustrious put to sea once again and on **1 November** patrolling Fulmars were vectored onto shadowing Z.506Bs. Lt Jackie Sewell (with L/Air Denis Tribe in the back seat of 6Y) intercepted two of the seaplanes and shot down one in flames, while the other escaped in a damaged condition. The remainder of the patrol of *Illustrious* was uneventful and she returned to port. However, further major naval operations were soon underway at both ends of the Mediterranean. A convoy from Gibraltar set out with reinforcements for the Malta garrison and, at the same time, another convoy of five cargo ships sailed from Alexandria for Malta under the codename MB.8, while other vessels headed for Greece and Crete. To provide cover for the convoy directly and for the other vessels indirectly, ships of the Mediterranean Fleet including *Illustrious* put to sea on **8 November.** Because considerable aerial reaction was expected, the carrier also embarked three of *Eagle's* Sea Gladiators (N5513, N5523 and N5549) as reinforcements for 806 Squadron's Fulmars on this occasion.

Action came almost immediately and it was two of the Gladiators that made the first kill, at 12:30, with Lts Nicolls (in N5549) and Sewell (N5513) catching and shooting down another of the ubiquitous seaplanes, Z.501 of the 186ª *Squadriglia RM* flown by *Tenente* Paolo Primatesta, which had left its base at Augusta at 09:00. A contemporary British report noted:

> It struck the water and two members of the crew of five were unable to extricate themselves; they were drowned. The other three, a Naval *sottotenente*, a *sergente maggiore* and a wireless operator, managed to scramble into the Cant's dinghy. The chance of survival was exceedingly remote as their dinghy quickly developed a leak. A Sunderland flying boat on patrol spotted the tiny boat and as it was far from land, decided to investigate. Although there was a nasty swell at the time, the Sunderland[5] alighted on the sea and rescued them.[6]

Mid-afternoon two formations of SM79s from the 34° *Stormo*, totalling fifteen aircraft, took-off from Catania to search for the vessels which were known to be approaching the area. 180 miles east of Malta one section made contact with *Illustrious'* fighters, directed to intercept them by the ship's radar. At 16:20 the Fulmars, Lt-Cdr Evans' Blue Section (Sub-Lts Lowe and Roberts) energetically attacked a formation of seven bombers. The CO claimed one SM79 shot down, while three parachutes were seen to come from a second aircraft but on this occasion, all apparently regained Sicilian soil, although one of the three damaged machines had to make an emergency landing at Reggio Calabria, on the toe of the mainland. Six crewmen had suffered wounds aboard the three machines. The second formation returned to base having seen nothing.

Next day (**9 November**), Italian reconnaissance aircraft made further searches, the British ships being spotted several times but without effect. A Z.506B seaplane from the 170ª *Squadriglia RM* from Augusta was caught by Sub-Lt Stan Orr/PO(A) Sam Muskett in Fulmar N1881 at 16:40, flying at 5,000 feet.

He made two stern attacks and one from the beam and the Cant crashed in flames, *Sottotenente* Tealdo Euria and his crew being lost. During this day convoy MB.8 reached Malta safely, followed next day by the troop-carrying warships from Gibraltar.

Reconnaissance by Malta's Marylands on **10 November**, had indicated the presence in Taranto harbour of six battleships together with many cruisers and destroyers. As these had not put to sea to challenge the British Fleets, a daring night torpedo attack was planned and in consequence *Illustrious* did not immediately head back to Alexandria. Searches and attacks by the units of 2ª *Squadra Aerea* in Sicily continued during the day, 806 Squadron's Fulmars making further interceptions. Lt Vincent-Jones wrote:

> It was vital for the Fulmars to make sure that the Italians should not become aware of *Illustrious* and her escort moving northwards and that the Fleet should not be detected getting away afterwards. Shadowing aircraft had to be eliminated at maximum range.

At 12:20, Lts Barnes and Sewell shot down a Z.501 of 144ª *Squadriglia RM* out from Stagnone, flown by *Sottotenente* Alfio Ferri, after chasing it down from 4,000 feet to sea level; it was then strafed. The crew was killed including observer *Sottotenente di Vascello* Umberto Gabrielli. At 13:10 Barnes' Yellow Section then intercepted a raid by nine SM79s from the 30° and 36° *Stormi*; they attacked one bomber which started losing height after being hit in the starboard engine and claimed it as damaged. In fact, *Tenente* Raffaele Brandi's aircraft failed to return.

Escaping further discovery by searching aircraft, *Illustrious* was able to launch her Swordfish during the night of **11/12 November**, for the historic attack on Taranto. Lt Vincent-Jones recalled:

> I did my best to appear enthusiastic when Charles [Evans] told me that it was possible that there might be a spare Swordfish—in which case we'd take it and tag along behind. I did not doubt his ability to fly a Swordfish although he had never done so before; what worried me was the thought of having to coil my large frame into the confines of a minute rear cockpit and sit there for four hours behind a large bare tank of petrol.

In the event, there was no spare aircraft. Immediately on recovery of her aircraft following the highly successful attack, the carrier made all speed towards Alexandria, Fulmars keeping a steady patrol overhead from first light in the expectation of massive air searches, followed inevitably by fierce bombing attacks. In fact, the combat air patrol proved spectacularly successful, catching several shadowers before, apparently, they could send accurate sighting reports and no attack developed. Lt Vincent-Jones wrote:

> By far the most successful of the 'Club Runs' was when, on the way back from Malta, *Illustrious* was detached from the Fleet to attack the Italian Fleet in Taranto. The official report states that:
>
> 'The efficiency of *Illustrious*' fighters in destroying Italian shadowers prevented the enemy from knowing the position and movements of the Fleet after 10 November and was responsible in a large measure for the surprise attained by the strike.'
>
> During the period of the night attack on Taranto, the aircrews of 806 Squadron were asleep in their bunks, preparing for reprisals which must surely come in the morning. At dawn two sections were flown off as CAP [combat air patrol] and it was not long before the air was buzzing with Cant shadowers, mainly Z.506B seaplanes. 806 Squadron Fulmars had a field day. In all, five were shot down. The CO's section accounted for three, one of which splashed alongside *Warspite*, giving the C-in-C an excellent view of proceedings.

Sub-Lts Orr and Clisby (N1940) were up on the first patrol on **12 November**, sighting a Z.501 at 5,000 feet at 11:55, which they shot down in flames. Ten minutes later Blue Section, led by Lt-Cdr Evans, engaged another from astern and this too was shot down in flames by the CO jointly with Sub-Lts Lowe (N1871) and Roberts. Within half an hour a Z.506B was sighted at 7,000 feet and following two attacks by Lt-Cdr Evans and Blue Section this also fell. Lowe noted:

> Shot down one Cant Z.501 flying boat and one Cant Z.506B seaplane. The Z.506B was intercepted three miles from the Fleet and when shot down crashed within 50 yards of one of the leading destroyers.

This slaughter led Lt Vincent-Jones to callously write:

> These Cants of both versions made ideal targets as, apart from being almost defenceless, they were well within our capacity to catch and usually exploded and descended like Roman Candles.

One of the Z.506Bs was an aircraft from 184ª *Squadriglia RM*, the other flown by *Tenente* Aldo Salvaneschi of 170ª *Squadriglia RM*—both Sicily-based. The identity of the other aircraft claimed has not been established. Of the day's action Admiral Cunningham wrote:

> The Italians made strenuous efforts to locate the Fleet, presumably to make a heavy bombing attack in retaliation. They did not have much luck, for three Cant flying boats were quickly shot down by fighters from *Illustrious*. The last air battle took place over the Fleet and we saw the large bulk of the Cant dodging in and out of the clouds with three Fulmars diving after her. There could only be one end and presently a flaming meteor with a long tail of black smoke fell out of the sky and splashed into the sea just ahead of the Fleet. One could not help feeling pity for the Italian airmen who had undertaken a hopeless task in their unwieldy aircraft.

Sub-Lts Orr and Clisby were successful again next day (**13 November**), when at 15:30 they jointly attacked another Z.506B at sea level, leaving it in a badly damaged condition after using up all their ammunition, it was then seen to fall in flames. By **19 November**, Gus Hogg was back on duty and recorded:

> Marshall and I were up fairly early and down to the flights before eight-thirty. I took-off with Orr for an interception exercise over Alexandria Harbour. This lasted two-and-a-half hours. After lunch we ferried two Gladiators over to Dekheila and had our tea there. The lorry came for us at five and we got back to Aboukir at seven.
>
> **Wednesday 20th**: Except for when I had to taxi an aircraft, I spent the morning watching the new 805 Squadron doing ADDLs [Aerodrome Dummy Deck-Landings].
>
> **Thursday 21st**: The ship is at sea today for deck landing training, so we had to do fighter patrols. At twelve-thirty, without lunch, I took-off in Barnes' section for a two-and-a-half-hour patrol, seeing nothing. Golden nearly killed me on landing.

A section of 805 Squadron Fulmars (N1932, N1934 and N1955) from Crete was now attached to 806 Squadron to boost their numbers, with Lt-Cdr Alan Black in charge and included Lt Rupert Brabner.[7] *Illustrious* put to sea once again on **25 November**, as noted by Gus:

> I got up at five this morning and at six we took-off for the ship. I made a jolly good landing considering how long it was since I did one. At two, I went on patrol with Orr and then did no more for the rest of the day.
>
> **Tuesday 26th**: Once again I got up at five and at six-thirty the whole squadron took-off. The CO's section and Orr and I patrolled over Suda Bay [Crete] for two hours and then landed at an aerodrome near Candia to refuel. It was a bad day so no further flying took place after we had landed on.

Two days later, in the morning of **28 November**, with the carrier now off Malta, came warning of approaching hostile aircraft and six patrolling Fulmars, three each from 805 and 806 Squadrons, were directed to intercept, meeting six CR42s of 23° *Gruppo*, on a reconnaissance mission to Malta. Lt-Cdr Black, leading the 805 Section, reported that although he expended 3,200 rounds in four bursts, he found the nimble biplanes far too manoeuvrable to gain any hits. His observer, Lt John Shuttleworth, recalled:

> During the engagement I fired 'smoke puffs' from the rear cockpit when the CR42s got on our tail … I certainly saw one if not two parachutes floating down.

While TAG L/Air T.A. *Bill* Bailey aboard Lt Rupert Brabner's aircraft (N1932) annotated his logbook thus:

> 09:55—engaged enemy CR42s. One shot down and two probables (confirmed).[8]

In fact, it was the experienced pilots of the 806 Squadron section who achieved, Sub-Lt Stan Orr claiming one down, while Gus Hogg and Bill Clisby (N1935) claimed two more as probably destroyed, although the latter's TAG, L/Air Harry Phillips, was wounded in one leg, hand and face by an explosive bullet, but not seriously hurt. In his logbook Stan Orr noted:

> While leading section on fighter patrol off Malta attacked by six CR42s. In dogfight that followed three CR42s were shot down. Information received later that Italian pilots were rescued from the sea.

Although *Sergente Maggiore* Arnaldo Sala's aircraft did crash into the sea some 30 miles off the Sicilian coast, he was lost. Possibly he had baled out and was one of the parachutes seen by Lt Shuttleworth. The Italian pilots believed their adversaries to have been Hurricanes and *Sergente Maggiore* Raffaele Marzocca claimed one, while *Capitano* Guido Bobba and *Tenente* Lorenzo Lorenzoni each claimed a probable. Of the fight, Gus wrote:

> We reached Malta today and we had patrols of two sections. We were up with [Lt-Cdr] Black's crowd and were sent off north-west. We were a bit behind the others and were suddenly attacked by about seven CR42s. We dived away to get up speed and as we pulled up I saw one on Orr's tail, so I gave him a burst and as he turned away, another [burst]. He disappeared into the sun and a second later I flew through a cloud a fabric. Then I turned to get two off my tail. After a few minutes Clisby shot one off my tail for me but it was not for a long time that I got rid of the other one.

During the early afternoon nine SM79s from 30° *Stormo* attempted to attack the British ships, while the escort provided by twelve CR42s of 23° *Gruppo* and ten MC200s of 6° *Gruppo* made a sweep in the same area. On this occasion Malta's Hurricanes were up in time and were able to dive through the Italian fighter escort onto the bombers one of which was shot down and another damaged. The latter force-landed on the volcanic island of Linosa and this aircraft was strafed by 806 Squadron Fulmars a few weeks later.

Gus Hogg's journal revealed a comparatively quiet period following the excitement of dogfighting the CR42s:

> **Friday 29th**: Our section was at readiness from 9:45 to 12:15. Then we did a two-and-a-half-hour patrol. There wasn't a thing to be seen anywhere and I was exceedingly bored.
>
> **Saturday 30th**: Today the Fleet is approaching Alexandria and at 11:30, Orr and I took-off for Aboukir. We got there in time for lunch.

Gus and Stan Orr and others had developed a passion for snooker and billiards and much of their spare time was thus occupied. Only occasionally were the junior officers required to undertake duties such as taxiing their aircraft and ensuring maintenance checks and servicing; the journal continues:

> **Tuesday 3rd**: There is a terrific wind blowing and it is bitterly cold. I took-off with Cullen to act as target for an RDF exercise. We were up for three hours and blind flying for two of them.
>
> **Wednesday 4th**: The cold spell is continuing with this bitter wind whistling through everything. I did no flying at all today.
>
> **Thursday 5th**: A press photographer came today and White Section (us) were his subjects. He took pictures of us getting into our cockpits, starting up, formation flying and fighter attacks.

Small-scale nuisance raids and reconnaissance flights over Alexandria were on the increase and as a result 806 Squadron was called upon to provide fighter patrols:

> **Friday 6th**: We have started fighter patrols over Alexandria now and we were at readiness most of the day from very early in the morning, about six.
>
> **Sunday 8th**: We had one patrol today, twelve-thirty to two and it was very quiet.

> **Monday 9th**: We had two patrols today, one from eleven to twelve-thirty and another from four to five and naturally we saw absolutely nothing.

On **16 December**, the Fleet sortied out once more to cover convoys while *Illustrious* launched a Swordfish bombing attack on Rhodes the next day. The whole Fleet put in at Suda Bay that evening to refuel, in preparation for a bombardment of Valona, the main supply port for the Italian army in Albania, which was planned for the night of **18 December.** It was intended for *Illustrious'* Swordfish to carry out a simultaneous bombing attack on the port but in the event the stormy weather was considered unsuitable for the Swordfish to be launched. Before heading back to Alexandria, *Illustrious* diverted towards Pantelleria where a convoy of three Italian merchant ships escorted by a destroyer was sighted on its way to Tripoli. Nine Swordfish attacked and one ship was seen to blow up while another sank.

To again build up numbers, 806 received replacements for those currently sick or otherwise indisposed, which included the CO, Lt-Cdr Evans, came Lt-Cdr Jimmy Garnett, a former Swordfish pilot but more recently in command of *Eagle's* Sea Gladiator Flight, who arrived to acclimatise himself with the Fulmar—and to later take command of 806 Squadron. Others included Lt John Shears and Sub-Lt(A) Stephen Griffith—a young man known as *Muscle*[9]—who transferred from 803 Squadron. As the year drew to a close, Lt Vincent-Jones summarised:

> This was almost the last we saw of the *Regia Aeronautica* and by this time the Squadron had accounted for more than thirty of Mussolini's flyers; not a bad record in the circumstances remembering the poor performance of the Fulmars. 806 Squadron spent the last two weeks of December peacefully and enjoyably at Aboukir, our favourite base, disturbed only by the occasional appearance of a high-flying recce aircraft usually followed by a small group of Italian bombers. These were left to the RAF and the artillery. Emphasis was put on modifying the Fulmars and bringing them back to peak fitness for combat.

At about Christmas-time, disturbing stories began to circulate round the bars of Alexandria and in the Egyptian newspapers about the movement of a Luftwaffe air-fleet from Northern Europe to Southern Italy and Sicily, the object being to isolate Malta and support the drive of the German Army into Greece. Our reasonably safe and comfortable lives were shortly to experience a dramatic change.

IV

Illustrious Blitz

On 7 **January**, a major portion of the Mediterranean Fleet put out from Alexandria, led by Admiral Cunningham in *Warspite*, joined by a second battleship, *Valiant* and by *Illustrious,* together with a covering screen of seven destroyers. A force of cruisers provided distant cover against any Italian reaction from the Aegean, also providing escort for the auxiliary *Breconshire* and a merchant vessel which were making the run from the east to Malta. Next day, as the vessels headed steadily westwards, *Illustrious* landed-on its air group, including 806 Squadron at its strongest yet and once again reinforced (for the fourth time) by three Fulmars of 805 Squadron. With the rumour of imminent German intervention, every possible fighter aircraft had been gathered together. On this occasion however, the CO was not present, as he had been taken ill and was in hospital. Command of the Squadron passed temporarily and slightly awkwardly into the hands of Lt Vincent-Jones:

> Being next in seniority the command of the Squadron devolved on me; it is a somewhat invidious position to lead a Squadron from an unarmed back seat. Shades of the 'Duke of Plaza-Toro'.[1] However, in a team like ours it didn't seem to matter and I had wonderful support from Roger Nicolls, the Senior Pilot [although also unwell]. To cause minimum disturbance and at the CO's suggestion, I flew as Bill Barnes' observer.

Lt Vincent-Jones continued:

> Our passage to Malta was cunningly quiet and we were not even disturbed by a Cant shadower. The Fleet steamed to the southward of Malta and picked up a small fast convoy in the Sicilian Narrows to escort on the eastern leg.

As this conglomeration of warships and merchant vessels all headed for the centre of the Mediterranean, much was afoot in the Axis camp which had still not been observed by British reconnaissance or intelligence. Ready for the approaching Allied shipping, 96° *Gruppo B.a'T.* had despatched some of its Ju87s to Sicily again, these flying from Lecce to Comiso. Of more ominous portent however, was the arrival at the same time of the first wave of a powerful German bomber contingent on the island. Hitler had indeed proposed aid to Mussolini before matters had started to go seriously wrong for the Italians either in Greece or North Africa. By early December the German offer had been accepted and airfields were allocated to the Luftwaffe. The first priority to the Germans was to neutralise Malta and the British Fleet, thereby safeguarding the sea lanes to Libya.

On the morning of **10 January**, accompanied by *Warspite* and *Valiant* and their escorts, *Illustrious* carried out a Swordfish bombing attack on an Italian convoy, while other Swordfish were undertaking anti-submarine patrols in pairs. Two sections of Fulmars totalling five aircraft were on patrol but the aircrew aboard ship were not entirely happy. Lt Vincent-Jones explained:

> *Illustrious* was stationed between the two battleships *Warspite* and *Valiant*. The Admiral may have had his reasons but we in *Illustrious* felt it would have been tactically sounder if the carrier had been detached to act independently and at speed some 20 to 30 miles to the southward of the main Fleet, thus keeping us further from the air threat in Sicily. The fighter CAP [Combat Air Patrol] could be maintained over the Fleet from a range of 20 miles with little greater difficulty than if the carrier were in company with the rest of the Fleet.

First off, at 10:15, was Red Section led by Lt Robert Henley (in 6F with Midshipman Cullen):

> Took-off from *Illustrious* in company with 6G (Sub-Lt Marshall and 6H (Sub-Lt Griffith). Proceeded to 15,000 feet for patrol. After several false alarms (friendly aircraft) we were directed, at 11:20, onto one SM79 at about 11,000 feet. Carried out a Section beam attack. Then attacked from astern and below until it burst into flames and dived in. Returned to patrol over Fleet with 6H and 6G, returned to land-on.

Meanwhile, Lt Henley and Sub-Lt Griffith continued their patrol, engaging two torpedo-armed SM79s from 279ª *Squadriglia* (flown by *Capitano* Orazi Bernadini and *Tenente* Angelo Caponetti) that came in very low, beneath the radar and made a courageous attack against *Illustrious*. Fortunately for the carrier the torpedoes missed; both torpedo-bombers were claimed damaged, as recalled by Henley:

> 12:10: Saw two SM79s making torpedo attack on Fleet. Dived after them and carried out stern attack about 5 miles from Fleet towards Linosa at a height of about 50 feet. Attack continued until ammunition was expended. Put starboard motor of leading SM79 out of action and silenced rear guns of both aircraft. Returned to Fleet to land-on but encountered barrage so sheared off. Carried out dummy attack on two Ju87s, which turned away and dived to sea level. Then proceeded to Malta as instructed by R/T and W/T. Landed 13:40.

Tenente Caponetti's aircraft eventually crashed at Trapani while attempting an emergency landing. Henley added:

> We landed at Hal Far with virtually no gas after 3 hours 40 minutes, which speaks well for the endurance of the Fulmar.

The other Fulmar section (White) on patrol—Sub-Lts Orr (6K with L/Air Paul Douet) and Gus Hogg (6Y with L/Air Arthur Oakes)—were also called down to give chase to the torpedo-bombers. A long stern chase followed but they were unable to close. By this time the Fulmars were more than 50 miles from the carrier and getting low on fuel. Stan Orr reported:

> Climbed to 15,000 feet. Directed to several false alarms. 12:10: Ship reported Fleet being attacked by torpedo-bombers. Sighted them closing the Fleet. When barrage opened up they turned away to westward towards Linosa. Unable to catch them by the time they reached this island. Observed an SM79, which had force-landed in a field—some troops were surrounding it. Opened-up on this SM79 and carried out ground strafing, repeatedly hitting the SM79 with tracer. Dived from 4,000 feet to sea level.[2]
>
> 12:20: Returning to ship, received order to resume patrol at full speed and climb. At 12:35 saw a large number (at least 20) Ju87s bombing Fleet with others above. Attacked Ju87s after they had pulled out from dive. First attack sent one spinning down into the sea. Attacked two others and caused them to lose height and disabled rear-gunners—consider it unlikely that either of them reached their base.

Gus Hogg in 6Y added:

> We took-off about 10:15 for a fighter patrol and spent the time chasing things. We chased two SM79s which Red Section were attacking. They made off to Linosa, which they reached before we got within range. At Linosa, we broke off and ground strafed one SM79 which had force-landed in a field—surrounded by a crowd of people. Light ground machine-gun fire encountered. Returned to Fleet climbing at full throttle. We came back in time to attack scores of Junkers

> 87s, which had just finished dropping bombs on *Illustrious.* Orr and I attacked about 20 Junkers and I believe I shot one down. However, one came up behind me and forced me to break off. Before breaking off, I noticed smoke pouring from the fuselage of my first target. My air gunner told me that this aircraft broke away and lost height. By this time, I got around onto the tail of the second Ju87 he was about half a mile away. I set a course for Malta due to lack of petrol and landed at 13:35 with about five gallons of petrol left.

At 12:35 four more Fulmars were scrambled just as the Ju87s commenced their attack but the fighters were unable to prevent the onslaught on the carrier. One of these was 6Q, flown by Lt Sewell, who reported:

> Took-off in company with 6C (Sub-Lt Roberts). Climbed up to 8,000 feet during which time I noted the ship being attacked by Ju87 dive-bombers. I counted 15 in the first wave and this was followed by two further waves, which appeared equal in size. These waves were peeling off from at least 10,000 feet. The air gunner confirmed that there were three distinct waves of about 12 aircraft per wave. I attacked one Ju87 at about 7,000 feet from the quarter, after it had pulled out from a dive and after a short burst it made a vertical dive to the sea. I then attacked another from the stern and followed it down to about 3,000 feet at about 15 miles from the Fleet, when I left it with a stream of liquid pouring from port wing root. The rear-gunner had ceased firing.

His TAG, L/Air Denis Tribe, added:

> We were at readiness on the flight deck and took-off before *Illustrious* was to wind. Before we were at 2,000 feet, the first bomb from a Ju87 hit the ship. It went into the open lift-well and exploded in the hangar—it was really horrific to watch as you realised how many would be blown to bits—also a very close escape. As we climbed to attack, the Stukas were diving to bomb. When we reached height, the air seemed full of aircraft. From the rear seat I saw one go down and another was damaged. It wasn't long before we were out of ammunition and landed at Hal Far.

Yellow 2, Sub-Lt Roberts, reported:

> Took-off in company with Lt Sewell (6Q). Unable to retract port wheel, while endeavouring to do this, observed the first wave of dive-bombers attacking the ship. Had climbed to 3,000 feet. I noticed some of these Ju87s making away to northward. Engaged one of these and saw it swerve, drop out of formation and continue down in a left-hand turn into the sea. Starboard wheel had come down

in this combat and with both wheels down speed and climb were very poor. Joined up with Lt Sewell and proceeded to Malta as ordered by R/T.

Even at this stage more Fulmars attempted to take-off but only Lts Barnes and Vincent-Jones in 6A succeeded:

There was no CAP overhead and there were only six serviceable Fulmars in the hangar, two of which were brought up on the after-lift. Barnes and I were leading the next section to take off and were on our way up to the bridge for briefing. I remember being told to get airborne as fast as possible as a huge formation was approaching from the northwards. There was no time for positioning us on the catapult and in any case the ship was steaming into wind so that we were free for a normal rolling take-off. As Barnes and I arrived at our Fulmar, it had just come up on the after-lift and was having its wings spread. As I leapt into the rear cockpit, I remember seeing what looked like a gigantic swarm of bees approaching from astern of the ship. There were in fact, well over 100 [*sic*] aircraft, the majority of which were Stukas.

One section was already airborne, but my own section was ranged on deck with our aircraft immediately behind the other aircraft in the section [this was Sub-Lt Jack Marshall and PO(A) Norman Tallack in 6G]. His engine refused to start and I recall standing up in the cockpit and waving at the flight deck party to drag him over to the starboard side of the deck, out of the way. By now the swarm was very close and beginning to fan out before starting to dive-bomb and there was no doubt which ship was to be the target. Barnes opened his throttle and we swerved round our unfortunate section-mate. Soon we were away down the deck and starting to climb off the bow of the ship. When we had reached a few hundred feet we found ourselves surrounded by Ju87s as they were pulling out of their dives and some of them were very close, one hundred yards or so and I could see clearly the rear-gunners firing at us. Two bullets went through my plotting board and others lodged in my seat. I looked down and saw the poor *Illustrious* passing through huge columns of water, her guns blazing and a fire and smoke coming from the after-end of the flight deck.

In his official report, Lt Barnes wrote:

12:35: Took-off with 6Z in company. HA guns opened fire immediately we left the deck. When at about 1,000 feet observed ship being heavily attacked by dive-bombers (Ju87s) which pulled out at about 1,000 feet. Chased two of these as they pulled out and they separated. Sub-Lt Lowe (6Z) attacked one while we attacked the other; the latter pulled up in a steep zoom and I was able to get in a short burst before my aircraft stalled. The enemy rear-gunner opened fire,

> obtaining one hit from above through hydraulic pipes in the rear cockpit. After this, we did not see this enemy aircraft again. Climbed to 6,000 feet and observed a single Ju87 slightly above us over convoy. Pursued it and as we approached it jettisoned its bomb and turned to northward. Got in long bursts astern—the first put the rear-gunner out of action and subsequent bursts caused it to go down in a shallow dive into the sea, the pilot having been hit. Ammunition being expended, we made for Malta landing at about 13:45.

Meanwhile, Sub-Lt Lowe in 6Z was not so fortunate; he annotated his logbook:

> Shot down in the sea 60 miles south-west of Malta during dive-bombing attack on *Illustrious*. N/A Kensett killed, self-wounded.

From his hospital bed, Lowe was able to dictate an official report:

> Took-off in company with 6A and was last seen engaging one of a pair of Ju87s. The enemy rear-gunner hit the water cooler of 6Z but was then shot down by Sub-Lt Lowe and seen to crash into the sea. At the same time another Ju87 got on his tail wounding Sub-Lt Lowe in the shoulder and killing L/Air Kensett. Sub-Lt Lowe immediately broke away but at the same time his engine stopped and he made a forced landing into the sea. Sub-Lt Lowe cleared himself with difficulty and went to the rear cockpit and found his air gunner under water and obviously dead. He was unable to release him before the machine sank. Sub-Lt Lowe was picked up after about 20 minutes by HMS *Jaguar*.[3]

Close to the action aboard *Illustrious* was a *Reuters* correspondent:

> Three Ju87s approached out of the clouds. Simultaneously the guns of all the British ships opened-up a terrific barrage. More planes swooped down. The sky was filled with a confused mass of bursting shells and twisting planes. The noise was appalling. As the leading plane dived through the inferno, I watched a single 1,000 lb bomb hurtle towards us. It fell in the sea slightly astern. Then a wave of 15 bombers dived on the fleet. My attention was divided between watching these and watching our own fighters taking off from the flight deck. A few seconds after our last machine had flown off, a tremendous explosion shook the ship. A 1,000 lb bomb released by one of the Junkers diving very low had scored a direct hit. The next moment the wing of a German plane fell across the after-lift. The hit was apparently immediately below the bridge. I have a vivid impression of a sudden sheet of flame and choking smoke. I felt a severe blow on my shoulder from the blast and then I was pulled into the wireless cabin and thrown on the floor. We lay coughing and listening to the sudden roar of aeroplane engines close overhead.

Another witness recalled:

> Through the flames and smoke shooting up from the after-lift they saw a stoker petty officer staggering under the weight of an officer's body. S2 pom-pom was a blackened, twisted wreck ... all that remained was a heap of smouldering clothes and a leg in a sea-boot. Men at S1 pom-pom were removing the remains of their oppos. In the middle of the flight deck lay the torso of a man. Captain Boyd noticed it from the bridge, caught the eye of the chief bosun's mate and nodded. The petty officer picked up the bloody object and heaved it overboard.[4]

The *Reuters* correspondent continued:

> The diving planes swooped so low that they sounded as though they were landing on the flight deck. Near misses sent shudder after shudder through the ship. The German bombers converged from all sides and then dived one after another in the face of blazing gunfire. They held their bombs until the last minute, then swerved quickly off. After what seemed an eternity, gunfire ceased. We opened the door. Splintered and riddled steel pipes and wires lay where we had been standing a few minutes before. The deck was covered with foam from the fire extinguishers. The flight deck was covered from end to end with debris from the bomb explosion. Further forward was a twisted crane, a heap of bomb splinters and empty shell cases. Through all the action the gun crews never ceased for a moment. Every man moved with precision. Spaces below decks, including the church, were cleared for casualty stations. Wounded were tended as fast as possible.

Admiral Cunningham, aboard *Warspite*, witnessed the assault with grudging admiration:

> There was no doubt that we were watching complete experts. Formed roughly in a large circle over the Fleet, they peeled of one by one when reaching the attacking position. We could not but admire the skill and precision of it all. The attacks were pressed home to point-blank range and as they pulled out of their dives, some were seen to fly along the flight deck of *Illustrious*, below the level of her funnel... at times she became almost completely hidden in a forest of great bomb splashes.

About a dozen of the Stukas targeted *Warspite* and *Valiant*, which flanked *Illustrious*. Admiral Cunningham's flagship was hit by one bomb that did not explode. The Admiral later commented:

> One of the staff officers who watched it hurtling over the bridge from astern told me it looked about the size of the wardroom sofa. One was too interested

> in this new form of dive-bombing attack really to be frightened. We opened-up with every AA gun we had as one by one the Stukas peeled off into their dives, concentrating almost the whole venom of their attack upon *Illustrious.*

The Stukas, from II./StG.2 led by Major Walter Enneccerus, had indeed pounded the carrier, diving from 12,000 feet down to 2,000 feet in a copy-book attack. All told, six bombs hit *Illustrious* (see Appendix IV) wrecking the armoured flight deck, destroying nine Swordfish and five Fulmars and putting half the guns out of action; casualties were heavy. Captain Boyd pulled her out of line. He was ordered to make for Malta but it would be three hours before she was able to proceed, steering by main engines as her steering gear had been put out of order. Meanwhile, Lt Barnes' Fulmar was climbing to engage, as Lt Vincent-Jones continued:

> Barnes had no shortage of close-range targets, he had in fact too many and contented himself with pumping bursts into Stuka after Stuka, as they came through his sights—and there was no question of not being able to see the whites of their eyes! I had a cine camera with me and having nothing better to do, apart from being a terrified spectator, I thought this might be a heaven-sent opportunity to 'shoot' a classic film of the wounded *Illustrious* and her assailants, which would make my fortune after the war. In the middle of my first 'take' a bullet tore into the canopy alongside me and I dropped the camera. Thereafter my thoughts of commercialism evaporated and I lost all interest in photography.
>
> From my rear seat I found it was difficult to see what was going on up front but I saw one Stuka go down with smoke pouring out of its engine. Despite their slow speed Stukas did not respond easily to .303 bullets as they bounced off a sheet of armour fitted at the rear of the back seat to protect the air gunners. The next thing I remember was Bill Barnes telling me we were out of ammo.
>
> Shortly afterwards I received my first message from the ship, although looking down at her, with smoke and flames pouring out of the length of her hull, I marvelled that anyone was alive to press a Morse-key. She was however, still manoeuvring at high speed. The message read 'All Fulmars proceed to Hal Far to refuel and rearm before returning over ship at best speed'. I gave Bill a course to steer and within 20 minutes we passed over the perimeter of Hal Far airfield with our undercarriage down. We were greeted by a burst from one of the Maltese Bofors but luckily this missed astern and we were soon taxiing in towards the control tower. Here we found the other four Fulmars who had landed just before us, after returning from the chase of the SM79s. They were being refuelled and rearmed and we soon joined them.

Damage to 6A was reported as (a) two gravity feed pipes shot away in rear cockpit; (b) bullet through port aileron.

Not only were Fulmars up and amongst the attacking Ju87s but the vulnerable Swordfish flown by Lt Charles Lamb of 815 Squadron, who had been about to land from an anti-submarine patrol when the attack began:

> At 12:30, I was in the waiting position over the port quarter of *Illustrious*, watching her turn into the wind. She flew off the Swordfish for the anti-submarine patrols and a gaggle of Fulmars. Breaking a little more to port I straightened up to approach the round-down of the flight deck, on my up-wind leg and saw that the after-lift was down. It would be up by the time I got there, or Haggis [Lt-Cdr Russell, the Deck Landing Control Officer] would wave me round again. Then a strange aircraft came into view, flying from port to starboard, right in front of me, across the flight-deck. Its huge swastika was painted red on the starboard side of the grey fuselage. As I pressed the trigger of my Vickers gun, the Stuka was right ahead in my sights but it dipped as though in salute and dropped an enormous great bomb right down the after-lift well, which was still gaping. The bomb looked like a GPO pillar-box, painted black. By the flames which shot out of the hole in the deck I realised that it had rolled off the lift and exploded in the hangar. Then the lift itself burst out of the deck, all three hundred tons of it and shot a few feet into the air and sunk back into the lift well on its side, like a giant wedge-shaped hunk of cheese. The first Stuka was followed by another, flying right through the barrage, dipping down low over the flight-deck and then soaring past the funnel and with my right thumb pressed on the trigger of the gun I opened the throttle wide and jinked to starboard and went around again.
>
> From the moment I opened the throttle and climbed to starboard I was amongst the Stukas—without the option—and although they were travelling at lightning speed, their spectacle of a sitting duck, spitting fire from both ends, was too provoking for the Germans and some of them paused for a pot-shot before speeding back to Sicily; a quick climbing turn, a half roll and a short dive—and they expected to find me sitting in their sights waiting to be shot down. Staggering along at about a hundred feet above the sea but well out to starboard of the ship, to avoid them I had to spin the aircraft like a top, in tight little circles at the point of stall, so that the fuselage and wings were hanging sideways from the propeller. In heaven-sent intervals between attacks, only by easing the stick forward and kicking on opposite rudder did I manage to stay in the air. The throttle was at maximum setting all the time and I had my thumb pressed on the firing button almost continuously, yet after the fourth attack I found that I was only a few hundred yards ahead of the ship's position, though a mile away to starboard. Our progress over the water had been minimal and the Stukas must have thought they were attacking some weird sort of hovering flying bedstead which could spin round within its own wing-span. There was no time to speak to either of the two in the rear cockpit but through the back of my head I could feel them firing the Lewis gun and was surprised that they weren't blacking out in those ghastly tight turns.[5]

Lt Lamb realised that it was now essential to retreat from the combat zone:

> I was receiving more punishment than I was dishing out; sprays of bullet holes and great gashes in the wings were appearing everywhere and one line of bullets which had started at the trailing edge of my starboard lower mainplane, had ended by shooting away the red handle of the locking-pin which kept the wings from folding and at that moment I expected the starboard wings to fold but it must have been only the handle that was shot away. The wings remained locked in the spread position—thank God!
>
> In a lull between these desperate turns I managed a quick look upwards to see where all the Stukas were coming from and saw several clusters in tight formation, circling very high in the sky, like wasps awaiting their turn to dive on a pot of jam. I saw them peeling off, one by one; tiny objects, their wings glinting in the sun. They rolled away from the formation slowly—almost casually—as though they were taking part in some air display and had all the time in the world. As each silvery dot sped downwards, it grew bigger with every fraction of a second and its dive became steeper until it was a huge blob of an aeroplane with a swastika on its side, diving vertically through the ship's barrage. Their flying was very skilled and they pressed home their attacks with no thought for their own safety.
>
> The difference between the Germans' method and those of the Italians could never have been demonstrated more clearly. They had only one bomb per aircraft, so they had to come right down to deliver it personally. Since it was enormous—it weighed 500kg—their determination not to waste their one big egg was understandable. They began their pull-out at about 5,000 feet, when they had built up their speed to the maximum, from a 10,000-foot start and they released their bomb while still diving, at about 500 feet, so that it followed after them with sickening accuracy. The Stuka was an ugly aircraft to look at but it was damned good at its job.
>
> Flying around the fore-end of the flight deck, feeling immeasurably sad at the sight of the running battle, I saw dozens of men rushing about the flight deck with hoses. Around them the 735-foot length and the 93-foot breadth of iron deck was a mass of steam; the heat from the hangar below immediately turned water into vapour as soon as it touched the hot steel beneath their scorched feet. But all the ship's guns were blazing away and I was in danger of being shot down by them and in any case I was probably in their way. I felt as though I was deserting my home and the people I loved when they were in peril but there was nothing to be gained by staying, so I turned to the north-east in the vague direction of Malta and concentrated on trying to keep the aircraft stable.[6]

Lt Lamb's aircraft was severely damaged while his two crewmen were up to their knees in petrol, which was pouring out where the tank had been holed.

Lamb decided to ditch the aircraft before it fell apart or went up in flames and brought the Swordfish down near the destroyer *Juno*, from which a whaler rowed to pick up the three airmen, who had climbed into a rubber dinghy. When they were picked up and the aircraft started to sink, Lamb took over from the coxswain of the dinghy and started shouting: 'Come on, row, you silly buggers … in … out … in … out …' He knew the sinking aircraft still carried its depth-charge which would explode at a certain depth and kill everybody unless they were able to climb into the scrambling net over the destroyer's side in double quick time.

On Malta, the first most personnel knew of the attack was when the first four Fulmars arrived at Hal Far, soon followed by two others. Lt Vincent-Jones continued:

> Refuelling and rearming, in particular, took much longer than usual as the ground crews at Hal Far were not familiar with Fulmars, neither did they have the right loading equipment. We waited with growing impatience as the fumbling went on and we heard reports of another big wave of enemy aircraft passing near Malta on its way to the Fleet.

As soon as the Stukas returned to Sicily refuelling and rearming took place as quickly as possible to allow a second strike to be made. Meanwhile, seven SM79s carried out a high-level attack but their bombs fell wide in the face of heavy AA fire. Three Ju87s of 236ª *Squadriglia*, led by *Tenente* Malvezzi, made a small contribution to the assault, one pilot claiming a hit on the carrier, before thirteen II./StG.2 Ju87s, with an escort of five Bf110s, returned to the affray at 17:15, diving into the intense ship's barrage to hit her once more. It was whilst returning from this attack that the dive-bombers were again engaged by the Fulmars. Lt Barnes reported:

> 16:50: Took-off from Hal Far in 6F with 6K (Sub-Lt Orr) and 6C (Sub-Lt Roberts). Controlled by W/T from *Valiant*. Immediately after crossing coast ran into eight or nine Ju87s steering north after having attacked Battle Fleet. Got in astern attack on one of these, putting rear-gunner out of action. My reflector sight went out during this attack, so I broke off to renew bulb. Reformed the section and remained in the air until 18:20, being controlled by *Valiant*. Did not encounter further enemy aircraft.

Lt Vincent-Jones, in the back seat of 6F, added:

> After an hour or so six Fulmars were ready, and Barnes and I got airborne with five others in company. We soon sighted *Illustrious* on her way towards Grand

> Harbour with smoke pouring out of her but still making a good 20 knots. She had parted company with the rest of the Fleet. We were not in time to intercept before the attack developed but we caught up with the enemy on their way back to Sicily. Again, there was no shortage of targets but instead of being in the middle of them, this time it devolved into a stern chase and we came in for a lot of well-directed cross fire from the enemy rear-gunners. We saw at least two Stukas drop out of formation but didn't have time to follow them down, moving as we did onto new targets. Ammunition expended, we returned to Hal Far and as we flew in over the coastline, I got a glimpse of poor old *Illustrious* rounding the point only a few miles from the entrance to the Grand Harbour of Valletta. Smoke was still pouring out of her hull.

His pilot, Lt Barnes, simply reported:

> I noticed some of these Ju87s making away to northward. Engaged one of these and saw it swerve, drop out of formation and continue down in a left-hand turn into the sea.

Despite the damage to his aircraft—two bullet holes in airscrew, one in hydraulic system, one explosive bullet in starboard tail root, one non-explosive in port tailplane elevator—Lt Jackie Sewell was also off again, as he later wrote:

> Almost immediately after crossing the coast encountered about seven Ju87s making away to the northward, having dropped their bombs. Attacked the left-hand aircraft of the formation. Two others dropped behind and came in on my tail. On completing the first attack, turned to attack one of the two who had dropped back. Registered large number of hits on his fuselage, which caused his rear-gunner to cease firing. Did not notice other damage. He continued away to northward.

Another to take to the air was Sub-Lt Roberts:

> Took-off with Lt Barnes and Sub-Lt Orr and proceeded southwards towards the Fleet. Almost immediately after crossing the coast, encountered about seven Ju87s making away to the northward, having dropped their bombs. Attacked the left-hand aircraft of the formation, two others dropped behind and came in on my tail. On completing the first attack, turned to attack one of the two who had dropped back. Registered large number of hits on his fuselage, which caused his rear-gunner to cease firing. Did not notice other damage. He continued away to northward. Climbed to 12,000 feet and patrolled until dark when the section returned to Hal Far.

Sub-Lt Orr experienced bad visibility but was still able to engage the Ju87s:

> 16:50: Took-off in company with 6F and 6C. Attacked formation of Ju87s (at least eight) immediately we passed over the coast. They were proceeding northward after having attacked the Fleet. Engaged in dogfight with these and definitely damaged two but did not see what happened to them in the bad visibility. Landed at Hal Far at 18:30.

As a result of the desperate action to protect *Illustrious*, 806 Squadron pilots were credited with the two SM79s shot down in the late morning and five Ju87s destroyed, two probables and others damaged, during the attacks on *Illustrious*. The ship's gunners were credited with bringing down a further three Stukas, with four more damaged. A flight of 261 Squadron Hurricanes from Malta had attempted to join the Fulmars but, as the Hurricane leader Flt Lt Jay MacLachlan commented:

> When at around 17,000 feet the Hurricanes were fired upon by *Illustrious*' pom-poms and 4.5s, some of which burst close by. If the Navy weren't so easy on the trigger, we might give them some sort of protection but they fire on us as soon as we fly within their range.[7]

Although the official war history mentions that the German figure for their losses on this date was six aircraft destroyed and one damaged, a study of the records lists only three Ju87s actually lost: Knights' Cross holder Ltn Gerhard Grenzel and his gunner in A5+DK of 2./StG.1; Uffz Karl Jagerman and gunner of 3./StG.1 in A5+LL and Ltn Helmut Leesch and gunner of 5./StG.2 in T6+DN. One further aircraft of 4./StG.2 crash-landed at Castelventrano with damage sustained from fighter attack.

Illustrious finally docked at 21:00 with 126 dead and 91 wounded aboard. Amongst the dead were the Fulmar crew whose aircraft (6G) had been hit at the start of the raid, Sub-Lt Jack Marshall and PO(A) Norman Tallack; Sub-Lt Henry Louden had also been killed (he had only arrived from Aboukir three days earlier), as had observer PO(A) John Bushell, while Sub-Lt Bill Clisby was seriously injured. Also killed was TAG L/Air Harry Fitzherbert. Nine members of 806 Squadron's non-flying personnel had also been killed including six RAF NCOs.[8] Of their flying personnel, 815 and 819 Squadrons lost eight dead and two seriously injured—most of whom had taken part in the Taranto raid. During the next few days the carrier's dead would be buried at sea from the minesweeper *Fermoy*, while many of the wounded were taken to Bighi Hospital by ambulance and others went to Mtarfa Hospital. Having been driven down to the dock, Lt Vincent-Jones reported to Captain Boyd:

> I was taken up to the Captain's cabin where I found Denis Boyd, sitting at his desk and I shall never forget the smile on his face as he said: 'Well, we finally made it. Have a gin. Now tell me what your boys have been up to.' I gave him a very brief account of our day, as he was clearly in the last stages of exhaustion and hurried off to see what I could find in the hangar. Barnes had already contacted the senior Flight Sergeant, who was fortunately still in one piece and told him to round up a nucleus of ground crews from the 50 or so survivors, together with essential equipment and stores to maintain the seven remaining Fulmars [in addition to Marshall's aircraft, four more had been destroyed in the hangar] and that we'd come and collect them the following morning with transport from Hal Far, which was to be our base for the next three or four weeks. There was no shortage of volunteers as little doubt existed that the ship would be the main target of the Luftwaffe as long as she remained in harbour.

Lt Vincent-Jones was informed that …

> The first 500-kilo bomb had scored a direct hit on the Fulmar which had failed to start—no sign of it or its crew [Marshall and Tallack] was ever seen again. The bomb went on down the after-lift well and exploded in the hangar deck killing about 30 of the maintenance crews including those of 806 Squadron who had been allocated the after end of the hangar. The blast went through the hangar and buckled the foremost lift, thus putting an end to any further chance of flying off other aircraft.

On his return to dry land, 815 Squadron's Lt Charles Lamb also visited *Illustrious*, seeking news of his friends:

> One RAF officer who had come with us as an interested spectator was unable to take any further interest; sitting in the anteroom, with all that hullabaloo going on outside, he must have thought himself reasonably secure from danger. Later, he was found sitting in a scorched armchair, headless but still clutching an open copy of *The Times* in both hands. The wardroom stanchions of tubular steel, about as thick as the average lamp-post, were twisted into spirals like ornamental candles, yet the wardroom clock was still ticking away, keeping accurate time. The effect of blast is always incalculable. It can kill a man yet only rustle the flowers in a vase. Worse things were happening in the hangar—some of them indescribable. Men lying with their brains spilling onto the deck were common-place. When the first bomb exploded after bouncing off the lift, all the metal fire-screen curtains were down, dividing the hangar into three separate fire-proof compartments. When subjected to a blast, which was capable of bending a 300-ton lift, they were useless and disintegrated at once, bursting apart in masses of red-hot steel

splinters about three or four feet long, which tore through every obstruction, setting all the aircraft on fire which weren't already burning as a result of the explosion itself and decapitating anyone standing in the way.

Poor [Lt] Neil Kemp was killed by one of them immediately. He had been standing in the centre of the hangar talking to [Lt-Cdr] Jackie Jago when the first sudden explosion occurred. Jackie found himself facing a headless body, which was all that was left of a fine chap who would have made a wonderful admiral had he lived. Even in death Neil refused to lie down, until Jackie gave his grim remains a little push. After the first attack, few of the ship's decks were recognizable and below the flight-deck there was just a gaping shell with dead bodies plastered against the bulkheads wherever one looked.[9]

Another of Lamb's colleagues, 815 Squadron pilot Lt George *Grubby* Going was on deck when the attack commenced. Finding that the officer in charge of the damage control party had been killed, he at once took over and he and his party worked feverishly for three and a half hours, putting out fires and opening compartment after compartment looking for the dead and wounded, as flames illuminated the water and cascaded down the lift-well making a terrible and eerie spectacle. When the fires were under control Going ordered everybody out and was just about to leave behind them when a bomb exploded in the lift-well, killing or grievously wounding everyone in the wardroom. Going was taken to hospital in Malta and was found to be so badly wounded that his right leg had to be amputated above the knee.[10]

That night, as *Illustrious* docked, an effort was made by Malta to hit back, six of the resident 830 Squadron's Swordfish bombing the port of Palermo, Sicily, where reconnaissance aircraft had reported a cruiser and other warships. Ten Swordfish departed Hal Far but four returned early with various problems. The remaining six dropped their bombs over the target area but failed to achieve any success. Next day Gus Hogg wrote:

Last night I went down to the ship and it is a terrific shamble. Marshall and Louden have been killed and Bill Clisby badly hurt. The ship will have to go into dock for about six months. We spent the day organising fighter patrols and getting settled in. In the evening I went to the ship and salved a certain amount of kit. My camera, photographs and diaries are alright. A lot of my clothes are written off. At Hal Far, I am sharing a room with Jackie.

Apart from the newly-arrived Fulmars,[11] Malta's strength at this moment in time to face the onslaught that all knew must now surely come, stood at fourteen RAF Hurricanes, some of which were not serviceable, plus a further twelve crated machines only just arrived by sea, which would take some days to offload and erect. But the feared attacks did not come immediately. Following five days of idly standing by their aircraft ready to scramble, the Hurricane and Fulmar pilots were again in action when the Luftwaffe eventually returned to the island on **16 January**, having been reinforced by the arrival of more Ju87s from I./StG.1 that had flown in to Trapani [Sicily] from France. These were commanded by Hptm Paul-Werner Hozzel.

At about 14:00, two large formations approached Malta from the north and east, comprising 17 Ju88s escorted by Bf110s and a total of 44 Ju87s from both *Gruppen*, in five waves escorted by ten MC200s and ten CR42s. From the ground the sight of the approaching raid was awesome:

> It was 1.55pm when the alarm sounded. The Stukas came in waves. More and more flew into sight. And as they drew into range the Malta barrage was heard in all its strength for the first time in history. The heavies from the forts opened-up with a reverberating roar. The guns round the Harbour area joined in with tremendous emphasis. The Navy's guns transformed the uproar into a stunning crescendo of sound. Through the symphony of gunfire could be heard the menacing drone of the Junkers as they raced towards their objective. The crash and clamour of the barrage was sharpened by a new note as the leading Stukas dipped their noses towards Parlatorio Wharf and dived into the maelstrom of steel, flame and smoke. With the whine of the dive ... came the accompanying rush of the bombs as the Germans released them from their racks in the direction of *Illustrious,* now hardly visible behind a pall of smoke and spouting columns of water.
>
> The entire island rocked to the shock of the battle. The thud of the heavy stuff which the Junkers were dropping, the roar of the bombs as they exploded and the rumbling crash of falling masonry as Senglea and Vittoriosa caught the weight of the enemy's attack, completed an unforgettable sound-picture. The Stukas followed their squadron leaders in the screaming plunge into the inferno that was raging over the Creek. Some of them did not emerge. Hardly one came out unscathed. The defenders were just as tough as the attackers. It required nerve to stick to your guns with those thousand-pounders thudding and bursting around you, with those screaming furies diving over you. In spite of this danger, people looked on fascinated, watching the suicide tactics of the Germans. Others, in their shelters, rocked and swayed and wondered if this was the end of it all.[12]

The Stuka leader commented:

> But now we got strict orders to do our best to make this ship sink. We went to Catania air station and there loaded 1,000 kg bombs. With these bombs under the belly we needed about one-and-half hours to reach an altitude of 3,000m [10,000 feet]. Four of these bombs we succeeded in dropping on the deck of *Illustrious* but

> she did not sink, for our bombs were not able to penetrate the armoured decks below and because of numerous bulkheads.[13]

Two large bombs fell between *Illustrious* and nearby HMAS *Perth*. One bomb passed between the cruiser and the wharf. The detonation lifted the cruiser's stern and buried her bow underwater. The blast bent propeller shafts, burst oil bunkers and knocked X and Y turrets off their roller bearings. Her Gunnery Officer wrote:[14]

> I pressed the action alarm signal and we went to full Action Stations. So, did the carrier and the little submarine. I was smoking my new pipe. Breaking it in. The army and Maltese defences opened fire. The bursts were out to sea but just visible above the rooftops of the houses, behind the dockyard crane and chimney stacks. The barrage increased in ferocity. Hundreds of shell bursts were dotting the sky—tracer from the 40 mm Bofors now criss-crossed the sky, the shells later exploding above 4,000 feet. That meant the enemy were coming in low. *Illustrious* opposite, suddenly opened fire with every gun she had—4.5-inch and 40 mm—right through our wireless aerials. She, with four higher decks, had seen them. Our wireless aerials came down, shot away by the carrier. Then we saw them. I counted four groups of five aircraft. Twenty Stukas with a high fighter cover of Me109s [*sic*], came weaving in over the rooftops kicking rudder bars right and left to put off our aim. Then we opened fire. The din was terrific. *Illustrious*' red tracer just clear of our masts. I turned to see the little submarine in dock. Sluice gates open—water flooding around her for some protection. Submarine captain and gun crew all exposed waiting for the ship to be floating so they too could fire their one 4-inch gun. Their twin Lewis guns were in action. The mad barrage increased, *Illustrious* fighting desperately to ward off these vicious dives. All ships were sitting duck targets. Then the bombs rained down. The shorts in the dockyard. Overs in the water. Enormous crumps, crashes and vibrations. Water spouts in Dockyard Creek. Blast waves. Debris. More targets coming in. God, how they could fly. I saw one come down in flames and blow up on hitting the ground but they came on and on.

Five Fulmars and four Hurricanes were scrambled at 14:55, Lts Bill Barnes and Jackie Sewell making up one section, with Sub-Lts Orr, Hogg and John Roberts the other. Gus Hogg (with L/Air Bob Roberts in the back seat of 6Y) had a busy and successful day:

> I went up with Stanley Orr and Roberts and attacked some Ju88s. I shot down two, landed for ammo, went up again but saw nothing.

Sub-Lt Orr (with Jimmy Beach in the back) also claimed a Ju88 and Sub-Lt John Roberts (6C) probably another. Meanwhile, Lt Barnes also claimed a Ju88 and a second as a probable, while Lt Sewell (6K) added a Ju87 and possibly two more as probably destroyed. It was recorded that one of the Fulmar pilots—presumably Sewell—followed a Ju87 through the AA barrage as the aircraft dropped its bombs and tried to get away at very low level through the harbour entrance. It was so low that it had to rise to clear a breakwater, wobbling badly as it did so; this gave the pursuing Fulmar time to catch it and open fire, sending it into the sea. Landing, the pilot later sent a message to the AA command stating that he did not think much of the accuracy of the guns' fire, which had missed the bomber and badly damaged his own aircraft! The army gunners received credit for three bombers of each type damaged but the Hurricanes, meantime, had been directed to the wrong area.

II./LG1 had taken the brunt of the fighters' attack, one aircraft (L1+CT) flown by Oblt Kurt Pichler, failed to return; three more—from the *Stab* (HQ Flight), 5. and 6.*Staffeln*—all crash-landed at Catania due to damage; a fifth bomber, from 8.*Staffel* and flown by Oblt Theodor Hagen, forced-landed at Pozzallo as a result of damage caused by anti-aircraft fire. Four members of the crews aboard these aircraft had suffered wounds, some serious and all four of the damaged aircraft were deemed beyond repair.[15]

During the attacks, dock installations and nearby houses suffered severe damage. The bombing on this date was like nothing the inhabitants of Malta had experienced before and during the previous seven months of war. Thirteen-year-old Philip Vella[16] recalled:

> During the raid I was at home in Valletta. When it became clear that this was no ordinary attack, my mother told me and my sister Doris to run for it and take cover in the crypt of a nearby church; there were no rock shelters in the vicinity. It is difficult to describe the din; it sounded as if hell had been let loose. The noise of exploding bombs, flak of all calibres and the screeching wail of the diving Stukas was so scaring that people just stood where they were and froze. Suddenly we heard a terrific explosion; a row of houses two blocks away was flattened, some said by an aerial torpedo and others mentioned two bombs chained together. At that stage people panicked as they realised that the only shelter we had above our heads was a big empty dome. I do not remember how long the attack lasted but it certainly seemed a long time. Our experience was insignificant compared to what people at Senglea went through—Willi Mizzi and 11 others were trapped for 48 hours under 40 feet of rubble.

Young Joseph Attard, in Cospicua on an errand for his father, had stopped to look at the stricken *Illustrious* when the air raid alert sounded. He watched as the dockyard workers ran for shelter, fascinated by the prospect of a German air raid:

> There seemed to be more than a hundred of them … the noise was so shattering that even from that height it felt as if it was going to rupture my ear drums. I stood where I was, intent on the straight-moving formations, as I had never seen anything like it and I was wondering how long those planes could endure the steel and explosive that was going up at them… First one, then the rest of the Stukas one at a time peeled off from the formations and dived straight onto the Dockyard below… a noise broke in from the guns which began firing to meet them half way. It takes a brave heart to dive from an inferno such as they had been in, straight into another one. But the Stukas did not falter and kept to their dive notwithstanding the one or two that were hit and exploded in mid-air. When they were past the second barrage of murderous fire, they went straight into the third barrage put up by the Bofors and pom-poms. But after that there was the whistling of bombs and whining planes pulled out of the dives, followed by tremendous explosions.[17]

When the debris was removed and bodies recovered, the final toll for the day's raids amounted to 53 killed and 36 injured, four of whom later died. There followed an anti-climactic day (**17 January**) when the anticipated follow-up onslaught failed to materialise, allowing both sides a brief respite. The dive-bombers returned in force on the afternoon of **18 January**, when the airfields at Hal Far and Luqa were targeted by more than 50 Ju87s from both I./StG.1 and II./StG.2 in an obvious attempt to cripple the fighter defences before further efforts were made to finish off *Illustrious*. As a result of these attacks, Luqa was for a time put out of action:

> 14:15 Air Raid Alarm sounded: a large number of dive-bombers appeared from the south-east and dive-bombed Hal Far; these planes flattened out over Luqa and were engaged by the ground defences. Several hits were claimed. Three Swordfish were destroyed at Hal Far and hangars were hit. The enemy planes left the island flying very low. A few minutes after these planes had left, a much larger number appeared and dive-bombed Luqa aerodrome. Four direct hits were made on hangars and one Wellington was destroyed by fire. Numerous hits were made on the main runway.[18]

Five Hurricanes and three Fulmars had been scrambled as the raid came in and in a series of swirling actions claimed seven Ju87s shot down and others damaged, mainly by the Hurricane pilots, although Lt Robert Henley (in 6F with N/Air Alf Rush) believed he got one before being shot down by another:

> I recall a fairly massive raid of Ju87s and Ju88s, with all available fighters scrambled—some four Fulmars—and we just graunced around, uncontrolled, shooting at anything which took our fancy/came within range. The poor old Fulmar had problems gaining height and in gaining speed against the Ju88s.

Nonetheless, he claimed a Ju88 shot down in flames and a second damaged, before claiming a Ju87 probably destroyed and a second damaged:

> My aircraft was hit—I think, of all degrading things, by a Ju87—which stopped the engine some miles east-south-east of Hal Far and I decided to glide as close to Malta as possible because (a) my TAG N/Air Rush told me, at this point, that he couldn't swim and (b) there seemed to be so many aircraft about and such chaos reigning that I doubted that two little parachutes five-ten miles out to sea would be noticed, much less noted as British, by the ASR boys who were already having to face something of a racket—and so we ditched some one mile off Kalafrana. A very brave Maltese AA gunner, who saw us go in, jumped into the sea and swam off to help us and arrived even before the ASR launch. Alas, I was never able to thank him.

Their saviour was Sapper Spiro Zammit, who was consequently awarded the British Empire Medal for his action. A second Fulmar (6H) also failed to return with the loss of recent arrival Sub-Lt Stephen Griffith. He may have accounted for one of the escorting MC200s of 6° *Gruppo* before his own demise, in which *Marescello* Persani was killed. Gus Hogg recorded:

> Henley and co [company] attacked a crowd of 87s. Shears landed all right, Henley landed in the drink and was packed up. Griffith is missing.

Despite the many claims for Ju87s shot down, only one failed to return although others were undoubtedly damaged. However, a Ju88 of III./LG1 that failed to return may have been Lt Henley's victim. L1+ER was forced to ditch although upon rescue Ltn Horst Dunkel reported that he thought his aircraft had been attacked by a Hurricane.

The first assault on the morning of **19 January** came in at about 08:30 and comprised an estimated 40 Ju87s and Ju88s, against which six Hurricanes and the single operational Fulmar were scrambled, the latter flown by Lt Bill Barnes. One of 830 Squadron's TAGs, Naval Airman Nat Gold was a witness:

> Driven by a furious need for revenge Barnes took-off alone in his Fulmar, without an observer or TAG and climbed high over Grand Harbour. Circling, he waited for the German bombers to dive, then followed straight through the box barrage of flak

> bursting from below. As the Stuka released his bomb and began to pull out of his dive, Barnes picked him off. Shortly after, he returned to Hal Far to rearm. While the armourers were busy preparing his Fulmar again, Barnes paced up and down, drawing deeply on a cigarette. As soon as his plane was ready, he sprang back into the cockpit and took-off again. Once more, I watched him circle above the harbour then dive through the hail of shrapnel after a Stuka and again pick off the plane. It was one of the bravest things I'd ever seen. How he got away with it, God only knows.[19]

When the first afternoon raid approached, at 12:55, the mixed bag of fighters were led off by 261 Squadron's Plt Off Jock Barber:

> I led what aircraft we had—six Hurricanes, one Fulmar and one Gladiator. This was quite amazing. We intercepted the bombers, which were Ju88s and Ju87s escorted by various fighters, right over Grand Harbour. They started the dives, with the 87s going down vertically and the 88s pretty steeply and we did the same thing—right through the barrage. Why none of us got hit by ack-ack, I'll never know. It was a pretty ding-dong battle that developed right down to sea level and various individual fights broke out.[20]

Gus Hogg was flying the Fulmar:

> At one fifteen [13:15] I took-off in the Fulmar and found scores of Ju88s all round. I attacked a formation of three. Two went down in flames, one went down on fire but did not go in. I attacked three more with no results.

It is not recorded as to who was flying the Gladiator (probably N5524 flown by a RAF pilot), nor is it clear whether Gus claimed all three Ju88s or just two. Total claims for the day by the defenders included nine Ju87s, eight Ju88s, one CR42 and the Z.506B, of which the guns optimistically claimed six of the Ju88s. One Hurricane and its pilot was lost and four more returned damaged.

Luftwaffe losses included three Ju87Rs, two of I./StG1 (Uffz Rudolf Vater of 1.*Staffel* and Obfw Kurt Zube of 2.*Staffel* and their gunners, in A5+EK and A5+BK respectively) and one aircraft of II./StG2 (T6+LP) flown by Obgfr Hans Kilisters. A further Ju87 of I.*Gruppe* returned badly damaged. Two Ju88s of 8./LG1 were also lost—L1+ES flown by *Staffelkapitän* Hptm Wilhelm Durbeck and L1+AS captained by Obfw Hans Schneider, one of these two bombers came down near Kordin, just inland from Grand Harbour. Another Ju88 of the *Stab* III./LG1 force-landed at Pozzallo with severe damage, while a Bf110D of III./ZG26 crashed-landed at Catania. In addition, both the CR42 and Red-Cross Z.506B, as claimed, were lost. The *Gruppenkommandeur* of I./StG.1 Hptm Paul-Werner Hozzel later recalled:

> We now lost our best crews in the attacks. When I rose in the morning, I knew with certainty that by sinking sun, some five or six crew would have gone. One day, after the last mission, the leader of my 2nd squadron, who was a very hard chap, could not report to me for tears; he was the last of his squadron—all his old chaps were lost.[21]

Despite the ferocity and intensity of the latest attacks, *Illustrious* escaped serious damage although the dockyard and surrounding area again bore the brunt of the bombing. During the three major attacks on *Illustrious* and the airfields, it was assessed that the defenders had accounted for 40 enemy aircraft destroyed, five probables and at least a dozen damaged, of which 16 were claimed by the guns and at least ten credited to the Fulmar pilots. Actual Axis losses were considerably less but nonetheless severe. In his diary Gus wrote:

> **Monday 20th**: This morning we took transport to Takali to fly Hurricanes for a short while with 261 Squadron. The morning was spent reading and, in the afternoon, I did a thirty-minute trip in a Hurricane.
>
> **Tuesday 21st**: Orr, Sewell and Barnes went back to fly Fulmars and I should think we will go soon, too. The afternoon was spent at readiness.
>
> **Wednesday 22nd**: This morning we returned to Hal Far to once again fly Fulmars and Gladiators. I was at readiness but nothing happened. I did a short trip in a Gladiator.

By **23 January** and by dint of many determined hands, *Illustrious* had been sufficiently patched up to allow her to slip quietly out of harbour and on towards Alexandria and safety.[22] Before she sailed, some of those who had known her as home for the last six months made a farewell visit, including Gus Hogg:

> We went down to the ship and said goodbye to everybody including the Captain and she sailed at six. Good luck, old ship!

On this occasion the eyes of the Luftwaffe failed to observe her departure and the carrier arrived at Alexandria without interference. However, six Ju88s of 8./LG1 had been despatched from Catania to search for her following reconnaissance reports that she was no longer at Malta. These carried out a fruitless search and by nightfall Ltn Hermann Böhmer's sub flight of three had become lost. Short of fuel but believing they were close to the southern coastline of the mainland, Böhmer ordered his crew of L1+KS to bale out and ordered the other crews to do likewise. Only the pilot of L1+CS, Obfw Herbert Isachsen, came down on *terra firma* when he landed near Cape Rizzutto, not far from Crotone. A number of corpses were later discovered on nearby beaches, while one body, believed to have been a member of the crew of the third aircraft, L1+JS, was eventually washed up on the coast of Albania, over 150 miles to the east. Eleven of the twelve airmen were lost. Next day (**24 January**), 806 Squadron scored an unusual victory, as Lt Vincent-Jones recorded:

> One morning, Lt Jackie Sewell was sitting in the cockpit of the Gladiator [N5524] with the barometer wedged firmly between his knees, writing down pressure readings. Suddenly he noticed a stream of bullets passing under his starboard wing, followed a moment later by a Ju88 diving past him towards Hal Far. The Luftwaffe, from time to time, used this tactic of sending in a single aircraft flying below radar cover, usually in the early morning, on a 'hit and run' mission. Sewell recovered in time to stay with the intruder and shot it down off Marsaxlokk harbour.

The Ju88 was almost certainly L1+HM of 4./LG1, captained by Uffz Gustav Ullrich, which failed to return from a sortie to Malta. Lt Vincent-Jones continued:

> On **27 January**, a small convoy was reported to be off Sfax (Tunisia). A detachment of six Swordfish took-off [at 12:15] with two Fulmars, including Henley and myself, to assist in searching and providing air cover if needed. We found the convoy as predicted; no air opposition was present but we had the satisfying experience of circling above the convoy and watching two small merchant ships disintegrate below us as the Swordfish' torpedoes went home. For once we had operated in our ordained role.

In fact, there were seven Swordfish of 830 Squadron involved in the attack, six with torpedoes while the leader carried bombs, while only one ship was sunk. Three German merchantmen were located, the 3,950-ton *Ingo*, which was sunk by torpedoes but the 2,950-ton *Inza* and the 7,500-ton motor vessel *Duisburg* escaped with damage. An Italian patrol boat rescued the survivors from the sunken ship. Lt Vincent-Jones recalled:

> The enemy operated night intruders fairly regularly, using mostly SM79s for the purpose. They had a nuisance value in keeping the inhabitants awake by circling over the island during the night and dropping their bombs before departing. The counter was to send up a Hurricane to lay off the island and then call it in when the intruder was held in the crossbeams of the searchlights. I believe quite a few successful interceptions were made in this manner. It was certainly impressive to watch. One night I flew with Lt Henley in a Fulmar to orbit off the south coast of Sicily in the hope that one of these intruders might switch on navigation lights as they approached the coast of their homeland but we never saw anything.

On the evening of **4 February,** another dusk raid was reported approaching at 18:45, Hal Far, Luqa and Kalafrana being the targets for three formations of Ju88s. Eight Hurricanes and two Fulmars were scrambled, the Hurricane pilots claiming one Ju88 shot down, with a second as probably destroyed and a third damaged; the AA defences claimed one more destroyed, while a another was credited to Sub-Lts Orr and Roberts but identified it as a Do17. Once again Lt Vincent-Jones provided an account, which in this case suggests that other types than the Ju88s may also have been present:

> A raid of more than 100 [*sic*] aircraft was detected one evening, shortly before dusk, crossing the 60-mile channel separating Malta from Sicily. Orders came through to get all serviceable Fulmars into the air. I was in my bath at the time when Stan Orr gave me the news. Telling him to get down to dispersal and get the remaining Fulmars started up. I dried myself and pulled on my jacket and trousers faster than ever previously. I rushed after him and leapt into the rear seat as the chocks were pulled away. I had no time to collect a parachute or 'Mae West' and apart from my uniform and a towel had nothing on except my flying helmet. Looking upwards the whole sky seemed covered with enemy aircraft, mostly Ju88s but also a fair number of Heinkel 111s and Dorniers. Cursing the slow rate of climb of the Fulmar, we proceeded out to sea to gain altitude to get on terms with the bombers which were coming in at about 5,000 feet. By this time, it was beginning to get darkish but we could clearly distinguish the bombs pouring down on Luqa.
>
> As we turned back towards the island, Orr sighted a Dornier silhouetted against the sunset to the westward and gave chase. We made our approach from his port quarter and another Fulmar came up opposite us (I believe Roberts was the pilot) and concentrated on his starboard engine. The enemy rear-gunner did not seem to be able to see us and was firing directly behind him. What looked like a stream of pink golf balls passed between the two Fulmars without doing any damage. It was not long before the Dornier went down into a shallow dive with a fire breaking out in the cabin. The crew were clearly visible against the flames as by this time it was fairly dark. Moments later the Dornier hit the water which soon put the fire out. Orr was so intent on his gunnery that he only remembered to pull out in time otherwise we might have dived in beside the Dornier, which I wouldn't have fancied, being 'Mae West-less'. At least there was no doubt about this one.

Despite these two eyewitness reports of crashes, available German records note that three Ju88s, all from II./LG1, were badly damaged during this action and that all three limped back to Catania where they crash-landed. A total of five crewmen were wounded. Lt Vincent-Jones found himself a victim of the bombing shortly afterwards:

> A week or so after this, the Luftwaffe returned in force for an evening raid on Hal Far. I was in the Sick Bay suffering from some Maltese virus and running a high temperature, when the alarm went. I was taken down to a shelter in the middle of the station and put on a trestle table. For the ensuing ten minutes the pandemonium was indescribable. The earth shook all round us and the ceiling of the shelter started to come down, which made me more grateful for the planks above me. After the All Clear was sounded we clambered up the steps and found an unexploded 1,000-kilo bomb lying in the shelter entrance! When I returned to what remained of the Sick Bay, my temperature was normal and I believe that every virus germ had died of fright!

The remaining three Fulmars had a close encounter with Bf109s on **2 March** and were fortunate to escape lightly and without casualties, as Lt Vincent-Jones again related:

> The day started auspiciously when a Heinkel 111 suddenly appeared out of the dawn mist with undercarriage down and started to make an approach to the main runway, presumably mistaking Hal Far for its own base airfield in Sicily. The aircraft was just about to touch down when the pilot found himself in unfamiliar surroundings and opened his throttle in time for his wheels to clear the cliff-edge at the end of the runway. He had achieved total surprise and there was complete silence until the first Bofors opened-up when he was out to sea and on his way back to the mainland.
>
> At about 11:00 hours a smallish raid was detected leaving Sicily on course for Malta. For some good reason no Hurricanes were available and orders were telephoned through for the Fulmars to get airborne and gain altitude over Hal Far. Bill Barnes took-off with two others, one I believe was Orr and had climbed to about 2,000 feet after making contact with the Malta Tower who told them the raid was coming in low and very fast.

The incoming raid consisted of four Bf109s of 7./JG26 led by the ace Oblt Joachim Müncheberg, who had established himself as the scourge of Malta's Hurricanes in the short time his *Staffel* had been in Sicily.[23] He and his *Kette* were out on another hunting expedition.

> Most of us were standing by the control tower when the fortress guns opened-up to the northward and coming through the flak we saw a series of black dots approaching directly towards us and as they closed, we recognised them as yellow-nosed Me109s. The Fulmars above us continued to circle totally oblivious and we on the ground were powerless to warn them. We watched in horror as the enemy opened fire and chunks of metal could be seen falling off the luckless

> victim's wings and fuselage. The Me109s swept away out to sea and made no attempt to turn for a further attack.
>
> When we looked upwards again, we were amazed to see all three Fulmars still flying but firing emergency landing signals. By some miracle all three aircraft landed safely and by an even greater miracle none of the three pilots were wounded. It had seemed to us like certain death from the beginning of this hideous drama we had just witnessed Barnes was laughing as he climbed out of his cockpit and pointed at the huge hole in one wing-root made by a cannon shell and another through the opposite wing. The other two aircraft had been damaged but got off with bullet holes only. It was the end of daylight flying over Malta for the Fulmars.

Oblt Müncheberg and his wingman Fw Hans Johannsen each claimed a Hurricane shot down at 10:45, both in the same location—obviously the Fulmars. But a tragic incident followed. Lt Vincent-Jones continued:

> We decided that some sort of celebration would not be out of order on the occasion of this remarkable escape. [Lt-Cdr] *Ginger* Hale, who had led 819 Squadron into Taranto harbour and had recently been appointed to command the Naval Section at Hal Far, suggested he should drive some of us, including the three lucky pilots into Valletta for dinner at the Union Club. This sounded a good idea. Malta was on short rations and the menu was sparse but we must have consumed most of the champagne remaining in the club cellars. At about midnight we set off on our way back to Hal Far. *Ginger* Hale was driving and Bill Barnes was sitting between Robert Henley and myself in the back seat. As we were crossing the plain of Birzebbugia nearing the air station, we were surprised to hear a sharp report.
>
> Someone said: 'We've had a blow-out rear tyre' and Hale pulled to the side of the road. My arm was along the top of the back seat and I felt Barnes' head fall back. I at once thought that the poor fellow had had a pretty rough day and had gone to sleep as he hadn't made a sound. There was a bright moon and on looking closer I saw a dark smear coming from his mouth. Getting alarmed I pushed my hand under his jacket and withdrew it covered with blood. He was stone dead. Seldom can fate have played a stranger trick. Having saved him from almost certain death in the morning at the hands of the enemy, fate had collected him the same evening by a stray bullet fired in error by a Maltese Army recruit. Barnes was undoubtedly one of the finest officers and most courageous aviators that the Royal Navy has ever produced.
>
> It was afterwards discovered that the young Maltese soldier was on his first night as a sentry, with instructions to stop any passing car with his lamp and if the car didn't stop to fire his rifle over the top of it. His lamp had gone out and while he was relighting it, our car must have passed and he fired his rifle vaguely in our direction. The bullet ricocheted off a stone in the road and then passed exactly through the centre of the rear seat.

Lt Bill Barnes DSC was duly laid to rest in Capuccini Naval Cemetery at Kalkara. Two days later the remaining three airworthy Fulmars, with rear seat double-banked to accommodate the maximum number of aircrew, took-off for Egypt, stopping en route to refuel at El Adem airfield in Libya. All three arrived safely, while the ground party was transported by sea aboard a destroyer. A new era in the Squadron was about to begin.

At Aboukir, the returning warriors found that 806 Squadron had been re-born. Replacement pilots had arrived and new Fulmars made available.24 Lt-Cdr Evans returned from his sickbed to resume command, while Lt-Cdr Garnett remained to learn the ropes as a fighter pilot, while Lt Robert Henley was now Senior Pilot. Among the new pilots were Lt Robert MacDonald-Hall (known as Sam), Lt Philip Touchbourne, a Canadian and Lt Anthony Howey, together with Sub-Lt Geoff Davie and observer Sub-Lt Eric Dixon, the latter a former County cricketer.

V

Operations from Eagle and Formidable

Illustrious' sister ship, the similarly configured HMS *Formidable*, had been commissioned on 24 November 1940. Following a brief work-up, she embarked two squadrons of Albacore torpedo-bombers (826 and 829 Squadrons) and a dozen Fulmars of 803 Squadron before she joined the Home Fleet at Scapa Flow on 12 December. Her stay there was short as she, escorted by the heavy cruisers *Dorsetshire* and *Norfolk*, sailed on 18 December to protect convoys and search for the German cruiser *Admiral Scheer*, which had recently attacked a major convoy in the North Atlantic but the raider was not located. The British ships then escorted a convoy to Cape Town, arriving on 22 January 1941. Four days later *Formidable* was ordered north to replace the damaged *Illustrious* with the Mediterranean Fleet. En route, she took the opportunity to attack Italian forces in Italian Somaliland and Eritrea, where her Albacores sank a steamer on 12 February, suffering the loss of two of her own aircraft.

With *Illustrious* on her way to the USA for repairs and *Formidable* still weeks away from replacing her, the Mediterranean Fleet's sole remaining carrier *Eagle* found herself in the forefront once again. Since she carried only a flight of Sea Gladiators for defence, sea trials were carried out to establish whether Skuas, of which there were a few at Aboukir, or one of the Buffaloes recently arrived for FAA use, would be acceptable. In the event, the Buffalo was not able to carry out a landing due to its high approach speed. As neither type was found to be suitable, it was decided to utilise the available 806 Squadron Fulmars.

Eagle sailed on 1 February in company with the Battle Squadron. Seven Fulmars were tasked to embark but three of these crashed on the deck whilst landing; the unidentified pilots were unhurt except for their pride. During its brief foray, the Fleet provided protection for local convoys before heading northwards next day but returned when spotted by an enemy reconnaissance aircraft. Three Fulmars were scrambled and chased away the snooper. *Eagle* was back in port at Alexandria by 4 February.

On **19 February**, *Eagle* departed Alexandria to meet two fast merchantmen, *Clan Macauley* and *Breconshire*, which were en route from the west. For her defence, *Eagle* embarked six Fulmars, three each from 805 and 806 Squadrons (including pilots Lt MacDonald-Hall and Touchbourne), to augment her small Sea Gladiator Flight. Two days out (**21 February**), the convoy came under attack by five He111s from 4./KG26 operating from Rhodes. Two of 805 Squadron's Fulmars were on patrol, flown by Lt-Cdr Alan Black and Lt(A) Alec Ramsay,[1] an Australian and these engaged just as the Heinkels commenced their attack. Lt-Cdr Black recalled:

> Before I was able to press home my attack, I saw one of the Heinkels release his bombs, one of which appeared to go right through the funnel of one of the ships (in fact one bomb did indeed pass straight through *Clan Macauley's* funnel and continued over the side into the sea without exploding). After Ramsay had discontinued his attacks, I concentrated on the starboard engine of one Heinkel and got so close that my aircraft was covered in oil from that engine before it stopped. The Heinkel then force-landed in the sea. I flew around it for a few minutes and saw the crew in the water. On return to *Eagle* I reported to the Captain. To attempt to rescue the crew was deemed to be inexpedient.

Meanwhile, two Fulmars of 806 Squadron had been scrambled from *Eagle* and these also intercepted the Heinkels, Lts MacDonald-Hall and Touchbourne sharing in the demise of one, which they also reported down in the sea. However, only one Heinkel was actually lost—IH+BM captained by Obfw Josef Prötsch,[2] although a second returned with an engine badly damaged and the rear-gunner dead. *Eagle* returned to Alexandria, where the Fulmar crews were delighted to learn of the imminent arrival of HMS *Formidable*. Having made a cautious transit of the recently mined Suez Canal, *Formidable* eventually reached Alexandria on **10 March**. The Mediterranean Fleet was thus greatly strengthened by the arrival of the new carrier as a replacement for *Illustrious*. 806 Squadron, now brought up to a strength of six Fulmars, went aboard *Formidable* to reinforce the carrier's meagre fighter complement, which comprised Fulmars of her sister 803 Squadron.

Ten days later (on **20 March**), *Formidable* escorted Convoy MW-6 to Malta and was also tasked to deliver two Fulmars and three Sea Gladiators for 805 Squadron based at Maleme in Crete. Two Ju88s of 5./LG1 carried out a bombing attack on one of the cruisers next day, L1+DM being shot down by the CO of 803 Squadron. Another section from 803 Squadron became lost but fortunately encountered a patrolling 805 Squadron Fulmar from Crete, which guided them to Maleme airfield. Somewhat later, two other Fulmars of 805 Squadron, flown by Capt Skeets Harris RM and Lt Peter Scott, landed on *Formidable* to aid the patrols over the convoy for the next two days. *Formidable's* duty to MW-6 was completed on **23 March** and she now headed back towards Alexandria. From a comfortable distance, the two Fulmars and Sea Gladiators were flown off to Crete. However, one of 803 Squadron's protecting Fulmars developed engine problems and force-landed on Kythera Island, from where the crew were taken to the mainland. Another of 803 Squadron's pilots encountered a Ju88, which was claimed shot down.

With *Formidable* back at Alexandria, on the morning of **27 March** came news that major elements of the Italian Fleet had put to sea, including the battleship *Vittorio Veneto* and eight cruisers. *Formidable* sailed later that afternoon as part of the Mediterranean Fleet to intercept them. Even though the resident 803 Squadron was reinforced by three pilots (including former 805 Squadron pilot Lt Rupert Brabner) and aircraft from 806 Squadron, her air group numbered only 13 Fulmars, 10 Albacores and four Swordfish. An Albacore spotted the leading Italian ships the next morning (**28 March**). A strike force of six Albacores, loaded with torpedoes, was launched to attack *Vittorio Veneto.* Two Ju88s attempted to intervene but were driven off by the escorting pair of Fulmars, one of which was crewed by PO(A) Alf Theobald and L/Air Freddy de Frias, who recalled:

> The enemy fleet was just about in sight when Theo spotted a Ju88 below us. The two Fulmars went into a diving attack (our only chance of getting a shot at a Ju88) and shot it down. At our speed of just over 200 knots you only got the one pass. I couldn't see much—there was practically no forward vision from the rear seat of a Fulmar and in any case, I was busy looking for other 88s. You didn't last long if you forgot to do that. The 88 must have got off a signal before he went down because we had no trouble finding the enemy fleet, which was firing everything into the air. But we made our dive without a scratch and as we pulled out, I had the satisfaction of letting off a pan from the Tommy-gun I carried. I claim to be the only man to take on a battleship with a Tommy-gun!

The Ju88 was probably an aircraft of I./LG1 flown by Uffz Georg Albrecht that crashed-landed in damaged condition at Krumovo on return. However, the Albacore attack was unsuccessful and another strike force of three Albacores and two Swordfish was prepared. Shortly after launching them at 12:22, *Formidable* was unsuccessfully attacked by a pair of torpedo-carrying SM79s from 281ª *Squadriglia*. Although both sustained AA damage they were able to get back to their airfield. At about 14:50, one Albacore succeeded in torpedoing *Vittorio Veneto.* The hit briefly knocked out her engines and caused heavy flooding. Another air strike of six Albacores and two Swordfish was launched at 17:30

to finish off the crippled battleship but they mistook the cruiser *Pola* for the battleship in the fading light. The cruiser was struck by a single torpedo from one of the aircraft, possibly from one of two Swordfish from Crete, that had linked up with *Formidable's* aircraft before the attack. The mistake allowed the battleship to reach port. One Albacore was shot down by *Vittorio Veneto* and two others were forced to ditch after running out of fuel during the day's operations. Although the battleship had slowed to a halt, her damage control party soon had two engines restarted and before long she was making 16 knots and safely reached Taranto. The battle was far from over, however and British naval forces continued a radar-controlled night attack on the other Italian warships, in what became known as the Battle of Cape Matapan. The heavy cruisers *Zara* and *Fiume* were sunk by gunfire from *Warspite* and *Valiant*, while the destroyer *Alfieri* fell to *Barham's* gunners. Another destroyer, the *Carducci,* was also sunk as was the damaged cruiser *Pola.* Although over 1,000 Italian sailors were rescued by Italian ships and a further 369 by the British, it was estimated that some 2,400 more lost their lives.

The anticipated retaliation did not materialise until 15:11 next day, when a dozen Ju88s from II./LG1 approached but were driven off by heavy ships' gunfire. An 803 Squadron Fulmar crew also engaged and shot down Uffz Georg Kunz's L1+EP of 6.*Staffel* but not before the rear-gunner had hit the attacking aircraft, which was obliged to ditch. Both the Fulmar crew and the German crew survived to be rescued, the former promptly by the destroyer *Hasty*, the latter the following day from their dinghy by a Z.506B out from Brindisi. Somewhat surprisingly there were no further attacks on the Fleet as it headed back towards Alexandria.

Most air/sea action during the next two weeks took place around the Greek coast and it was not until **18 April** that a major naval action involving the Mediterranean Fleet materialised again, when it sortied out from Alexandria to bombard the major supply port of Tripoli, the main Axis supply port in Libya. A screen of three battleships, three cruisers and eight destroyers surrounded *Formidable.* Because heavy losses of fighters were deemed possible, the carrier had aboard 15 Fulmars when she sailed, including six aircraft and crews of 806 Squadron. At 18:20, the Fleet was sighted by two SM79s of 281ª *Squadriglia* operating from Rhodes and although pursued by a Fulmar patrol from 803 Squadron, no success was seen. Indeed, Lt Donald Gibson, pilot of the leading Fulmar, was wounded in an arm by return fire and almost completely blinded by hot oil; he recalled:

> I was shot down by three Cant bombers [*sic*]. I got too close in and a lot of explosive shells came into my cockpit. The aircraft was hit in the oil cleaner (I should think); the oil came into my cockpit. We were 40 miles from the Fleet. The engine finally

> stopped when I was about 2,000 feet over *Formidable*. I knew I could catch a wire when she was into wind. I caught a wire very fast; this tore the bottom out of the aeroplane. I collided with the island and set fire to the petrol refilling station; the tail folded over my head. I skidded on, hit 'A' turret and somersaulted into the sea. I was run over by the whole length of the ship; had a great struggle to get out and was picked up in the wake by *Hereward*. Alas Peter Ashbrooke [the observer] was lost. I was very young and foolish and should have ditched.

Meanwhile, Red 2 continued attacking *Tenente* Rodolfo Guza's bomber, wounding three members of the crew before it escaped. The badly damaged aircraft struggled back to Gadurra where it force-landed with the torpedo still beneath the fuselage. Next day (**19 April**), the Fleet put into Suda Bay to allow the destroyers to top-up on fuel. As *Formidable* entered the Bay at 12:25, radar picked up a hostile plot; a Fulmar was on the booster catapult but not manned. 803 Squadron's L/Air de Frias happened to be on the flight deck with helmet and Mae West when Lt Gibson, wounded arm in plaster, came rushing up and urged the TAG to join him in the Fulmar:

> I just had time to tighten my harness when we were sent off with the ship out of wind, hardly any way on, high ground in front of us ... and with a pilot on the sick list. Why did I have to get tangled up with a hero? But we made it OK, though the attack did not develop.

With the Fleet on its way again on **20 April**, heading for Tripoli, at 10:43, an unidentified aircraft blip appeared on the radar. A section of Fulmars from 806 Squadron was on patrol, flown by Lt-Cdr Evans and Lt Jackie Sewell and they were vectored onto a lone Z.1007bis, apparently on passage from Cyrenaica to Sicily. This aircraft was shot down by the Fulmars at 11:15. Some two hours later, a small formation of aircraft was reported at a distance of about 25 miles, two more sections of 806 Squadron Fulmars being scrambled to intercept. This proved not to be a bombing raid but a formation of five Ju52/3m transports from I./KGzbV.9 on their way to Africa. Brown Section (Lts John Shears and Julian Sparke) spotted them first and were quickly joined by Grey Section, led by Lt Robert Henley. One of the tri-motors escaped northwards but the others were engaged, two of them exploding in the air, suggesting that they were loaded with fuel. It appears that one of these fell to Lt Shears but his aircraft (N1985) was hit by return fire and spun into the sea; he and his observer, Sub-Lt Eric Dixon, were killed. Lt Henley recalled:

> After I had made my first attack on a lone Ju52, I pulled into the sun and watched Johnny Shears close from dead astern to within 50 yards or so when he was

> obviously hit and nosed vertically into the sea. I made another pass and claimed a possible, then returned to where Johnny had gone in, to search for him, in vain.

As four Ju52/3ms were officially credited to the Fulmars, it would seem that Lt Henley received credit for one, as did Lt Shears, whilst it is believed that Lt Sparke was credited with the other two. In fact, it seems that only two Junkers were actually lost, Ofw Josef Kastl and Fw Walter Heyer and their crews,[3] plus two passengers, being reported missing. It would seem that both Ju52s had been attacked by Sparke and that Shears and Henley had attacked one of the aircraft before Sparke delivered the *coup de grâce.*

As night fell the Fleet split up, *Formidable*, two cruisers and four destroyers drawing away to fly off air support, whilst the three battleships and close escort headed inshore for the bombardment. During the early hours of 21 April, Wellingtons from Malta bombed the port, while flares were dropped by Malta-based Swordfish, other Swordfish and Albacores from the carrier followed to drop more flares for the naval gunners and at 05:03 fire was opened by the 15-inch and 6-inch guns. After twenty minutes the Fleet changed course to withdraw, firing for a further twenty minutes. Only during this latter phase was any return fire experienced from the shore and that achieved no hits. One Swordfish crashed while landing-on but the Fleet was soon well away. Following this audacious enterprise, heavy air attack was expected but none developed—a sure sign of the complete surprise that had been achieved. During the assault on Tripoli about ten tons of bombs and 553 tons of shells had been expended, air reconnaissance later reporting that some destroyer berths had been hit and one destroyer badly damaged, while five merchant vessels were burnt out and at least four others had been set on fire

At 11:10, a shadower appeared and was intercepted by Orange Section of 803 Squadron; it turned out to be another Z.1007bis. Half-an-hour after interception, Orange 2 (Sub-Lt Simpson) returned, reporting that the aircraft had been damaged but that Orange 1, Royal Marine pilot Lt Al Wright, had lost contact. At last, at 13:40 contact was resumed and White Section of 806 Squadron [Sub-Lts Stan Orr and Gus Hogg] was directed to find Lt Wright and lead him back. However, after flying 20 miles, this pair spotted a Do24N flying boat from 6.*Seenotstaffel*, out from Syracuse [Sicily], heading south at 1,000 feet, too low to be picked up on the ship's radar at that range. This was attacked at once and forced down onto the sea with its port engine on fire. It made two attempts to take-off again but hit each time the Fulmars attacked, it settled in the water streaming a trail of petrol and oil; it was claimed destroyed. However, it was not badly damaged and managed to take off again and reach safety, although two members of the crew, Fw Walter Bender and Gfr Fred Weingärtner had suffered wounds. Meanwhile, Lt Wright had at last found his own way back

18-year-old Midshipman Graham *Gus* Hogg—future ace.

Above left: Midshipmen *Lew* Ayres and *Daisy* Day.

Above right: Midshipman *Gus* Hogg.

Newly promoted Sub-Lts Stan Orr and *Daisy* Day.

Above: Training Carrier HMS *Argus*.

Right: Sea Gladiator, *Argus* Training Flight (either Midshipman *Lew* Ayres or *Daisy* Day in cockpit).

Sea Gladiator of *Argus* Training Flight about to land on the carrier.

Sea Gladiator N5540/B, probably the aircraft on which Midshipman *Gus* Hogg trained.

806's CO Lt-Cdr Charles Evans with Senior Observer Lt Desmond Vincent-Jones.

806's leaders—Lt Bill Barnes, Lt Roger Nicolls, Lt-Cdr Charles Evans.

Roc L6R (L3075) of 806 Squadron.

Skua L6G (L3011) of 806 Squadron.

Right: Lt Bill Barnes resplendent in whites.

Below: Sub-Lts Stan Orr and *Lew* Ayres enjoying the warmth with Midshipman *Daisy* Day.

CO's Skua A (believed L2989).

A near thing! Lt Robert Henley's lucky escape.

Skua K in the drink—Sub-Lt Eric Buttle evacuating cockpit.

Skua K being salvaged.

Left: Skuas dive-bombing Bergen.

Below: Unusual shot of Skua landing.

Above: Newly arrived Fulmar.

Right: Fulmar 'office'.

Above: HMS *Illustrious*—home for 806 Squadron for six months.

Left: Recovering Fulmar—probably Sub-Lt *Pappy* Hill's ditching.

Z.501—one of 806 Squadron's frequent opponents.

Z.501 following shoot-down.

One of the ubiquitous Z.506Bs displaying its dazzling camouflage.

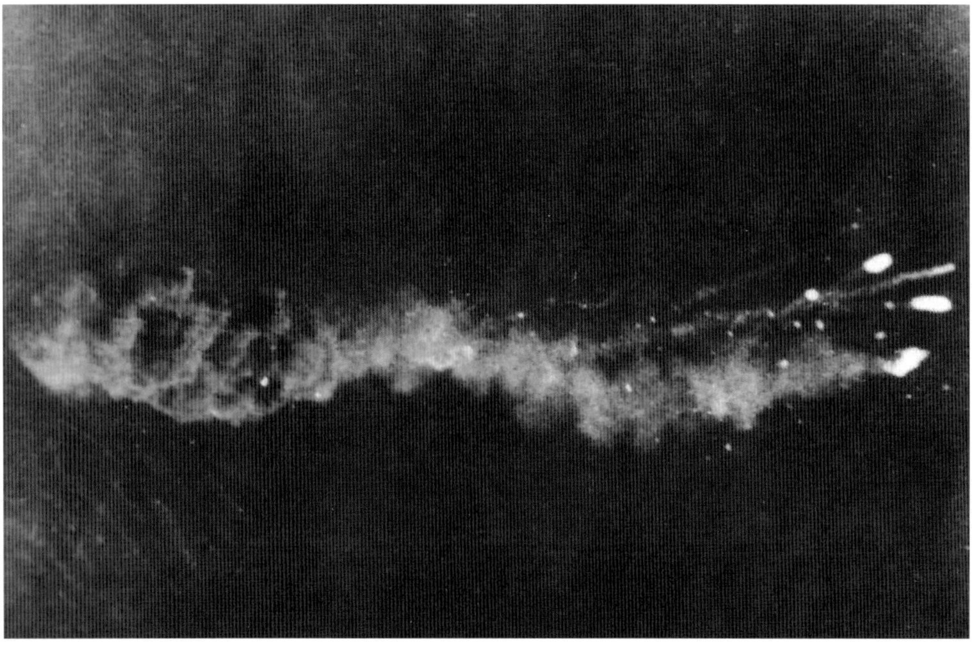

The demise of a Z.506B following combat with Sub-Lt Stan Orr.

Cdr Robin Kilroy shared 806's first Mediterranean victory.

Fulmars G and P at low level over the sea.

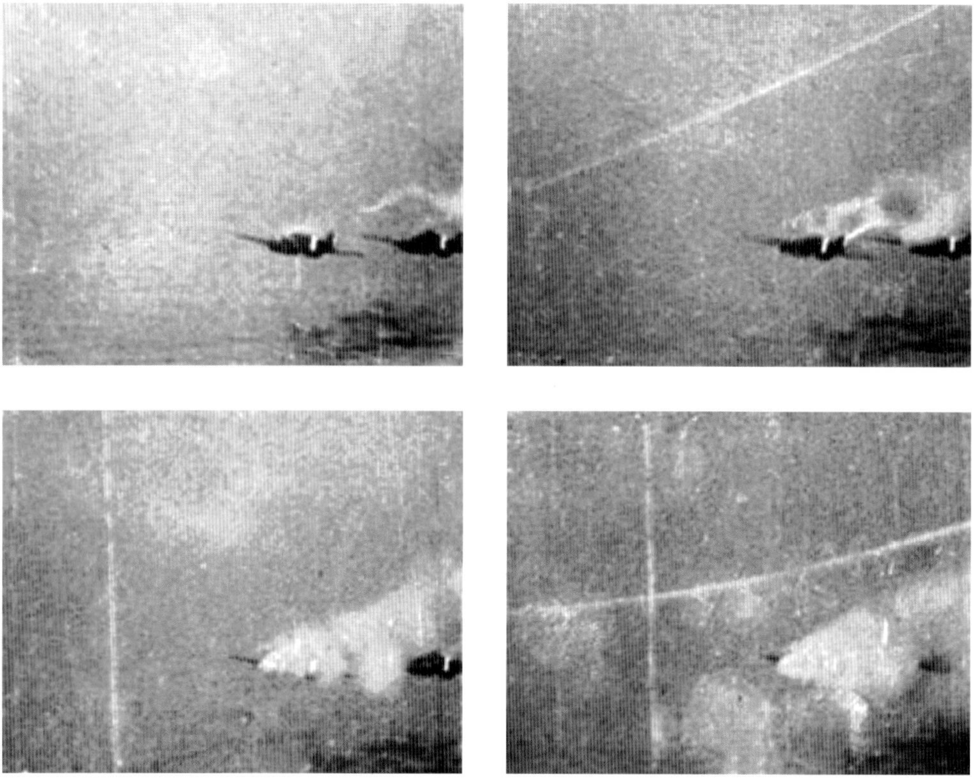

Sequence from Fulmar gun-camera film of a brace of SM79s under attack.

SM79.

Leading ace Lt Jackie Sewell.

Low-level attack by SM79.

Sea Gladiator (N5513) aboard *Illustrious*—one of three loaned to 806 Squadron.

Seen from another perspective.

Lt-Cdr Charles Evans poses with members of the maintenance crew, probably at Dekheila.

Fulmar R (N1886) temporarily interned at Crete following emergency landing.

Fulmar being refuelled by Italian prisoners, probably at Dekheila.

Above: 806 acquired the logo of a leaping Black Panther whilst at Dekheila.

Right: L/Airman Harry Phillips posing beside the newly-painted logo.

Although poor reproduction, Fulmars A and B can be seen displaying the new logo.

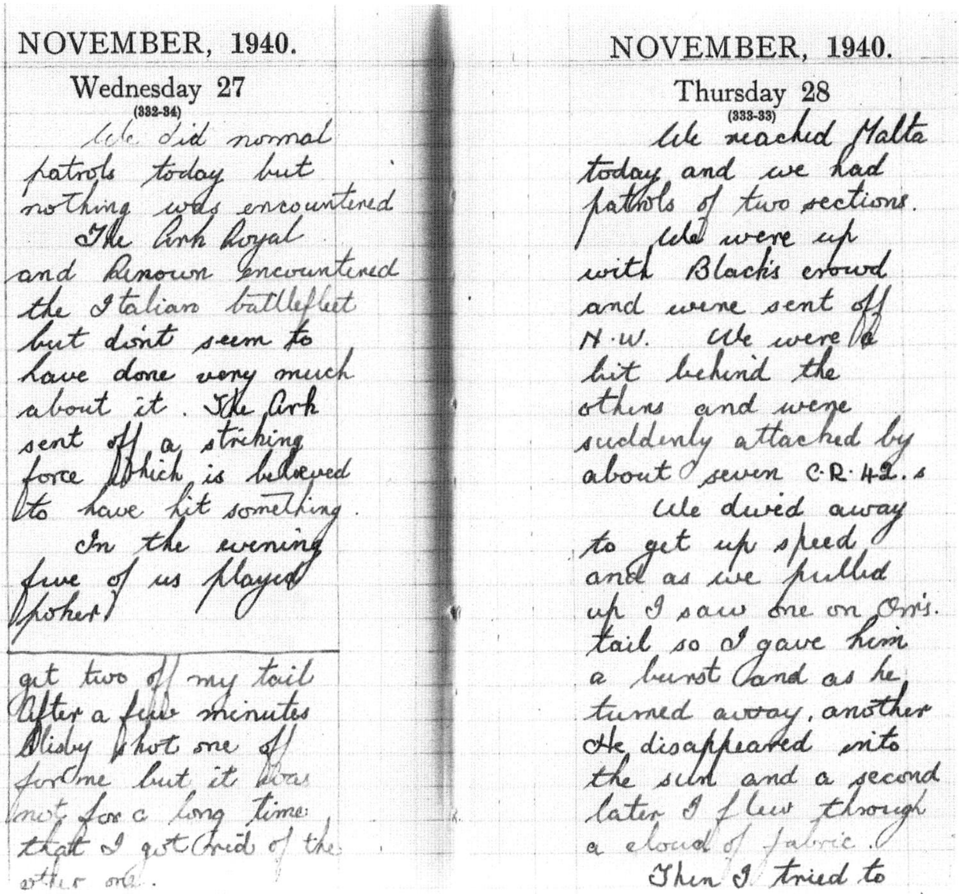

NOVEMBER, 1940.

Wednesday 27

(332-34)

We did normal patrols today but nothing was encountered.

The Ark Royal and Renown encountered the Italian battlefleet but dont seem to have done very much about it. The Ark sent off a striking force which is believed to have hit something.

In the evening five of us played poker.

got two off my tail. After a few minutes Blisby shot one off for me but it was not for a long time that I got rid of the other one.

NOVEMBER, 1940.

Thursday 28

(333-33)

We reached Malta today and we had patrols of two sections.

We were up with Black's crowd and were sent off N.W. We were a bit behind the others and were suddenly attacked by about seven C.R.42.s

We dived away to get up speed and as we pulled up I saw one on Orr's tail so I gave him a burst and as he turned away, another. He disappeared into the sun and a second later I flew through a cloud of fabric.

Then I tried to

Reproduction of *Gus* Hogg's journal pages include his action against CR.42s on 28 November 1940.

CR.42

Explosions of bombs aimed at HMS *Illustrious* while berthed at Parlatorio Wharf in Grand Harbour, Malta, January 1941.

German aerial photograph of *Illustrious* under attack in Grand Harbour.

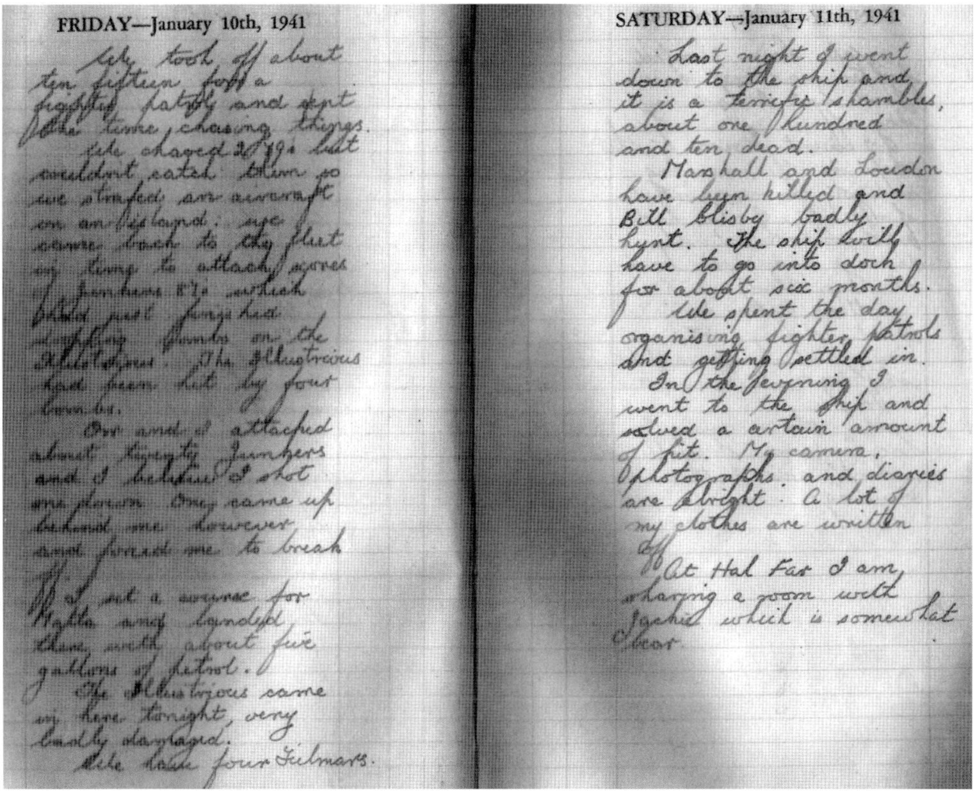

FRIDAY—January 10th, 1941

We took off about ten fifteen for a fighter patrol and spent the time chasing things. We chased 2 79s but couldn't catch them so we strafed an aircraft on an island. We came back to the fleet in time to attack scores of Junkers 87s which had just finished dropping bombs on the Illustrious. The Illustrious had been hit by four bombs.

Orr and I attacked about twenty Junkers and I believe I shot one down. One came up behind me however and forced me to break off. I set a course for Malta and landed there with about five gallons of petrol.

The Illustrious came in here tonight, very badly damaged.

We lost four Fulmars.

SATURDAY—January 11th, 1941

Last night I went down to the ship and it is a terrific shambles, about one hundred and ten dead.

Marshall and Loudon have been killed and Bill Clisby badly hurt. The ship will have to go into dock for about six months.

We spent the day organising fighter patrols and getting settled in.

In the evening I went to the ship and salved a certain amount of kit. My camera, photographs and diaries are alright. A lot of my clothes are written off.

At Hal Far I am sharing a room with Jackie which is somewhat bear.

Reproduction of a page from *Gus* Hogg's journal covering the attack against *Illustrious* 10 January 1941.

Illustrious berthed at Parlatorio Wharf, Grand Harbour – Valletta in the background

806's Fulmars aboard their new home—HMS *Formidable.*

Weather-beaten Fulmar K (N1931) resting at Dekheila.

Lt *Sam* MacDonald-Hall.

Lt MacDonald-Hall's Fulmar Y (N1866).

Triple DSC winner Lt Julian Sparke.

L/Airman Alf Rush killed in action with Lt Sparke.

Lt Pat Massy DSC.

N/Airman Colin Hearnshaw DSM.

Right: Sub-Lt *Gus* Hogg with his RNAS Hurricane.

Middle: Lt Henry Allingham's Hurricane OL-H (Z4245).

Bottom: Lt Robert Johnston's Z4932/OL-B photographed by German troops following shoot-down (Lt Johnston was captured but escaped).

Above left: Lt Robert Johnston, acting CO 1941-42—killed in action during the Pedestal convoy.

Above right: Sub-Lt Barry Nation was credited with shooting down a dive-bomber at Ceylon, April 1942.

Sub-Lt John Sykes was shot down at Ceylon but survived, April 1942.

Martlet aboard *Indomitable.*

Above left: Damage to *Indomitable* August 1942.

Above right: Indomitable's scoreboard following 12 August action, of which 806 Squadron pilots contributed 6 'confirmed'.

Post-war Spitfire XV 116 of 806 Squadron at Kai Tak, Hong Kong.

Sea Fury VR932 of 806's Aerobatic Display Team.

Sea Hawk FGA.6 XE451 at Kai Tak, Hong Kong.

The end! Sea Hawk 180 on the scrap heap.

806 Legends

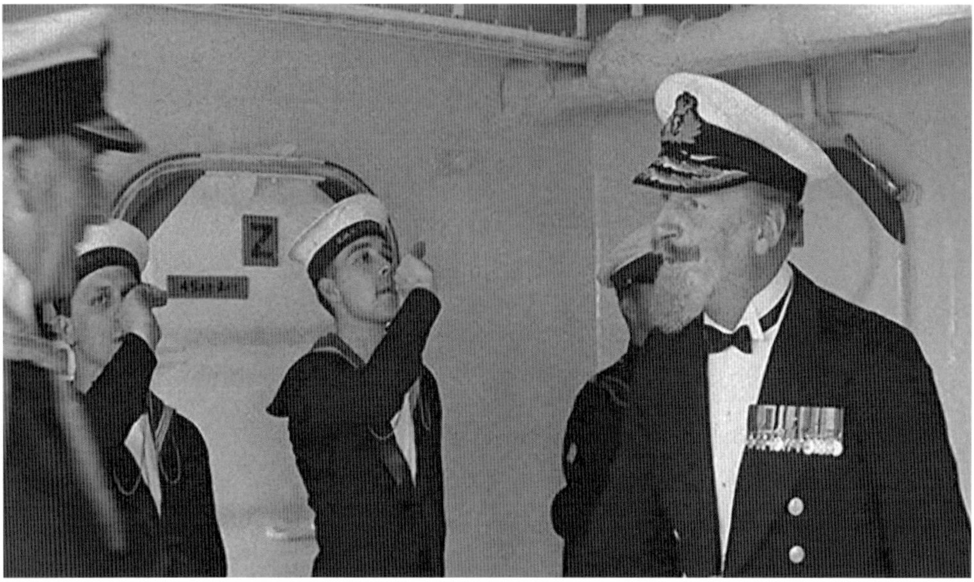

Vice-Admiral Sir Charles Evans CBE DSO DSC (died 1981).

Left: Captain Desmond Vincent-Jones DSC+ (died 1992).

Middle: Commander Stan Orr, DSC++ AFC (died 2003).

Right: Lt(A) *Gus* Hogg DSC+ (died 1942).

to *Formidable*, landing onto report that the Z.1007bis he and Simpson had attacked had, in fact, been shot down.

The situation in Crete was now deteriorating to such an extent, that the evacuation of redundant aircraft, such as the Swordfish, was implemented. The first three Swordfish were ordered to leave for Egypt on **22 April.** This was a 300-mile flight to Mersa Matruh. After about an hour's flight Sub-Lt Martin Rudolf's engine began to play up and sighting a convoy through a gap in the clouds, he headed down intending to ditch near one of the ships. On emerging into clear air directly over the vessels, he spotted a section of Fulmars climbing towards him and fearing that these might consider his aircraft to be hostile, he climbed back into cloud, thereby losing sight of the convoy. As a result, he decided to head on for Mersa Matruh, landing there safely after some four hours and ten minutes over the sea; despite his faulty engine he was reunited with his two companions. The Fulmars seen by Rudorf had come from *Formidable*, now well on her way back to Alexandria after the actions over Tripoli.

Fighter patrols had been maintained all day as the presence of shadowers had constantly been reported but it was 17:24 before a raid was finally detected approaching. Two sections of Fulmars intercepted two Ju88s some 30 miles out, as more groups appeared on the radar screens. All available interceptors were scrambled and by the time the attackers got near, 14 Fulmars were in the air. The first pair of bombers (aircraft of 8./LG1) were attacked by Green Section of 803 Squadron and Grey Section of 806 Squadron (Lts Henley and Sparke). Green Section forced one Junkers to jettison its bombs and make off into clouds, possibly damaged, while the second raider, flown by Uffz Gerhard Pfeil,[4] was also seen to jettison its bombs before it was shot down into the sea by Julian Sparke; Henley's guns had failed to operate. Black and White Sections of 806 Squadron also intercepted a lone Ju88, reported to be a shadower and this was claimed probably destroyed by Lt-Cdr Evans, Lt Sewell and Sub-Lt Orr. No damage was caused to the Fleet. 803 Squadron observer Lt Jasper Godden recalled:

> We saw nothing until the Fleet was well on its way back to Alexandria. At about 17:00 hours, we spent 30 minutes in combat with two Ju88s. One was shot down—not by us. All I had was a Thompson sub-machine gun—you could see the .45 bullets trickling out of the muzzle—the muzzle velocity was so low! During the Tripoli operation Bill (Lt Bruen, the CO) and I flew ten sorties totalling 23 hours—fighter patrols over the Fleet. Very monotonous indeed, especially for the non-driver. The average sortie was two and a half hours, spent scanning the (mostly blue) skies with binoculars and supping oxygen.

As the Fleet headed back towards Alexandria, it was about to enter a new phase of action with Greek-based units of the Luftwaffe.

The Battle Squadron with *Formidable* was out again on **29 April**, escorting another Alexandria-bound evacuation convoy, GA-15, carrying aboard some 11,000 evacuees to safety. These included many wounded and sick troops, merchant seamen rescued from sunken vessels, nurses, women and children and even Italian prisoners of war. Only a single Ju88 appeared and this was claimed shot down by an escorting destroyer. Next day (**30 April**), White Section of 806 Squadron encountered five CR42s, obviously from Rhodes but after a brief engagement without any damage to either side, the Italians broke off and departed. Somewhat later, an 803 Squadron patrol encountered what they took to be a trio of Ju88s but were in fact Blenheims of 203 Squadron from Crete, evacuating to Egypt. L/Air de Frias (in PO(A) Alf Theobald's Fulmar) explained:

> With our Ju88 complex, they were fair game—fortunately we only damaged them on our first run and realised, as we turned in for another go, they couldn't be 88s if we could have two goes at them!

Orders required aircraft approaching the Fleet to do so in line astern with the leader firing the colours of the day but the Blenheim leader had not been so informed. The Blenheim attacked was only slightly damaged. The other Fulmars had broken away when Very lights were fired and the Blenheims continued on their way. However, on return to *Formidable* both Theobald and de Frias were grounded pending a possible court-martial but this was apparently forgotten when action intensified in the weeks to follow.

The start of May found a tense air of expectant calm pervading the skies around Crete following the conclusion of the evacuation. That Crete would be invaded was already known via Ultra. Now was the time to despatch supplies of tanks and aircraft, desperately needed in the Middle East and a convoy comprising five heavily-escorted large freighters put to sea. Known as *Tiger* Convoy, the freighters carried 295 tanks and 53 crated Hurricanes and on their safe arrival depended any future plans for the area. Meanwhile, in the Eastern Mediterranean, the First Battle Squadron, together with *Formidable*, was patrolling southern waters on **1 May**. During the course of the day, a section of Fulmars of 803 Squadron was vectored onto a hostile plot, which turned out to be a reconnaissance Ju88. One Fulmar was hit by return fire, though both crewmen were unhurt. The other Fulmar carried out an attack but the Ju88 escaped unharmed. *Formidable* was out again on **6 May**, with five cruisers of the First Battle Squadron, to assist the *Tiger* Convoy operation. Having joined the destroyer escort outside harbour, *Formidable* flew on her Air Group, which included Fulmars of both 803 and 806 Squadrons. The initial task of the Squadron was to escort four large merchant vessels and two tankers, carrying 24,000 tons of fuel, to Malta. *Tiger* Convoy was approaching from the west meanwhile, escorted by Force H from Gibraltar. Rendezvous was to be made near Malta and the freighters escorted to Alexandria.

Halfway to the island rendezvous, the cruiser *Ajax* and three destroyers were detached to bombard Benghazi by night, harbour installations and shipping being successfully shot-up. While returning to re-join the main force, these warships encountered two Axis transports, one of which blew up violently when attacked, the second running ashore and being left in flames. Very poor visibility and occasional rain frustrated many efforts by the Luftwaffe's reconnaissance aircraft to find the Fleet on **8 May**, following the bombardment. Frequent radar plots indicated the presence of the searchers, radio intercepts indicating the occasional fleeting sightings which were achieved. During the early part of the morning Blue Section of 803 Squadron was vectored onto two Italian bombers, identified as Z.1007s. Both were engaged and both believed shot down but one Fulmar failed to return and was assumed shot down by return fire from its victim. Early in the afternoon radar indicated that a number of enemy aircraft were approaching and two sections of Fulmars were scrambled to join 806 Squadron's White Section (Lt MacDonald-Hall and his TAG, L/Air Harry Phillips, in N1990, with Lt Philip Touchbourne flying as White 2 in N1865) which was already airborne. MacDonald-Hall recalled:

> We came across two He111s, the first of which I rather stupidly flew in formation with some 50 yards behind but managed to blow-up the Heinkel's starboard engine, the debris of which being glycol and fuel, smothered my cockpit and I watched it cartwheel down and hit the sea. I then re-joined Touchbourne and we harassed, attacked and shot down the other Heinkel prior to returning to *Formidable*. My hydraulics had been damaged and the starboard wheel would not come down and the port wing was badly damaged by the rear-gunner's fire, as was the port tyre. I landed with one leg down, the other retracted and the wheel deflated.

Meanwhile Green Section of 803 Squadron intercepted another Heinkel, which they shot down. A fourth Heinkel was claimed by another 806 Squadron section and shot down into the sea by Lt Les Hill and Sub-Lt Geoff Davie (N1870); the latter crashed into the sea on returning to the carrier and was lost though his TAG was rescued. The claims made were very accurate and it appears that White Section's victims were probably both aircraft of 6.*Staffel* of KG26—1H+AP flown by Obfw Willi Kleinknecht and 1H+FP (Oblt Hermann Pfeil). There were no survivors. One of the other Heinkels was from 4.*Staffel* (Oblt Eberhard Stüwe's 1H+BC), the other from 5.*Staffel*, 1H+FN flown by Oblt Max Voigt; the crews perished.[5] These bombers had in fact been despatched to attack the Suez area.

Later in the afternoon two sections from 806 Squadron encountered Ju88 snoopers, Lts Henley and Sparke believing they had shot down one off

Cape Passero. In fact the damaged aircraft, 4U+LK from 2.(F)/123, had been able to regain its base at Catania with two wounded crewmen (Uffz Konrad Heyde and Uffz Karl Holtz) on board. Lts MacDonald-Hall and Touchbourne were up again towards the end of the day and they too engaged a lone Ju88, reporting that it had crashed into the sea with no survivors following their attack. Although bad weather had saved the Fleet from sustained air attack it also had tragic consequences for a number of *Formidable's* aircraft. Two Albacores on anti-submarine and reconnaissance patrols were lost, only one crew being rescued, while an 803 Squadron Fulmar crashed into the sea with the loss of both crewmen.

Far to the west *Tiger* Convoy and Force H had also come under intense attack by German and Italian aircraft from Sardinia and Sicily. During these actions, five Axis aircraft were claimed shot down by Fulmars from *Ark Royal* for the loss of two fighters and one crew. That night however one of the freighters was badly damaged by a mine and blew up some hours later. The crew were taken-off but 57 tanks and ten crated Hurricanes went down with the ship. A second vessel was slightly damaged by the explosion of a mine caught by her mine-sweeping paravane.

By 08:00 on **9 May**, the First Battle Squadron was 120 miles to the south of Malta, while *Tiger* Convoy was 90 miles to the west. The weather remained uncertain, with many fog patches and visibility less than two miles. By early afternoon the fuel convoy from Alexandria had safely reached the island and at 15:15, *Tiger* Convoy and escorting destroyers joined forces with the Battle Squadron some 40 miles off Malta. Axis aircraft searched all day but the only contact came when Lts Bob Henley and Julian Sparke of 806 Squadron again caught a reconnaissance Ju88, this time a machine from 1.(F)/121, which they attacked and badly damaged; the Junkers crashed on return to Catania and was totally destroyed, although the crew survived. At 16:00, one of the searchers at last located the ships but no attack developed before darkness fell.

The snoopers were out in force next morning but in variable visibility they experienced trouble in maintaining contact when sightings were made. Similarly, patrolling Fulmars were unable to achieve any effective interceptions. A He111 sighted and pursued by Lts MacDonald-Hall and Touchbourne disappeared into the murk before they could get within range. A little later the approach of another hostile caused a scramble to be ordered but as Lt Philip Touchbourne's N1865 was boosted off by catapult the aircraft crashed over the starboard side, both the pilot and his TAG, L/Air Cliff Thompson, perishing. As a result of this fatal accident, the remaining crews were not keen to make use of the booster in spite of assurances from engineers. In an effort to raise morale and restore confidence, Commander (Flying) Charles Atkinson allowed himself to be boosted off even though he had not flown a Fulmar before.

Not long after this there was warning of enemy aircraft in the area and three sections of Fulmars were ranged for take-off, the booster being used. The last aircraft was crewed by Sub-Lt Basil Sinclair and TAG L/Air Freddy de Frias, who recalled:

> I asked him (Sinclair) if we were to be boosted—'Shouldn't think so. I've only got eight hours on Fulmars and I've never done a booster. They'll probably shoot off the others and then we'll do a normal take-off.' I relaxed but was soon shaken when we were waved up to the loading position. Sinclair must have made some frantic signals because he throttled back and the Flight Deck Officer hopped up onto the stub plane. I heard everything through the intercom which Sinclair had left on. 'What's the snag?' (enquired the FDO) 'None except I've never been boosted or even had a briefing' (replied Sinclair) 'No time to argue, there's a gaggle (of enemy aircraft) on the plot. Listen, when you are on the trolley, I'll wind you up. Get your straps as tight as you can. Normal take-off flaps and coarse pitch. Let the stick centre itself, put your hand behind it and tuck your elbow into your guts. Open the throttle to full take-off power and tighten up the screw. Then lift your left hand and put your head back against the pad. When you drop your hand, I'll give you a moment to put it at the back of the throttle, so it won't close, then off you go!
>
> I sat there horrified. In my mind I still had the picture of the Fulmar which had pranged off the booster floating down the starboard side with the TAG [L/Air Thompson] strapped in the rear seat, which had come adrift, with his head at an odd angle and obviously dead. The pilot [Lt Touchbourne] had slumped forward but appeared to be moving a bit. Then it sank as it reached the stern and the plane-guard hadn't picked up anything. We were now mounted on the booster carriage and the engine roared. I saw the operator push the lever and felt the usual rush of blood to my face. There was a yell from up front and my hand flew to the canopy-jettison handle. But it was only Sinclair yelling 'It works! It works!'

Still bad visibility continued to protect the Fleet and only one further engagement was to occur as the vessels neared Alexandria on **11 May**. Once again Lts Bob Henley and Julian Sparke were involved, this intrepid pair attacking a formation of Ju88s from II. and III./LG1. Each selected a target, Henley attacking an aircraft from 5.*Staffel*, his fire wounding the gunner, Obgfr Horst Goldner; his aircraft was severely damaged but managed to reach base. Sparke (N1990) meanwhile closed to very short range on Obfw Otto Engel's L1+IR from 7.*Staffel* but either collided with, or was simultaneously shot down by the bomber, the two aircraft falling together into the sea.[6] Only one parachute was seen by Henley who then failed to locate its occupant in the sea. A search was made as sea conditions were very slight and oily calm. It was believed that if Julian Sparke or his TAG, L/Air Alf Rush, had baled out, or if their aircraft had force-landed, there was a very good chance that they would be found. However, *Formidable's* Captain Bisset refused to allow such a search as it was already late afternoon and the dangers inherent in allowing the carrier to slow down while a search was made required him to put the safety of the ship, its escorts and the convoy first. The morale of the aircrew aboard was badly affected by this ruling. It is believed that Lt-Cdr Charles Evans made his feelings strongly known to Captain Bisset. On the ship's return to Alexandria the CO took his leave of 806 Squadron and again handed over the reins to Lt-Cdr Jimmy Garnett although Lt Vincent-Jones still remained the effective leader.[7]

Late on the morning of **12 May**, the remaining ships of *Tiger* Convoy and the First Battle Squadron steamed into Alexandria. The relatively heavy attrition suffered by the Fulmars during this operation left only a few serviceable aboard the carrier and until others could be rendered so, *Formidable* would be unable to put to sea to escort warships and convoys between Egypt and Crete.

With the invasion of Crete well under way, there was little that *Formidable* could do to help, even if she had a full complement of fighters. Therefore, it was not until midday on **25 May** that the carrier and the First Battle Squadron departed Alexandria for operations around Crete. On this occasion *Formidable* was accompanied by the battleships *Queen Elizabeth* and *Barham* as well as eight destroyers. The carrier had aboard 12 Fulmars, crewed by a hotchpotch of whoever was available from 803, 805 and 806 Squadrons; some of the aircraft were of doubtful serviceability but all that could be made available, plus 15 Albacores and Swordfish. One of the pilots to join 806 Squadron was Lt(A) Pat Massy, who had been flying Sea Gladiators from *Eagle* the previous year.

The Air Group's first task was to be a dawn raid on the Dodecanese island of Scarpanto, since it was obvious that the airfield there was being extensively used for operations against Crete and the south coast ports. At 03:30 on the morning of **26 May**, six Albacores took-off from *Formidable* and while two were forced to return early, the other four gained complete surprise at dawn, finding rows of closely-parked CR42s and Ju87s; two were claimed destroyed and several damaged. The bombers were followed in by four 803 Squadron Fulmars, led by Lt Bruen. Their strafing attack was considered to be very successful and it was believed that at least a dozen aircraft had been put out of action and others damaged. Commented Lt Godden, Bruen's observer:

> We shot up a number of Ju87s and CR42s. This was a very economical way of destroying enemy aircraft.

In fact, there is no record of any Ju87s being damaged, although one Ju88 was recorded as destroyed and two more damaged, damage also being caused to one SM81 and six CR42s. One Luftwaffe airman was killed, the only casualty. All the

Naval aircraft returned safely to the carrier. Reprisal raids were anticipated and the four Fulmars were refuelled and rearmed as quickly as possible, taking off at 07:10 with two other sections as plots appeared on the ships' radars. Odd reconnaissance aircraft were seen but interceptions proved abortive and the Fulmars returned to refuel. Four sections were again launched at 09:05 and once more at 11:48, as intruders became more aggressive. One section comprising 806 Squadron's new commander, Lt-Cdr Garnett, with Lt Vincent-Jones in the back seat and Lt Sewell as his No.2, encountered a pair of II./KG26 He111s, the experienced Sewell swiftly shooting down Oblt Oskar Klapproth's 1H+CN into the sea.[8] Within minutes two Ju88s of II./LG1 were spotted and Garnett at once attacked, observing hits. Sewell joined the attack and soon the bomber was in trouble but at that moment Garnett's Fulmar was hit by return fire. Lt Vincent-Jones wrote:

> It was Garnett's first combat and he scored a few hits on the engine. Jackie Sewell joined in and the Ju88 went down into the sea, although Garnett also went after it hoping to inflict the *coup de grâce*. But we were hit in the engine by the rear-gunner [Gfr Günther Peschke] and ditched. The Ju88 ditched about 200 yards away—their dinghy worked, ours didn't! This was embarrassing. There we were swimming around in the sea and the Germans were laughing at us. But we had the last laugh since Jackie Sewell remained in company and orbited over us until the destroyer *Hereward* saw us. We were plucked from the sea.

Uffz Heinrich Geisenhoff and his crew from L1+CV[9] were also rescued. Meanwhile another section of 806 Squadron Fulmars, flown by Lt MacDonald-Hall (N1957) and Sub-Lt Gus Hogg, also reported intercepting a pair of Ju88s—possibly the same pair as attacked by Garnett and Sewell. They attacked together, reporting that the first bomber—in all probability Oblt Wolfgang Meissner's L1+QV[10]—burst into flames at about 7,000 feet and that the second was followed down until it hit the water with an almighty splash. No survivors were seen from either aircraft but since LG1 reported the loss of only two Ju88s it seems likely that the second aircraft was that flown by Uffz Geisenhoff. Meantime, Green Section of 803 Squadron skirmished with another Ju88.

During this forenoon period the fighters had flown 23 sorties, engaging in 20 combats and skirmishes, during which four aircraft had been claimed shot down and one damaged. At 13:10, by which time the force was 150 miles from the Kaso Strait, a formation of Ju87s was detected approaching from the North African coast. These were from II./StG2, led by Major Walter Enneccerus, who had led the attack on *Illustrious* off Malta four months previously. The dive-bombers were not taking part in the Cretan operations, nor were they hunting for the carrier; they were searching for supply shipping making for Tobruk. Thus it was pure chance that Oblt Bernhard Hamester's 5.*Staffel* crews spotted *Formidable* and took advantage of this chance encounter to attack at once, followed by 4.*Staffel* (Oblt Eberhard Jakob) and Oblt Fritz Eyer's 6.*Staffel*. Two direct hits were scored on the flight deck, fore and aft, as well as several near-misses, one of which created a gaping hole in the carrier's starboard side underwater. Fires broke out, 12 men were killed and ten wounded—a relatively low number of casualties, given the very severe damage inflicted.

Two Fulmars flown by Sub-Lt John Sykes and Sub-Lt Basil Sinclair had just landed when the attack commenced and the two TAGs—L/Airmen Freddy de Frias and Reg Northfield—had just entered their Mess, where they were moaning that no lunch had been saved for them. Suddenly, recalled de Frias:

> The bomb penetrated the flight deck aft of our mess and blew out part of the bows underneath us. We were both dazed by the explosion but unhurt; even the mess was undamaged apart from a bulge in the deck and lockers and other furniture strewn all over the place. We gathered ourselves up and left. A damage control party was squirting hoses into the hole the bomb had passed through. Really, we had a miraculous escape because had the bomb exploded a fraction of a second earlier it would have blown out the mess. As it was, it exploded (as far as I recall) almost on the waterline, right in the stern, which was why our casualties were so light.

Two relieving Fulmars flown by Lt Pat Massy and Sub-Lt Ken Wood had been launched as the Stukas approached but these had not gained sufficient altitude to intervene. Now, as the dive-bombers retired, they attacked and each claimed one Ju87 shot down and a further two damaged. Only one Ju87, an aircraft of 5.*Staffel*, was actually lost, the gunner, Obfw Ewald Kruger, being wounded. Massy's aircraft was hit by return fire, L/Air Colin Hearnshaw, the TAG, receiving four wounds in one leg. Despite the damage to the carrier (see Appendix V) both Fulmars were able to land-on and the wounded air gunner was soon receiving attention to his wounds. *Formidable* was not the only ship hit, for the escorting destroyer *Nubian* also had her bows blown off and her aft guns put out of action, 15 of her crew being killed and six others seriously wounded.

As soon as the attack had developed, the carrier had sent out urgent signals requesting air cover, the initial response being the arrival of a solitary Blenheim, which remained on station for ten minutes. Three Hurricanes from Sidi Barrani then arrived but were treated as hostile and met initially by a barrage of AA fire. These were relieved by three more Hurricanes from Gerewala and then by three more from Sidi Haneish. Another three of this unit's aircraft appeared an hour later, these engaging a single reconnaissance Ju88 which suffered minor damage.

By 18:00, Cdr (Flying) Atkinson considered that launches of Fulmars could recommence, although the catapult was out of action. Two aircraft were ordered off to patrol, bouncing over the battered, bumpy deck before becoming airborne, followed by two more 25 minutes later. No further attacks transpired and when Lt Bruen and Sub-Lt Richards landed after two hours *Formidable* had recorded the last operational flights by her Air Group in the Eastern Mediterranean. She would arrive in Alexandria next day, her aircraft disembarking to Dekheila and Aboukir. For 806 Squadron it meant that the unit had lost its second home within six months. For the pilots it would mean a period of operating from land bases.[11]

Despite the successes achieved, *Formidable's* Captain Bissett would write in his report on the operation:

> From daylight onwards on Monday 26th May, there were frequent calls for fighters to drive off enemy reconnaissance aircraft. Three of these were shot down. The small number of fighters available on board made it impossible to answer the above calls and maintain an adequate number in reserve to deal with bombing attacks. As a result, when the main attack developed on the Fleet, only two fighters were in the air and no more were available until the attack was over.

Although *Formidable* was now out of the battle, other ships of the Battle Squadron continued to escort evacuating vessels from Crete and on **28 May**, the Fulmars at Aboukir were called into action once again. The cruiser *Dido* was targeted by Stukas, which put her forward guns out of action; 46 men were killed and 38 seriously wounded in this attack. The already damaged cruiser *Orion* was then hit again, fires breaking out and many casualties being sustained. Witnesses reported that one of the dive-bombers responsible was also apparently hit, failed to pull out of its dive and crashed into the sea just off *Dido's* bows. A second attack commenced at 10:45 and caught the ships just before they would pass out of range of the Stukas. *Orion* was again attacked, one bomb passing through her bridge and exploding in the stoker's mess, which was crowded with troops. The carnage was indescribable and during these attacks 262 men were killed, including 155 soldiers, mainly men of the Black Watch; 300 more were wounded. Despite these conditions, the fires were contained, the wounded tended and the cruiser continued her way at much reduced speed towards Alexandria.

On receipt of signals informing him of the air attacks and continued lack of fighter cover, Admiral Sir Andrew Cunningham ordered that the standby Fulmar flight at Aboukir be despatched immediately. Two Fulmars of 806 Squadron scrambled, led by Lt MacDonald-Hall who recalled:

> We received a signal from the C-in-C to the effect that because of the evacuation and the heavy losses of ships, we were to provide the maximum air cover until relieved and if not relieved, to ditch. As we were flying from shore the air gunner was strictly not necessary for navigational purposes and in view of the signal, we thought it prudent to dispense with all air gunners.

It seems that the Fulmars arrived at the tail-end of the Stuka attack:

> On two occasions I engaged a Ju87. The first time it was considered a probable—smoke issuing from the engine and it pulled away from its bombing dive. On the second occasion it was very much a doubtful—it broke off its bombing run and beetled off towards Crete.

The series of attacks cost the Stuka force just one aircraft, 2./StG.3's Uffz Martin Kretschmar and his gunner, Uffz Erwin Moritsch, being killed when their Ju87 crashed into the sea—probably the aircraft seen to crash near *Dido* and possibly the same machine attacked by Lt MacDonald-Hall. The two Fulmars finally arrived over the ships at about noon, the first friendly aircraft actually seen by the sailors since their departure from Alexandria on the previous day.

In order to support the last of the evacuating ships, the AA cruisers *Coventry* and *Calcutta* were sent out from Alexandria on the morning of **1 June**. At 09:00, when 100 miles out to sea, radars detected hostile aircraft approaching. Twenty minutes later two Ju88s dived out of the sun, the stick of bombs from one aircraft narrowly missing *Coventry,* while two bombs from the other hit *Calcutta* with deadly effect; she sank within a few minutes with the loss of 117 of her crew; 255 survivors were picked up by her sister ship. This was to be the last Royal Navy loss of the campaign.

At about this time a reconnaissance Ju88 had been briefed to fly a sortie to Alexandria. It failed to return and two members of the crew who were subsequently picked up were under the impression that they had been shot down by AA fire. The aircraft may possibly have fallen to 806 Squadron Fulmars however, for Lt MacDonald-Hall and Gus Hogg had been sent out from Aboukir, encountering a lone bomber which they took to be a reconnaissance Ju88:

> We came across an 88 which appeared to be a reconnaissance machine and on that occasion, we had considerable height advantage and although it turned towards Crete we both attacked it and watched it spiral down and hit the water.

As the evacuation of Crete ended, some 12,500 troops had been left behind, of whom 226 were RAF personnel. Many of these had already been captured but to those still free General Wavell gave discretion to surrender, fight on, or escape if they might. The majority did surrender but many attempted to evade and escape. Indeed, by the end of 1941 over 1,000 escapees from Crete—as well as from the Greek mainland and the Aegean islands—had arrived back in Egypt by various means and routes.

VI

Royal Navy Fighter Squadron

With the loss of the services of both *Illustrious* and *Formidable* due to bomb damage, the Royal Navy lacked a suitable carrier from which the FAA fighters and torpedo strike aircraft could operate in the Mediterranean. Hence, the Navy's aircraft in the area were obliged to operate from North African airfields in conjunction with their RAF comrades. Their presence was a boost to the RAF, which was struggling to build up sufficient forces to combat both the Italians and Afrika Korps—and now against the Vichy French in Syria. The Allied offensive against the Vichy in Syria at the beginning of June was aimed at preventing the Germans from using the Syrian and Lebanon airfields as springboards for attacks on Egypt. After a *coup d'etat*, neighbouring Iraq fell under the control of pro-German rebel forces. This eventually led to the outbreak of the brief Anglo-Iraqi War, which ended in British control over Iraq. Syria was now to be subjugated and ground forces began crossing the border from Palestine. British and Commonwealth squadrons began preparing for ops from bases in Palestine, Transjordan, Cyprus and Egypt, including a flight of 803 Squadron Fulmars at Lydda and a flight from 806 Squadron (including Lt MacDonald-Hall, Sub-Lts Orr and Hogg) at Aboukir now re-equipped with ex-RAF Hurricanes, on loan from 33 Squadron and re-coded OL, as was 803 Squadron when it also received Hurricanes.

The Naval fighters were initially tasked to fly patrols over the British warships operating off the coast. Although clashes with Vichy fighters was anticipated, the outcome of the first meeting, on **9 June**, between D.520s and 803 Flight's Fulmars turned out to be disastrous for the Allies. Lt Donald Gibson of the 803 Flight remembered:

> We therefore flew to Lydda and camped in the control tower. The airport at Lydda was modern with good runways. There were deep drainage ditches on each side

> of the runways, which contained the wreckage of the Tomahawks of an Australian squadron [3RAAF]. British warships were patrolling off the Syrian coast and the Vichy French were very active. We carried out combat air patrol over the British ships who had little idea of effective fighter control and they may have had no radar. We, in our slow Fulmars, were at the mercy of the infuriated Frenchmen. During the operation we lost four of our best people.[1]

803's Senior pilot Lt John Christian was lost in N1950 together with 806 Squadron observer, Sub-Lt Norman Cullen, while PO(A) Jimmy Gardner and L/Air Harry Pickering were also shot down (in N1956), a third Fulmar went down although both crew were rescued from the sea including TAG L/Air Brian Dearnley. A fourth aircraft was so badly damaged that it had to be written off and a fifth suffered less severe damage. The French pilots, from GCIII/6, lost one aircraft to the Fulmars but the pilot was able to bale out and was taken prisoner. Several of the French fighters also suffered damage in the action, some having been hit by ships' gunfire. Two French destroyers fired on the advancing Australians before being driven off by shore-based artillery fire. The French destroyers then exchanged fire with the British destroyer *Janus*. The New Zealand light cruiser *Leander* came to the aid of *Janus* along with six additional British destroyers and the French wisely retired.

With or without French approval, the Luftwaffe attempted to come to the aid of the hard-pressed French naval forces on **15 June**. Ju88s of II./LG1 attacked British warships off the Syrian coast and hits were scored on the destroyers *Ilex* and *Isis*. That evening, French aircraft bombed the British naval units off the Syrian coast. On **16 June**, Cyprus-based Swordfish sank the French destroyer *Chevalier Paul*, which had been en route from Toulon to Syria carrying ammunition from France. Shortly afterwards, the French tanker *Adour* was attacked by Swordfish and was badly damaged. *Adour* was carrying the entire fuel supply for the French forces in Syria.

As a consequence of 803 Flight's losses in the scrap with the D.520s, the RAF was requested to provide additional fighter cover over the warships. Shortly after this disaster, 803 Flight was withdrawn to Amiyra, where the unit was also re-equipped with a dozen ex-RAF Hurricanes. On **18 June**, Lt Bill Bruen led six Hurricanes from Dekheila to Sidi Haneish, where they were to co-operate with the Hurricanes of 33 Squadron. But there occurred an incident that soured the relationship, as Lt Donald Gibson later wrote:

> My Squadron was briefed for a patrol and army support over a tank battle in the region of Sidi Omar, while the others were to attack a German airfield called Gerrala [*sic*—Gerewala]. They were to fly west and approach Gerrala from the sea. Both squadrons were to refuel at Sidi Barrani on the return journey. My squadron

> did its duty, which involved strafing but while refuelling at Sidi Barrani we were strafed by our colleagues. Fortunately, they concentrated their fire on a wrecked Maryland in the centre of the airfield but they also set fire to a Hurricane near me and caused me to dive into a slit trench. This party was led by a junior pilot who had got his navigation fouled up. Bill Bruen broke our party away and tried to call them off; realising their error, they landed and asked for fuel. Whatever disciplinary action was taken I never heard about it. I had sympathy for the perpetrator of this boob, as the desert has few features and a strong wind from the west led him astray.[2]

803 Flight was recalled to Dekheila next day, primarily because Operation *Battleaxe* had effectively failed. The three errant 33 Squadron pilots were also summoned to Dekheila, no doubt to explain their *faux pas*.

Meanwhile, the remnants of the third fighter unit, 805 Squadron, back from defending Crete, was reformed on Martlets. Whilst operating from Crete, 805 Squadron had used a variety of aircraft—Fulmars, Sea Gladiators and three Buffaloes, while some of the pilots assisted the defending RAF units by flying their Hurricanes to relieve pressure on the RAF pilots. The Buffaloes were of little use, however. The Squadron had only recently suffered the loss of two of its pilots while flying Buffaloes, within a few days of each other. Sub-Lt(A) John Busson flew AX817 into the ground at Dekheila while low flying on **11 June** and six days later the experienced Lt Lloyd Keith, a Canadian and recipient of the DSC for services with the Sea Gladiator Flight aboard *Eagle* earlier in the war and in the defence of Crete, was shot down. On **17 June**, he had been instructed to fly from Dekheila to Mersa Matruh in Buffalo AX813 and from there to relieve a Beaufighter on convoy patrol. Unfortunately, his aircraft was intercepted and shot down by a Bf109 from Sidi Barrani, flown by Obfw Hermann Förster of 2./JG27. The Buffalo crashed north-west of Sidi Barrani and Keith was badly injured; recovered by German troops and taken to hospital, where he died ten days later.

To bind these units into a cohesive fighting force, the Royal Navy Fighter Squadron (RNFS) came into existence in **July 1941**, once sufficient numbers of pilots and aircraft had been assembled at Dekheila, the FAA's main base near Alexandria. Command of the RNFS went to Lt-Cdr Alan Black, former CO of 805 Squadron. Both the 803 and 806 Squadron pilots, mainly newly posted to their respective units, were to fly Hurricanes, while 805 Squadron was equipped with Martlets. A first success—and loss—for the new unit was not long in coming. While flying from Haifa on **14 July**, Lt Al Wright RM of 803 Squadron (V7816/OL-V) intercepted an SM79. When last seen it was diving towards the sea with its starboard engine stopped and smoke pouring from the port engine. It was classed as probably destroyed. But on **23 July**, a Martlet

(AX724) of 805 Squadron ditched in the sea one mile off the coast of Mersa Matruh after running out of fuel while pursuing a suspected enemy intruder and Lt Paul Woods was lost.

Of the 806 Squadron survivors from Malta, it seems that only temporary CO Lt Vincent-Jones,[3] Sub-Lts Stan Orr and Gus Hogg[4] were attached to the RNFS in an operational capacity, albeit briefly, Gus leading four others to Ma'aten Gerewala LG on **7 August**. The records state that they were to carry out a patrol over the Fleet but were recalled without patrolling. War-weary Gus Hogg was then transferred to non-operational duties, as was his friend Stan Orr. Others posted out at this time were 803's CO Lt Bill Bruen DSC and shortly thereafter Lt Donald Gibson, both tour-expired.

Three days later (**10 August**), three Martlets of 805 Flight accompanied Hurricanes and Tomahawks to escort eight SAAF Marylands on a raid. All returned safely. The RNFS was now deemed ready for operations and, on **17 August**, Lt-Cdr Black (Z4171/OL-Q) led the first six Hurricanes—a flight of 803 Squadron—from Dekheila to Sidi Haneish South, the landing ground from where the RNFS was to operate under the control of 258 Wing. The other five were flown by Lt Al Wallace (Z4177), Royal Marine Lt Al Wright (V7816) and Sub-Lts(A) John Hancock (Z4236), Duncan Richards (W9327) and Bill Simpson (V7107/OL-R). Meanwhile, four Martlets of 805 Flight also arrived; two of these were off early next morning to search for a missing oiler which had been anticipated coming in from Greece, but no sightings were made. At dawn, the first six Hurricanes of 806 Squadron flew in to Sidi Haneish from Dekheila led by the new acting CO, former Walrus pilot Lt Robert Johnston (Z4560/OL-A), with Lts Henry Allingham (Z4245/OL-H), *Zac* Cox (Z4370) and Sub-Lts Peter Fell (Z4227), Ken Talbot (V7308) and Ken Wood (V7328). More Hurricanes would arrive at Sidi Haneish within the next few days, including 803 Squadron's new CO, Lt Bruce McEwen (who had shared with Lt-Cdr Charles Evans in shooting down the first German aircraft of the war, a Do18, way back in September 1939), plus Sub-Lts(A) George Henderson, Alf Astin and Basil Sinclair followed by 806's Sub-Lts(A) George Dennison, Geoff Pudney, Tony Willis, George Warren, Bill Tench and John Knee.

All twelve Hurricanes were airborne at 13:30 on the 18th, together with the four Martlets as top cover to provide protection for two 'A' lighters proceeding to Tobruk with supplies for the garrison. No enemy aircraft were sighted, and all returned to Sidi Haneish via Sidi Barrani for refuelling, where there were four landing grounds and three other fighter squadrons—33 RAF and 1SAAF with Hurricanes and 2SAAF with Tomahawks. Protection for three destroyers on course for Tobruk was provided by all RNFS fighters next day (**19 August**) and as they approached the destroyers the pilots saw seven Bf110s, of which two proceeded to bomb the ships, scoring a near miss but the Hurricanes and

Martlets were unable to intercept. The protection operation was repeated next morning (**20 August**) at 07:30, as the destroyers returned from their mission to Tobruk. These duties were again the order of the day at 17:15 but with a dozen Tomahawks of 250 Squadron providing top cover, their charges including two cruisers and several destroyers making for Tobruk. Although no enemy aircraft were sighted, one of the destroyers informed the patrolling fighters that radar had detected a plot some 20 miles away but Lt-Cdr Black (Z4370), who was leading the Hurricanes, was instructed not to obey the destroyer's instructions and to return to base.

On **21 August**, 805 Flight's four Martlets, which had stayed overnight at Sidi Barrani, were off at 06:00 for a convoy patrol, returned, refuelled and then departed for another sea patrol, covering the cruisers and destroyers returning from Tobruk. The ships had been protected earlier by Tomahawks of 2SAAF but an enemy aircraft had succeeded in bombing the destroyer *Nizam,* which was damaged. Whilst on patrol, the Martlet flown by Sub-Lt John Macdonald was attacked by two Bf109s but was not hit. Macdonald was able to pursue and get his sights on one but then found his guns failed to fire since the master switch was not on. At 17:20, two Hurricanes flown by 806 Flight's Lt Henry Allingham (Z4245/OL-H) and Sub-Lt Geoff Pudney were scrambled to intercept a shadower reported by the ships. However, Pudney became separated from his leader and returned to Sidi Haneish leaving Allingham to carry on alone; he reported:

> Flying at 20,000 feet, 15 miles ahead of the Fleet, I saw two bombs fall ahead of the starboard destroyer. I dived to 15,000 feet and then saw ten 110s ahead of me, in the sun and about 5,000 feet below me. They could have had no connection with the bomb explosions I observed. I positioned myself between the enemy and the sun and then dived down to engage. They saw me coming and went into a defensive circle, so I picked the nearest and did a bow attack, following through to the beam and quarter. I fired five bursts into the port side of the enemy and pieces fell off the port side of the port engine. Engaged aircraft went over on its back and dived vertically down towards the sea. On breaking away I noticed another 110 on my tail firing at me, so was unable to watch the first aircraft to know whether it hit the sea or not. My own aircraft was damaged around the tail unit, port mainplane, port longeron and cockpit hood.

Lt Allingham was given credit for the destruction of the Bf110, which was undoubtedly an aircraft of 8./ZG26 and may have been that (3U+AS) crewed by Uffz Werner Seiler and Obgfr Hermann Schmidt which came down in the sea; the pilot was rescued but the gunner was killed. Allingham's attacker was probably Oblt Kurt Rosenkranz, who claimed a Hurricane at about this time. The Bf110s were also engaged by Tomahawks of 2SAAF Squadron that had been acting as escort to SAAF Marylands on a bombing raid, losing another aircraft in return for one Tomahawk. Patrols over convoys and warships by all RNFS Hurricanes and Martlets was the order of the day on **22 August**, from dawn to dusk. Apart from one Martlet bursting a tyre on take-off, causing damage to a wingtip, there was little else to report. Similar duties were carried out for the next three days, the only excitement being an accident to a landing Hurricane, which hit a poorly-filled bomb crater and tipped onto its nose; the pilot was unhurt.

Action resumed on **26 August**, with the RNFS losing a Hurricane and its pilot. Early in the morning six Martlets were to be guided to a convoy by a Maryland but this crashed on take-off. Only three Martlets were able to get airborne—and completed an uneventful patrol. At 17:00, ten Hurricanes and two Martlets were tasked to undertake another convoy patrol, with the Martlets providing top cover but unknown to the Hurricane leaders, the latter were recalled, as Lt Robert Johnston recorded:

> Two Martlets, which were to have joined me in the air, were recalled without my knowledge. Consequently, I fell astern of the remainder of the formation while looking for them. Just before reaching the Fleet I heard gunfire; turned sharply and saw my top weaver [Pudney], who had dropped slightly astern, was going down in flames. By then the enemy had climbed out of range.

Sub-Lt Geoff Pudney (Z4052) was killed, his victor either Ltn Hans Remmer or Fw Peter Werfft of 1./JG27. Meanwhile, Lt Bruce McEwen was leading his 803 Flight, unaware of the drama behind but soon experienced another. He sighted a lone RAF Hurricane (identified as coming from 73 Squadron) being pursued by two Bf109s (possibly the same pair that had shot down Pudney):

> Two Messerschmitt 109s in line astern after a Hurricane, diving from up sun. Put Hurricanes in defensive circle and 73 Squadron Hurricane able to save himself by diving through centre of circle. One 109 fired at defensive circle and both climbed away.

This may have been the occasion when a target-towing Swordfish flown by PO(A) Geoff Peacock, a former 803 Squadron pilot, narrowly escaped being shot down off Dekheila by a marauding Bf109, as recalled by N/Air Alan Armstrong:

> Flying out to sea the red drogue was streamed and paid out on its wire the better part of half-a-mile. Bang, bang went the guns and a few moments later the flash and black puff balls of exploding shells. If the drogue had been an enemy aircraft need not have worried himself unduly ... but suddenly I was brought sharply to

> my senses by the unmistakable sight of tracer whipping past much too close for comfort. Looking up I could see shells bursting over our head and some even in front of us. I had no great opinion of army ack-ack gunners, Egyptian or otherwise but this was ridiculous. Surely their gunnery couldn't be that bad.

The reason for the intense AA fire became apparent when a Bf109 was observed heading straight at the unarmed Swordfish:

> The pilot spotted it at the same time and almost burst the tubing yelling 'Cut the bloody wire!' I made a quick snip with my pliers ... down drooped the drogue like a pigeon in mid-flight. Relieved of its burden the Swordfish shot forward from its normal plodding 80 knots to something over 100 knots, helped no doubt by the steep dive. The only damage to the aircraft was part of the towing-arm shot away but whether this was done by the Messerschmitt or by our own shrapnel, it was not possible to tell.

Sub-Lts Tony Willis in Z4560/OL-A and George Warren (Z4269) were scrambled at 11:50 on **31 August,** when a snooper was reported approaching Sidi Haneish. They sighted an unidentified aircraft and gave chase but gave up due to lack of speed. Presumably another of the fast Ju88 reconnaissance aircraft that were difficult to catch unless the pursuers had height and speed.

At the beginning of September all serviceable Martlets at Sidi Haneish returned to Dekheila for minor local modifications to their carburettor intakes. This proved to be a relatively quiet period with mainly routine patrols but even then, the pilots had little time to relax. For example, at 04:55 on **5 September,** orders were received at Sidi Haneish that six Hurricanes were required to standby as there were believed to be enemy aircraft in the vicinity. At 05:10, control called to say at least three enemy aircraft were over Fuka aerodrome. Orders were given to scramble four aircraft, two to patrol over Fuka and two to patrol over LG9; two more were to standby for further instruction. No enemy aircraft were sighted and all four were back by 08:00. Six more Hurricanes were then placed at readiness, two of which were scrambled at 14:50 and were ordered to orbit Mersa Matruh. Again, no enemy aircraft were seen and the Hurricanes were back at 15:35. Two more were scrambled at 16:30 but were back within the hour. The whole effort was repeated next day, again without contact with enemy aircraft.

But, on **7 September,** Italian fighters were able to carry out a successful strafe of the Sidi Barrani airstrips. At 05:55 three Hurricanes departed Sidi Haneish for Sidi Barrani East and were flown by Lt-Cdr Black (OL-E), Lt Allingham (OL-H) and Lt Johnston (OL-G). Having refuelled they were in the process of taxying to dispersal, when approximately ten G.50s (actually 15 aircraft of 155°

Gruppo with top cover provided by 22 MC200s of 153° *Gruppo*) appeared at low level and began strafing. The Hurricane pilots were only just able to clamber out of their cockpits in a great hurry and were fortunate not to have been hit. One Hurricane (OL-G) went up in flames and the CO's was badly damaged, while Allingham's OL-H suffered only minor damage. Nine Hurricanes of 33 Squadron were also strafed, four of which were burnt out. None of the five 33 Squadron Hurricanes on patrol at the time of the attack were sufficiently close to intercept the attackers but two 806 Flight Hurricanes flown by Sub-Lts George Dennison (OL-C) and Peter Fell (OL-J), arriving from Sidi Haneish at the crucial moment of the attack, were able to engage. The latter reported in detail:

> At 07:50 flying No.2 in formation from Sidi Haneish South to join rest of Flight which had flown up at dawn and landed at Sidi Barrani, I observed from a height of 600 feet when approximately a mile from Sidi Barrani PAC and AA fire and later three aircraft in line astern flying low over the aerodrome and pulling up steeply into a climb and heading out to sea. We were approaching the aerodrome from north to east and course of enemy aircraft was roughly south to north. I turned with my leader on a course roughly parallel to that of the enemy aircraft. As my leader broke away, I engaged the nearest aircraft at long range, closing slowly, with a quarter attack moving to astern. After third burst enemy aircraft turned right; as I turned to follow, I saw astern of me an aircraft and firing. I broke off the attack and climbed up-sun to the east of Sidi Barrani. I circled for some minutes when I received by R/T a message to 'pancake'. This message was repeated three times in exactly the same manner. On landing I checked this message with the Controller and he had not sent this order.

Sub-Lt Dennison, of his attack, simply noted:

> Quarter to astern, long range, closing slowly. Right hand turn after third burst. Probable hits on enemy aircraft, no damage to own. Attack broken off owing to astern attack by an unidentified aircraft.

Both G.50s of 378ª *Squadriglia* suffered minor damage and *Tenente* Ugo Palli and *Sergente* Roberto Gaucci got safely back to Gars el-Ahrad. The Italian pilots claimed a Baltimore (probably a SAAF Maryland), five Hurricanes, two of which were left burning, three Gladiators and a large biplane damaged. Apart from the two G.50s damaged by the RNFS Hurricanes, a third returned with damage to its starboard wing and tail unit, inflicted by a PAC device (parachute and cable), though *Sergente* Giovanni Del Fabbro was unhurt. For the remainder of the morning, patrols were carried out by RNFS Hurricanes but no further activity occurred until later in the afternoon, at 17:27, when four Navy Hurricanes and five from 33 Squadron were ordered to scramble just as six G.50s more appeared over the aerodrome, again catching some pilots in their cockpits while others were still running to their aircraft. Fortunately, only one pilot was wounded (a Sgt of 33 Squadron) but two Hurricanes including Z4086 of 803 Flight (Sub-Lt Richard's aircraft) were burnt out; four others were damaged including V7107/OL-R and Z4171/OL-Q of 803 Flight. Within half-an-hour the order was given to evacuate Sidi Barrani. The two Italian fighter attacks had cost 258 Wing at least 21 fighters either burnt out or damaged (three Hurricanes and two Tomahawks destroyed, 15 Hurricanes and one Tomahawk damaged). There was some bitterness towards personnel of the AA defences who were dubbed by one of the SAAF squadrons as 'useless'. Sidi Barrani could once more be used only as a refuelling base.

For the RNFS the following two weeks was devoid of any confrontation with enemy aircraft. The occasional scramble to investigate bogies usually turned out to be friendly aircraft not showing IFF. Six Martlets led by Lt *Tubby* Shaw returned to Sidi Haneish on **9 September** following their modifications and three Hurricanes fitted with long-range tanks arrived to replace the aircraft lost. Two days later, the RNFS was able to put up six Martlets and three Hurricanes to patrol over three destroyers bound for Tobruk, while next day five Martlets provided cover for a tug and three A Lighters making for the same destination; six Martlets and seven Hurricanes patrolled a gunboat and a tug on **14 September.** An incident occurred next morning when Sub-Lt Leslie Harper took-off from Sidi Barrani North in Martlet AX731 to fly to Sidi Barrani South at 00:05 to avoid a threatened enemy advance but spun in and crashed; he was killed. With daylight, two Hurricanes departed Haneish to cover Wellingtons taking off for a raid from Fuka satellite. Later, two Hurricanes (Lt Johnston and newly arrived Lt Walter Pangbourne) were scrambled when information received that He111 and a Ju88 (or the same aircraft) was reported in the vicinity but nothing was sighted. Shortly thereafter, two Hurricanes of 803 Flight and a Martlet left Haneish to escort a Lysander to Thalata to collect a wounded pilot.

On the morning of **17 September**, five Martlets led by Lt Shaw and four Hurricanes (Lt Allingham), that had landed at Sidi Barrani to refuel, were ordered off to intercept a force of seven Bf110s and two Ju87s reported south-west of Maddalena. However, before they became airborne the order was cancelled. Instead, they were tasked to patrol RN vessels making for Tobruk. Such patrols were daily routine with little incident apart from one Hurricane—Z4560/OL-A flown by Sub-Lt Ken Talbot—making a heavy landing that resulted in a broken tail wheel and a burst tyre. The aircraft was soon back in line however, following a replacement wheel from a burnt-out Hurricane. Five Martlets were ordered to patrol shipping on **25 September** and were forming up over Sidi Barrani when one aircraft was attacked in error by a Hurricane of 33 Squadron (possibly that flown by Flg Off Tofield, the patrol leader) one of six that were flying a defensive patrol. A few bullet holes in one wing of the victim were inflicted before the errant pilot realised his error.

The air war returned in earnest on **28 September,** when 258 Wing assembled a 38-aircraft escort comprising six Martlets and six RNFS Hurricanes (three from each Flight), plus additional Hurricanes from 33 Squadron and Tomahawks from 112 and 250 Squadrons, to escort 18 Marylands tasked to bomb an estimated 2,000-ton patrol ship reported to be off Bardia. This was actually the 1,500-ton former Danish cargo ship named *Almena* (renamed *Bengasi* by the Germans following its capture the previous year). Heavy AA over the harbour resulted in all three Hurricanes of 806 Flight (Allingham, Pangbourne and Fell) sustaining slight damage but two Bf109s that dived from above failed to score any hits and were too fast to pursue. However, one of the Tomahawks was damaged by the Bf109 attack, the pilot later baling out. Three G.50s of 351ª *Squadriglia* led by *Capitano* Riccardo Spagnolini from Benghazi then appeared and one attacked Sub-Lt Dickie Law's Martlet (B), scoring four hits on its wings and tail unit. Law outmanoeuvred his attacker and engaged one with a short burst but observed no hits. Meanwhile, Sub-Lt Reg Walsh (Martlet C) was able to engage the same aircraft:

> I was flying second from right in a formation of six Martlets which were stepped up on the port quarter of the Marylands. Whilst over the target, Hurricanes of 33 Squadron cut across in front of our formation and caused some disorder. For a short time, Sub-Lt Watson (on my right) and I were about 200 yards behind the main formation. Whilst overtaking them I saw a G.50 about 150 yards behind the other four Martlets, firing at them. I immediately turned and delivered a beam attack. He turned away to the left and came back for another attack on the main Martlet formation. I again fired on his beam and observed pieces of his tail unit breaking away. He then turned over and dived vertically with pieces still falling away. After this I was attacked by two other G.50s and was able to fire a short burst at each but broke off when both were in a position to fire at me. I evaded them by turning sharply and made my way back to base.

Although the G.50 was not seen to crash—and 351ª *Squadriglia* did not report any losses—confirmation was later received by 258 Wing HQ and Walsh was credited accordingly. All the Italian pilots (the other two being *Tenente* Vittorio Galfetti and *Sottotenente* Corrado Sarti) fired at the Martlets but did not make any claims. It is probable that Walsh had seen Law's Martlet falling away shedding pieces.

The *Almena/Bengasi* escaped damage, even though there was a follow-up attack by Blenheims and she set out that night for home base. There followed a strange sequel to this episode a few days later. On **30 September**, the British 400-ton auxiliary schooner *Tiberio,* on a routine supply trip from Alexandria to Tobruk, was attacked in error by RAF Blenheims of 203 Squadron, the crews of which believed that she was the *Almena/Bengasi,* since she had an escort of enemy fighters, whose pilots evidently also believed they were escorting the German vessel. In the event, *Tiberio* (captured from the Italians earlier in the year) was slightly damaged by a near-miss but arrived safely at Tobruk.

Following this limited action, the next few weeks were somewhat of an anti-climax for the Naval pilots, with only mundane convoy and ship patrols interspersed with flying training for some of the new arrivals. A highlight of the month occurred on **12 October,** when ten Hurricanes from both Flights and five Martlets were ordered to fly to LG07 in preparation for a patrol in company with the Tomahawks of 112 Squadron. On arrival at LG07 a ground mist made landing difficult to judge, causing Lt Allingham in Z4227 to land short. His Hurricane ran over a slit trench and crashed, though no injuries were incurred. Lt-Cdr Black (Z4388) punctured his tailwheel. Another Hurricane was rendered unserviceable on **15 October**, Sub-Lt Richards of 803 Flight having to carry out a forced landing at Ma'aten Bugush when his engine failed. On his approach in Z7416/OL-L, one wheel hit the top of a car on the edge of the aerodrome and the Hurricane crashed but without injury to the pilot. Six days later (**21 October**), the Hurricanes were called up onto provide constant patrols over the gunboat HMS *Gnat*, which had been damaged in a torpedo attack some 30 miles off Sidi Barrani. Having suffered no casualties, the gunboat was able to reach Alexandria safely without further interference. The relatively quiet month for the RNFS almost ended in catastrophe when, during fighter interception practice between the two Hurricane Flights, two aircraft collided head-on. Only minor damage fortunately occurred and both were able to land safely, albeit *sans* wingtips but without injury to the otherwise shaken pilots.

There was some shuffling within the RAFME Authority behind the frontline scenes, with 264 Wing being formed at Sidi Haneish towards the end of the month, with responsibility for 30 and 33 Squadrons and the RNFS. However, within days this was replaced by 269 Wing under the command of Wg Cdr Harold Fenton DFC, former CO of 238 Squadron. Also, during the month, the RNFS's redundant Fulmars at Dekheila were assembled into a new unit named RN Fulmar Flight, formed for shipping protection; one Flight was based at Dekheila and the other at Fuka, with an initial total of twelve aircraft on strength.

With the next British and Commonwealth push against the Axis forces in the desert about to commence—Operation *Crusader*—there followed two weeks of intensive training for the RNAS Hurricane pilots in close escort simulated operational flying with Blenheims and Tomahawks, honing particularly the new arrivals in preparation for the battles to come. Meanwhile, two Martlets were scrambled on **10 November** on the approach of an intruder. Despite the Ju88 passing within a mile of the searching Martlets, the aircraft was not sighted in the failing light. Next day (**11 November**), all 16 RNFS Hurricanes were ordered to LG109 in readiness for forthcoming operations, while the Martlets remained at LG13 for coastal patrols.

16 November saw a 269 Wing sweep carried out by a dozen Hurricanes (six/806 and five/803) led by Lt-Cdr Black. Tomahawks of 112 Squadron flew as top cover over Sidi Omar, Gabri Saleh and Fort Maddalena but nothing untoward transpired. At 14:45 on the next afternoon (**17 November**, the eve of *Crusader*), the Hurricanes were off again (six of 806 flown by Lts Johnston, Cox and Pangbourne, Sub-Lts Fell, Diggens and Wood), again led by Lt-Cdr Black, as close escort for 14 Squadron Blenheims, with Tomahawks from 112 and 3RAAF Squadrons flying as top cover. The formation flew northwards from LG109 and crossed the coast, then turned westwards over the sea before turning south and re-crossing the coast in the region of Mersa Lucch. They made one circuit down to ground level and carried out an attack on Bir el-Baheira aerodrome about one minute after the Blenheims had bombed. Pilots reported seeing two Henschels destroyed and two M/T on fire; a third full of troops was strafed. Sub-Lt Alf Astin's 803 Flight Hurricane (Z4177/OL-Q) experienced engine trouble and he aborted the attack and landed at LG05, followed by all the other Hurricanes for refuelling.

18 November saw the commencement of Operation *Crusader* but in the air all was relatively quiet despite five offensive sweeps carried out during the day by a total of eleven Hurricane and Tomahawk squadrons; Hurricanes of 33 Squadron clashed with CR42s of 393ª *Squadriglia* over Gialo airfield and Bf109s of 1./JG27 shot down two SAAF Marylands near Gazala, while Beaufighters strafed Tmimi airfield but the RNFS Hurricanes failed to sight any targets and routinely patrolled over advance ground units. With little Axis reaction on the ground or in the air, next day again witnessed Beaufighters strafe Tmimi and Sidi Rezegh and Blenheims and Marylands bomb a variety of targets; three of the bombers fell to flak. The RNFS again patrolled over an Allied armoured division in the area of Fort Maddalena.

For the FAA pilots the air war re-started in earnest on **20 November**, when eleven Hurricanes joined forces with Tomahawks of 250 Squadron for a Wing sweep over the Gambut-El Adem area, where a dozen Ju87s were sighted at the same height as the Allied formation. Initially only six escorting fighters were seen but Bf109s dived from above and a series of swirling dogfights ensued. For the RNFS only 806 Flight leader Lt Johnston (Z4560/OL-A) and 803 Flight's Sub-Lt *Freddy* Charlton (W9327/OL-M) were able to engage the Stukas, as were three or four of the Tomahawk pilots. Lt Johnston claimed a probable:

> While on a fighter sweep in the vicinity of El Adem, I observed a large formation of aircraft to starboard and slightly above on a converging course. I lost sight of them for a short while and then saw several Me109s diving at the formation. I turned and became involved in a general dogfight. During this action I saw nine Ju87s below me and selected one vic of three as target. Dived on them intending to carry out beam attack. However, as I approached, the three turned away and dived, committing me to an astern attack and forcing me to steepen my dive. I fired three short bursts at one of them while closing from 300 to 100 yards and then overshot him. As I passed, I saw white vapour coming apparently from his port wing strut. I blacked out in recovering from my dive and did not see the 87s again but just below the action several large bomb bursts in apparently uninhabited country, which led me to believe that some, at least, of the enemy had jettisoned their bombs.

But Charlton was the star of the day and recorded two kills and a probable:

> I observed Ju87 formation below, so I dived down towards them, violently weaving on the way. I made diving attack on port rear bomber and after short burst the 87 continued vertical dive into the ground, where the bombs exploded on impact. Then the leader of the formation increased their dive and they jettisoned their bombs and as they levelled out, I attacked the starboard rear bomber from beam quarter. After about five two-second bursts the bomber dropped behind in a dive towards the ground, pouring smoke from him. After seeing him hit the ground, I observed hits on another bomber attacked from astern. On breaking away from this attack I felt a slight jolt.

Charlton's aircraft had been erroneously attacked by a Tomahawk (probably that flown by Australian Sgt Dick Nitschke of 250 Squadron) in mistake for a Bf109. With his engine faltering he was able to make a forced-landing in friendly territory. Meeting up with an army unit, he was soon on his way back courtesy of a Lysander alerted to his misfortune. On the negative side, 806 Flight's Lt Walter Pangbourne (V7858) was also shot down but killed. He was possibly the victim of Uffz Hans Niederhöfer of 5./JG27 who claimed a Hurricane (unconfirmed) south of El Adem. The accompanying Tomahawks lost one pilot killed (probably the victim of 1./JG27) and three aircraft damaged, one of which was flown by the errant Sgt Nitschke. A total of eight of the dive-bombers were claimed and a further five probably so—mainly by 250 Squadron pilots—but in fact only two were totally lost with their crews, one each from 2./StG1 (Ltn Jochen Hiddessen/Gfr Franz Schaffranek) and the other from 5./StG2 (Uffz Friedrich Figge/Gfr Alfred Heinse); others may have force-landed. All bombers were seen to jettison their bombs over a salt pan and thus were unable to inflict any damage or casualties amongst the Allied ground forces.

Next day (**21 November**) a dozen RNFS Hurricanes took-off at 14:00 on a Wing sweep in company with Tomahawks from 250 Squadron. On approaching Gambut, AA fire was seen well to the rear and on the airfield five Bf109s were observed taking-off or about to take-off. These were not engaged by the Naval pilots however, but the Tomahawks engaged without known results. Further east, pairs of Fulmars from the Fulmar Flight provided cover for a convoy proceeding towards Tobruk. At dusk, six He111s approached the convoy, one at 7,000 feet and the others low over the water. One Fulmar pilot climbed to engage the high aircraft while the other went for the five lower aircraft, which jettisoned their torpedoes. Apart from this success that undoubtedly saved the convoy from possible attack, there were no engagements. **23 November** again witnessed a clash between RNFS Hurricanes and Bf109s and G.50s (the latter escort six Ju88s) during a mid-morning patrol over the Gabr Saleh area, two Hurricanes being shot down in return for one Bf109 probably destroyed and two G.50s damaged. A dozen Tomahawks from 250 Squadron made up the Wing formation. Sub-Lt George Henderson of 803 Flight in Z4555/OL-T claimed the Messerschmitt:

> On sighting the enemy, the Hurricanes went into a defensive circle. While going around this circle I saw a Tomahawk dive into our circle with a 109 firing at it and on its tail. I pulled up my nose and got a long burst into the 109. It stopped firing immediately. The Tomahawk pulled out of the dive and joined the circle. The 109 continued straight down in its dive into cloud and was lost from view.

Meanwhile, Sub-Lts Peter Fell (Z4189/OL-D) and John Knee (Z4834/OL-S) each claimed damage inflicted on a pair of G.50s but Sub-Lts Ken Talbot (W9359) and Tony Willis (V7308/OL-C) failed to return. Talbot, who had initially been allocated Z4698, had suffered a port undercarriage collapse on taking off, so jumped into W9359 only to be shot down by a Bf109; he forced-landed and was rescued by retreating troops and was back two days later. But Tony Willis was not so fortunate and was killed, believed also to have been a victim of the Bf109s. Further misfortune befell the RNFS during an afternoon bomber escort, the formation being attacked by an estimated 12–15 Bf109s both before and after reaching the objective but none of their charges were lost. One Hurricane failed to return, probably the victim of Hptm Wolfgang Redlich of 1./JG27, although Lt *Zac* Cox was able to bale out of his burning aircraft. (Z4267/OL-G). He was found by British troops and taken to hospital.[5] In return, Sub-Lt Alf Astin (Z4177/OL-Q) claimed a Bf109 probably destroyed, mainly on the basis of seeing a parachute shortly after his combat but it was most likely Cox's.

More bomber escorts and sweeps followed but of Axis aircraft very little was seen. However, Afrika Korps forces were pushing back British and

Commonwealth forces on the ground, causing much confusion for the Hurricane and Tomahawk units operating from various advance landing grounds. The RNFS Hurricanes had arrived at LG123 from LG109. Now reports were coming in of German forces rapidly approaching the area. At 16:45 on 24th, all Hurricanes were ordered to evacuate to LG128 and at 11:00 on the morning of **25 November**, 806 Flight's CO Lt Johnston took-off to carry out a recce (believed in Z4932/OL-B) and soon sighted an M/T convoy. Flying low to properly identify it, he promptly got his answer when a burst of light flak hit his engine, forcing him to crash-land. He was immediately taken prisoner by troops from a German convoy. He was put in a car together with a tank officer under guard by an Uffz and for three hours headed west with the M/T convoy, which was then attacked by Blenheims:

> It was very good bombing but highly unpleasant. Bombs rained down on the column, hitting trucks and lorries. We were taken out of the car to make room for some wounded and in the confusion resulting from the raid and despite the number still around us, we walked quietly away and lay down in the camel scrub. The enemy column moved away without us—what was left of the column—and we started walking south.

They reached safety next day and became members of the semi-official Late Arrivals Club. Patrols and escorts continued as the month drew to a close, Ju87s and Bf109s being sighted but not engaged on one occasion. Following the scare, RNFS returned to LG123 the following day, causing many headaches for the bemused ground personnel who were trying to keep up with all the moves and threats of being overrun.

Lt Henry Allingham (Z4245) led eight Hurricanes on a Wing sweep together with a dozen Tomahawks from 250 Squadron to the El Duda-Gabr Saleh area on **1 December**, as he reported:

> At 09:30, I was leading the squadron … and sighted a formation of nine Ju88s in vics, escorted by six or more G.50s and Me109s flying in line escort 1,000 feet above and astern of bombers. Enemy formation was sighted right ahead at 800 yards range—consider our squadron unobserved. Bombers jettisoned bombs and incendiaries and dived at full throttle to ground level on westerly course. I pulled the tit and followed and held bombers in dive at 310mph, approximately 500 yards. Close range at ground level and fired six short bursts from right astern at port bomber of last vic at range 400–300 yards. Following last burst enemy aircraft lurched to starboard and starboard wing hit ground. Aircraft crashed. I then climbed and while gaining height was attacked by one G.50 who dived on my tail. I turned sharply and put a full deflection shot into G.50 as it broke

> away from me. He broke upwards and outwards and exposed whole belly. Enemy aircraft burst into flames and crashed.

Lt Allingham's victim was 4U+JK, which fell 30 miles south-east of Fort Maddalena. Both Ltn Franz-Heinrich von Gablenz and Fw Gerhard Letz survived to be taken prisoner but Uffz Felix Flemming, the gunner, was killed. Another Ju88 was attacked by Sub-Lt Ken Wood (OL-E), who claimed his victim as probably damaged. He also claimed a G.50 probably destroyed, while Sub-Lts Harry Diggens (V7017) and George Dennison (OL-C) each claimed one destroyed. In addition, Sub-Lt Charlton (Z4177/OL-Q) engaged two Bf109s, claiming one probably destroyed and the other damaged, while Sub-Lt Darrell Dick (OL-Y) also claimed a probable. It seems probable that the G.50s were in fact MC200s of 153° *Gruppo CT*, operating from Derna, *Tenente* Renzo Sappa of 373ª *Squadriglia* being reported shot down and killed. Two more Messerschmitts were damaged by Tomahawk pilots; in return, two Tomahawk pilots were shot down though both returned next day. Successes continued and on **3 December** Lt Tristram Winstanley, originally a Swordfish pilot but now flying with 803 Squadron, claimed a Bf109 damaged while flying Hurricane Z4535 during a Gazala patrol.

RNFS fighters experienced a busy day on **28 December**, claiming two aircraft shot down for the loss of a Martlet and a Fulmar; one pilot being killed. Whilst escorting a coastal convoy, Sub-Lt Royston Griffin intercepted four torpedo-carrying SM79s of 281ª *Squadriglia AS* some 50 miles north of Ras el Mih, shooting down the aircraft (MM24089) flown by *Tenente* Luigi Rovelli and forcing two others to jettison their torpedoes. Whilst so engaged his Martlet (3895) was hit by return fire and crashed into the sea. Lost with *Tenente* Rovelli were co-pilot *Sergente Maggiorre* Ugo Scardapane and two others.

Meanwhile near Tobruk, Sub-Lt Peter Fell encountered a He111 which he claimed probably destroyed. Further east, near Sidi Barrani, two Fulmars from the Fulmar Flight became engaged with a Ju88 but Sub-Lt Frank Sanderson's aircraft was hit by return fire, forcing him to ditch in the sea from where he was subsequently rescued.

Two days later (**30 December**), Kittyhawks of 4SAAF had just begun taking off for a sweep, with two RNFS Hurricanes as top cover, when Ju88D 4U+HK, a reconnaissance aircraft of 2.(F)/123 appeared overhead. Two Kittyhawks and the Hurricane flown by Sub-Lt David Langdon gave chase and shot it down near Msus. Ltn Karl-Heinz Renner, Fw Potthast and Uffz von Moltke were killed.

On **25 January**, 806 Squadron's Lt Henry Allingham and Sub-Lt Barry Nation reported engaging a He111 off the coast and claimed it damaged. This proved to be 806's final action with the RNAS, which was now disbanded.[6]

Shortly before the turn of the year, awards had been announced for a number of 806 Squadron aircrew, relating to earlier service during the Crete operations. Long overdue DSCs were awarded to Lt Jackie Sewell, Lt Pat Massy,[7] Lt Robert Henley[8] and observer Sub-Lt Norman Cullen (since deceased). Surprisingly there was no recognition for the successful Lt MacDonald-Hall[9] apart from a Mention in Despatches. Long-serving TAG L/Air Colin Hearnshaw[10] received the DSM and promotion. Lt John Shears and his observer Sub-Lt Eric Dixon (both deceased) were awarded posthumous Mention in Despatches, a similar award going to Lt-Cdr Charles Evans DSO DSC.

VII

Ceylon

Until February 1942, the air defence of Ceylon had rested almost entirely in the hands of the Royal Navy but until the arrival of 803 and 806 Squadrons from Egypt, eight Hurricanes, which had been assembled at Karachi, were also flown to Ceylon, six by pilots of 136 Squadron—who were in transit, their original destination being Burma—arriving at Ratmalana late February. A Fleet Requirements Unit, 788 Squadron, had been impressed for coastal reconnaissance, torpedo-bombing and general duties, for which it was equipped with Swordfish. At China Bay airfield was 273 Squadron, which operated antiquated Seal and Vildebeest biplanes for general purpose duties, though later a few Fulmars were borrowed from the Navy.

The two RNAS units arrived in the Colombo area after re-equipping with Fulmar IIs,[1] 803 Squadron under Lt Bruce McEwen and 806 Squadron still under the temporary command of Lt Robert Johnston. Flying with Lt McEwen on the cross-continent trip from Egypt as his observer was Sub-Lt Roy Hinton, a veteran of the battle of Crete the previous year, who recalled:

> We proceeded overland in four batches of six aircraft. I flew with McEwen and we had a hilarious flight out, arriving at Bangalore (southern India), which we liked so much we decided to spend a week in relaxing. Another flight lost their way and came down in the grounds of the Maharaja of Hyderabad and became guests for several days. All aircraft, by a miracle, arrived at Ratmalana, more or less, in flying trim. Accommodation was very poor. McEwen, myself and a few other chaps decided that the Galle Face Hotel in Colombo was more in keeping with our status, so we moved in, spending most of the daylight hours relaxing in the sea. Sure enough, we were rudely awakened by the C-in-C, who could not find any responsible person at Ratmalana and eventually tracked us down. Back to base and work!

The 806 Squadron contingent comprised:

Pilots	**Observers**
Lt R. L. Johnston	Lt A. T. Shaw
Lt H. P. Allingham	Sub-Lt(A) F. W. Ponting
Lt N. A. Bartlett	Sub-Lt(A) A. Peace
Lt S. J. Hall	Sub-Lt(A) L. W. Peck
Lt M. Hordern	Sub-Lt(A) F. W. Bonnell
Sub-Lt(A) J. H. C. Sykes	
Sub-Lt(A) B. H. C. Nation	
Sub-Lt(A) K. J. M. Pettitt	
Sub-Lt(A) G. M. Warren	
Sub-Lt(A) E. S. Marshall	
Sub-Lt(A) D. W. Langdon	
Sub-Lt(A) F. W. Leng	
Sub-Lt(A) R. A. Peacock	
Sub-Lt(A) H. S. Diggens	

The main defence of Ceylon rested on the Eastern Fleet, which was itself maintaining a primarily defensive role in the Indian Ocean. The loss of several modern units in the East Indies was felt by the cruiser and destroyer forces and the battle line represented all that could be spared from the Home and Mediterranean Fleets. Only one battleship, *Warspite*, had been modernised to the extent that it could match the Japanese. The cruiser situation was even more desperate, with only two relatively modern heavy cruisers—*Cornwall* and *Dorsetshire*—and a miscellany of four small, old, six-inch gun cruisers. The major strength of the Fleet lay (on paper) in the number of aircraft carriers, three of which had assembled by late March. Of the carriers, *Indomitable* was the newest and largest in the Royal Navy. She had been intended to join *Prince of Wales* and *Repulse* at Singapore in late 1941 but an accident while working up in the West Indies had delayed her arrival in the Indian Ocean until the New Year. Proceeding to Aden to continue working-up, *Indomitable* had been ordered to disembark her Fulmar squadron and one of her two Albacore squadrons in order to make room for two squadrons of Hurricanes, which were to be delivered to Java. Following a successful ferry run, *Indomitable* returned to Aden to embark two more RAF Hurricane squadrons intended for Java but by the time the carrier was due to leave, Java had been invaded and the Hurricanes diverted to Ceylon. These fighters were dispersed to Ratmalana and the hurriedly constructed airfield at Racecourse.

On **24 March**, more Fulmars began arriving at China Bay for 273 Squadron, the first batch being flown in from RNAS Cochin—an aerodrome on the south-west coast of the mainland—by FAA pilots led by Lt Val Bailey. Most of these pilots had served with 808 Squadron but were now 'homeless' following the loss of their aircraft carrier, *Ark Royal*, in the Mediterranean the previous November. On arrival at China Bay the Naval pilots were attached to 273 Squadron. The Fulmars had been delivered to Cochin in crates and had been closely followed by the arrival from Karachi of Cdr Robin Kilroy, piloting another Fulmar, who had been instructed to supervise the assembling and testing of these fighters. Lt Bailey recalled:

> I had just finished assembling and testing some Fulmars. These were not the world's best fighters and my recollection is that the RAF pilots of 273 Squadron were not that keen to fly them against what we were certain would be *Zeros*. Anyway, I had arrived with a number of pilots from that ship and we were sent to China Bay where we were attached to 273 Squadron. I recall two very sporting RAF (ex-Army) pilots who remained with us.

With the arrival of further Fulmars, 273 Squadron now had a total of 16 of these fighters on hand, ostensibly under the command of Flt Lt R. M. Pimm but, as this unit now had a larger proportion of naval aircrew than of RAF personnel, Lt Bailey was effectively in charge. Thus, the beginning of April found Ceylon greatly reinforced in a period of just one month. The Hurricanes were reasonably competent to handle the opposition but only a handful of the pilots could be considered to have any depth of operational experience and some had none at all. The Fulmars could not be expected to cope with modern fighter opposition but, given the chance, would be able to deal with most bombers they were likely to meet with a reasonable chance of success; the experience of their pilots was generally comparable with that of the members of the Hurricane squadrons. So far as the bombers were concerned, a number of the Blenheim crews had adequate recent experience of bombing land targets in the Western Desert but had received no training, nor any experience in attacking shipping.

Following Japanese successes with the invasion and capture of Singapore and the whole of the Dutch East Indies and the inroads made into Burma by the Japanese army, the threat of a Japanese foray into the Indian Ocean was anticipated by the British authorities. In the light of this threat, the Admiralty ordered that the main ports—India's Calcutta and Madras and Ceylon's Trincomalee and Colombo—should be cleared of as much shipping as possible. Although more than 70 ships departed Calcutta, some of these would later fall foul to air and sea attack. The Japanese had indeed assembled a mighty naval strike force, comprising five large aircraft carriers (*Akagi, Soryu, Hirya, Skokaku* and *Zuikaku*), four battleships, two heavy cruisers and 11 destroyers, under the command of Admiral Nagumo. Aboard the carriers, ready for the assault were 125 dive-bombers and fighters. However, the main intention of the Japanese was to neutralise any British fleet in the area and to disrupt Allied shipping in the Bay of Biscay. Invasion of Ceylon was never seriously entertained at this stage. The presence of a strong British naval force in the Indian Ocean posed a threat to Japanese convoys carrying supplies to the newly-captured main Burmese port of Rangoon. On the morning of **4 April**, as Nagumo's Strike Force was approaching Ceylon, it was spotted when some 350 miles off the south-east of the island by a patrolling Catalina, which managed to transmit a warning signal to Ceylon before being shot down by A6M *Zeros* from the carriers. Fearing an invasion, all shipping in harbour at Trincomalee and Colombo was ordered to scatter. These included the small aircraft carrier *Hermes* (*sans* her Swordfish) and the old cruisers *Dorsetshire* and *Cornwall.*

Dawn of **5 April**—Easter Sunday—thus found the island's defences fully alerted and ready to repel an expected invasion. However, the Japanese carriers began launching aircraft for a strike on Colombo at 06:00, while still 120 miles out to sea: 53 B5N *Kates* and 38 DA3 *Vals*—all dive-bombers with an escort comprising 36 A6Ms. The fighters were the first to arrive at 07:32, encountering a flight of six Swordfish, all of which were shot down (four killed and four others died from their injuries). While this one-sided action was in progress, a total of 35 Hurricanes and six Fulmars—three each from 803 and 806 Squadrons—were scrambling as fast as they could from Ratmalana and Racecourse. At Ratmalana, L/Air Bert Holt of 803 Squadron was Duty TAG in the Ops Room—a thatched hut—and recalled:

> At about 07:40, a large number of planes came over from the seaward side—the ones I saw seemed to be Navy 97s and *Zeros*, flying in V formation. At the same time the phone rang—it was the RAF asking if we knew of any carriers sending off aircraft. I answered: 'Yes, Japs! Get your bods airborne!' I then ran outside, screaming as loud as possible: 'Scramble! Scramble!' I don't suppose anyone knew who gave that alarm. The most vivid thing I remember then was a sub-lieutenant, towel in hand and wearing only his black beard, belting out of the showers, heading for his flying gear. I ran into the Ops Room, grabbed my pads and other gear, then to the parachute store looking for my chute, which was missing. Someone else, no doubt, had it so I grabbed another but by this time everyone else was on the jeep and it was moving out; I was left behind. Getting the armoury open, I took one of the Vickers 'K' guns, which had only just arrived the week before and mounted it on top of a mound but then along came Sub-Lt Peck, who took over the gun! When I pointed to a Jap coming low over the trees, he fired but only three shots, as the pans had not been wound up.

The leader of the 803 Squadron section was Sub-Lt Bill Anderson:

> Just as we reached the airfield perimeter by truck, the second wave of aircraft were arriving at a much lower height, dropping what appeared to be enormous bombs (which were, in fact, long-range fuel tanks made of *papier-mâché*), strafing the airfield and taking an incredible toll of the Hurricanes as they scrambled ahead of us. One of the only TAGs (N/Air Fred Johnson) to reach the airfield in time for the scramble, jumped into the back of my Fulmar and used the only weapon available—a Very pistol and cartridges—to frighten off any Jap getting a bit too close!

He added:

> The only way that we could mix it with the Japs was to dive from a great height out of the sun, have a go and get the hell out of it. These conditions unfortunately were not present as the Japs already had a 10,000 feet advantage and the Fulmar was a painfully slow climber, even at full boost.

Anderson's two companions were immediately pursued as they climbed away from the airfield, Sub-Lt Ian White-Smith's Fulmar (X8555) diving into the sea while Sub-Lt Harry Diggens (806 Squadron) crashed into the jungle; he too was killed; his body was later recovered from the wreck of his aircraft. The 806 Squadron section was marginally more successful, although Sub-Lt Ken Pettitt was also shot down and killed, his Fulmar (X8569) seen to dive in flames into the jungle. Apparently, he was coming in to land when he was caught by an A6M. Lt Mike Hordern, the section leader, recalled:

> We were caught on the ground for a start and not many of us even got airborne. A Petty Officer with a sub-machine gun leapt in the back of my aircraft and I believe even fired it with wild abandon! I was on my own and saw a number of enemy aircraft circling over the sea—possibly reforming or in defensive orbit against some other aircraft. I approached through broken cloud cover at about 5,000 feet and made one pass before breaking off at high speed and seeing one aircraft burning on the surface of the sea. I was credited with one Navy 96 shot down, seen and confirmed by a Naval officer standing outside the Mount Lavinia Hotel.

The third Fulmar (possibly X8640) of the section, flown by Sub-Lt John Sykes, was also shot down:

> Having seen some of our boys getting into trouble almost immediately on take-off, I thought I would do a quick, tight circuit and protect anybody who was still on the ground or in the process of getting airborne. This wasn't such a bright idea—I was jumped by two Nips who got on with the business of shooting me down. I

> was frightened, bloody frightened. Tracer bullets were hammering me from the rear, the instrument panel shattered, the right-hand side of my head—by my right eye—was blistered by a tracer which came a bit too close and the controls of the Fulmar stiffened. If I cried out to God, would He hear? I cried out. I heard later that the gunners, entrenched round the airfield, shot the first Nip out of the sky. The second Nip got through their fire but by this time I was heading for a paddy field. I came to a halt in the mud in the middle of the field and was unstrapped and out of the aircraft in a matter of seconds! There was the roar of an engine. I looked up. There was this Nippon bastard coming to finish me off whilst I was up to my knees in mud! Bullet holes all round me but nothing hit me! I ran, or tried to run, for the side of the field. My enemy came back three times. There were bullet holes in the mud all round my footprints but I did not even get a scratch.

The Fulmars' attackers included A6Ms from *Soryu*, whose leader Lt Iyozo Fujita personally claimed one shot down. The RAF Hurricanes were overwhelmed and equally mauled by the Japanese fighters, no fewer than 21 being shot down (at least one by the island's own guns), a number of which crash-landed. Nine pilots were killed and a tenth died of his wounds. Eighteen Japanese aircraft, mainly dive-bombers were claimed in return. In fact, six D3As were lost, as was one A6M, while a further twelve dive-bombers landed on the carriers with combat damaged, as did three A6Ms. Japanese fighter pilots claimed 33 British fighters shot down, plus eight Swordfish (six lost). A further six fighters were claimed by the dive-bomber crews. As the Japanese formations returned to their carriers, a flight of Fulmars from 803 Squadron was just returning from an uneventful patrol, the crews unaware of the assault on their airfield; recalled observer Sub-Lt Roy Hinton:

> We had flown down the coast at 2,000 feet to Bentota, a distance of about 30 miles and directly across the island to Batticalo and were on our way back for breakfast. About 20 minutes flying time from base we saw a number of aircraft flying out to sea. Although all aircraft were fitted with radio, no signals whatsoever were received of impending trouble. Japanese aircraft were farthest from our minds on the return flight that morning and we dismissed the aircraft seen by thinking they were another unscheduled FAA flight. Arriving back at base it was so obvious that all hell had been let loose only minutes before. It transpired that all the wireless operators at Ratmalana had sought shelter as soon as the first bombs were dropped.

Although losses in the air had been heavy for the defenders, the fighters clearly had an effect on the efficiency of the attack and the timely removal of all possible shipping had kept losses in this respect to a minimum. However, the harbour workshops at Colombo were seriously damaged and an armed merchant cruiser and a destroyer were sunk; the submarine depot vessel and a 6,000-ton merchant ship sustained damage. Thirty-nine naval personnel had been killed, together a dozen Goanese and Lascars. Tragically, 15 civilian inmates of a nearby mental hospital were also killed and a further 22 injured when a bomb hit the building.

From Ceylon an attempt was made at retaliation, ten Blenheims being despatched at 08:30 to attack Nagumo's carriers but fortunately for the crews on this potential suicide mission they were given incorrect directions and failed to find the fleet. The carrier fighter pilots instead contented themselves by shooting down a searching Catalina. The day was young however. Scouting planes from Japanese cruisers were searching the sea south of Ceylon for signs of fleeing ships which they had expected to find in harbour and, just after 11:00, an aircraft from the cruiser *Tone* discovered the *Dorsetshire* and *Cornwall.* Three formations of D3A dive-bombers were despatched to the area and within 15 minutes both cruisers had been sunk, although 1,222 survivors from the two ships were later rescued by Australian warships, over 450 had been lost.

Over the next four days the Nagumo Strike Force was carrying out manoeuvres that would eventually bring the ships onto a north-westerly course for an intended strike at Trincomalee, at the same time its aircraft attacking any shipping that came within range. Many Allied ships were sunk during this period but mainly fell victim to a second Japanese naval force sent specifically for this task.

By early morning of **9 April**, Nagumo's Strike Force was nearing Trincomalee, where radar had picked up a mass of aircraft rapidly approaching—in fact 91 B5N *Kates* escorted by 41 A6Ms. Three patrolling Hurricanes were the first to encounter the armada and gained success by shooting down two of the escort, including *Zuikaku's* fighter leader. Six more Hurricanes were scrambled and engaged in a series of swirling dogfights, two of these being shot down although both pilots were able to crash-land. Four Fulmars from China Bay's *ad hoc* Staff Flight had narrowly avoided encountering the approaching raiders. Swordfish observer Lt Jack Smith was flying in a Fulmar piloted by an RAF officer and recalled:

> Our task was to try to locate the Jap fleet. My pilot was a former Hurricane pilot from the Middle East. To him, flying a Fulmar was like driving a London bus and he had never navigated before—steady course and speed and height were all anathema to him. But he did very well and I navigated by averaging! The radio did not work and the compasses had not been swung for ages. Our search was unsuccessful but only three of the four Fulmars returned. We returned just in time to park in dispersal under the trees. We got to the Ops Room for debriefing when the Japs arrived.

The missing Fulmar (X8769/K) was crewed by Flg Off Arthur Gregg and Sub-Lt Aubrey Mass; having apparently suffered engine trouble, it crashed into dense jungle just inland of Foul Point and both Gregg and Mass were killed. Amongst the many who witnessed the attack on the airfield from close quarters was RAF Flt Sgt George Mothersdale:

> A beat of engines at the south-west end of the airfield was heard and a formation of six single-engined bombers had come into view, flying in a tight vic of five with one in the box. Against the solid blue sky and bright sunshine, with their red disks prominent on their near-white surface finish, they looked impressive! They came in over the ridge behind me—their altitude was only about 1,500 feet—crossed the airfield on a curving track in a matter of seconds and were on their way over the jungle north-eastwards. As I stood watching it seemed unreal—they had the sky over China Bay to themselves—and the Bofors guns on the airfield had not fired (the time the gunners had them in view must have been very limited). A short period lapsed then a fighter, followed by another, came into view from behind a headland just beyond the south-west end of the airfield.
>
> They came in from over the sea at about 100 feet and were soon recognised in their near-white finish. One came down low, banked steeply round the two refuellers and steamroller, quickly zoomed, quickly dived, firing a short burst at a refueller. The second fighter followed the first, firing a short burst at the other refueller and the steamroller. They then rapidly flew low over the airfield, searching for ground targets. One was nearing where I stood—I promptly slid down and crouched in the shelter trench amid the protests of those huddled in the bottom. From behind came the whistling sound of falling bombs. Down into the trench I crouched in the standard drill—steel helmet across the back of the head—teeth clenched—until the ear-stunning bangs of near bomb bursts ended as abruptly as they all began. I stood up and looked around.

A scene of devastation greeted him. Black smoke was rising with mounting flames from the M/T yard and a corner of the RAF hangar had been hit, where two or three of 273 Squadron's remaining Vildebeests were housed; these were effectively damaged beyond repair. The Sergeants' Mess and a number of other Station buildings were also damaged. By now more Hurricanes had been scrambled and engaged both dive-bombers and fighters. When the final scoresheet was drawn up, the Hurricane pilots were credited with four B4Ns and four A6Ms, while eight Hurricanes were shot down or crash-landed (one pilot killed and another mortally wounded on the ground). Trincomalee harboured mainly naval vessels but one merchantman was anchored in the middle of the harbour and had not been able to escape. Her deck cargo included a Walrus amphibian and three dismantled Albacores, as well as ammunition for the Hurricanes; it was reputed that her holds also contained copious quantities of whisky! With her decks ablaze, the flames consumed her cargo of aircraft and whisky alike.

Meanwhile, spotter planes from Nagumo Force had located the small carrier *Hermes* and a strike force comprising 85 dive-bombers was launched. In the opposite direction came 11 Blenheims, the crews tasked to attack any Japanese warships they could find and independently, six Fulmars of 273 Squadron led by Lt Val Bailey:

> The first intimation of excitement was when a Hurricane from China Bay landed at Kokkilai with a wounded RAF officer, who said the Japanese were attacking. I scrambled my flight and with my No.2, *Twinkle* Neal flew off in the general direction of whence the Hurricane had come. I had had the back-seat gear from all the Fulmars removed to save weight. We did not have enough parachutes and used engine covers to give us the necessary height in the seat. I climbed as fast as I could, which was not very fast in a Fulmar and at about 18,000 feet I saw *Hermes* ahead. As we approached, I saw more aircraft than I had ever seen in one place before and, as I had no wireless communication (none of us did), I rolled over—and believing that the best chance was to have maximum speed—kept pointing downhill into the mêlée. The Fulmar had a terminal velocity, so we believed, of about 270 knots and at that speed I arrived in the middle of a lot of aircraft—fortunately all opposition! I remember noting that *Hermes* was not on fire but seemed to be very full of holes. There was an escort of some sort.
>
> I found a Navy 96 in front of me and was about to fire when there was the most-almighty noise in my cockpit. I pushed the tit and to my surprise, whilst continuing to overtake the 96, it flipped over. The noise, I then discovered, had been my cockpit hood blowing off, doubtless due to the unexpected speed the thing had been doing. There was an extraordinary number of aircraft still about and I was now at about 1,000 feet. I headed for land, being uncomfortable in the presence of the Zeros. There were several aircraft in front of me and once again a 96 got in the way. It wasn't possible to miss a 96. I knocked bits off it. Thereafter, life became chaotic. I kept the throttle fully open whilst weaving about, by now very low and more anxious to avoid a collision than find a target.
>
> I regret to say that I continued landwards after that as I had no ammunition and was nervous! Nothing pursued me and I arrived back at Kokkilai to find Major Norrie Martin, RM (CO of 814 Squadron) and his Swordfish alone on the strip. We had no refuelling facilities there so after a short stay I went to China Bay. There the armoury was on fire but nobody seemed very interested! We refuelled and headed out to *Hermes* again. On arrival there was no enemy and *Hermes* was sinking fast. We flew around and then returned to China Bay.

Lt Bailey was credited with one D3A shot down and another damaged, whilst two probables were claimed by Sub-Lt Norman Neal and Royal Marine pilot Lt Peter Nelson-Gracie and two others were claimed damaged. But they could not prevent a devastating attack on *Hermes* and escorting destroyer. An officer aboard the carrier later wrote:

> Their bombing was pretty deadly. We caught fire and started blazing furiously. The one thing we expected, however, did not materialise. There we no torpedoes. Some of the raiders came in low despite our AA. They paid for their audacity. We reckon at least four never reached their bases—three staggered away and one came hurtling into the sea.

Hermes went down at 10:55, with the loss of over 300 of her crew including the captain. The escorting destroyer was also sunk. As this attack was under way, the Blenheims came across the Nugamo Force and began bombing the nearest warships, the carrier *Akagi* and cruiser *Tome*. Although near-misses were seen, no hits were achieved. Before the bombers could make good their escape, the A6Ms were upon them. Four were promptly shot down before the others evaded and headed home but their ordeal was not yet over. At 11:05, they encountered more Zeros returning from the attack on *Hermes* and the Blenheim leader's aircraft was shot down; three more were damaged of which one crash-landed on return to Racecourse. On board two of the missing Blenheims were observers from 806 Squadron, Sub-Lt Tony Peace and Sub-Lt Frank Bonnell.

At Ratmalana the message to go to the aid of *Hermes* and her consort was received too late to help, due to damage suffered by the telephone system inflicted earlier. Notwithstanding, 806 Squadron's Lt Johnston mustered his available pilots.[2] On this occasion, observers and TAGs were ordered to stand down, as noted by L/Air Bert Holt:

> We—that is all the TAGs—went to our planes but were sent away again by the pilots, who said it was only a top cover routine patrol and we were just 'excess baggage'.

Finally, eight Fulmars of 803 and 806 Squadrons got off but by the time they arrived over the east coast the carrier had already sunk. The D3As of *Soryu* which had arrived, only to see *Hermes* sinking and which had set up a search further north, had discovered a hospital ship, two cargo ships and a patrol boat at 12:00, attacking three minutes later. The hospital ship was not attacked but the other vessels were sunk. Just before the attack ended around 12:15, the Fulmars arrived and engaged the dive-bombers, becoming involved in a 25-minute battle; for the loss of two of their number, they claimed three D3As shot down, one apiece being credited to 806 Squadron's Lt Robert Johnston and Sub-Lt Barry Nation and Sub-Lt Paul Peirano (803 Squadron). L/Air Holt continued:

> When the Fulmars arrived at *Hermes*' position, she had already received her *coup de grâce* and the Japs were there, greatly outnumbering them. In the ensuing fight two were lost including Paul Peirano, 'my' pilot; he was a fine type. He got at least one.

The Japanese in fact reported losing four of their D3As and five more damaged in combat near the carrier; they recorded that they had been attacked by 19 fighters, claiming to have shot down five, with two more probables. Apart from the Fulmar (X8535) flown by Sub-Lt Peirano, a second Fulmar (X8538) failed to return from this action, Sub-Lt Dick Jacob of 803 Squadron also losing is life. The remaining Fulmars landed at China Bay, ostensibly to refuel and re-arm but the Station Commander commandeered them for defence of his own airfield, where they were to remain for the next few days. One of the Fulmars may have fallen victim to future ace Naval Airman 1/C Sadamu Komaki, flying an A6M from the carrier *Shokaku*, who wrote:

> Behind and to the right of my flight leader, I entered combat with enemy fighters for the first time. In the midst of the battle, I became separated from the flight and found myself the target of attack from above and behind by a 'Spitfire'. This was the end! But luckily for me the 'Spitfire' overshot, losing its opportunity for an attack and hung instead in front of my sights. I shot it down with my first burst, attaining my first victory in the process.

Thus, ended the Nagumo Strike Force attack on Ceylon. The fleet was already steaming south-east. Bearing gradually southwards during the next 36 hours, the serried ranks of warships passed through the Andaman Sea and entered the Malacca Strait. By nightfall on **13 April** they had slipped between Malaya and Sumatra, passed Singapore and swept into the South China Sea, bound for home. The Japanese were jubilant: for the first time, carrier-borne aircraft had sunk an opposing aircraft carrier, albeit small and practically defenceless. Two cruisers and numerous other vessels had also been sunk and, they believed, that two major ports had been rendered unserviceable. However, the Japanese never again attacked Ceylon.

As for the Fulmar pilots, they had acquitted themselves well under the circumstances, being out-performed as they were by the supreme A6M *Zero*. For the loss of only five aircraft in combat (although four pilots were killed), the pilots of 803 and 806 Squadrons had claimed four of their opponents, albeit dive-bombers and those with 273 Squadron a further one destroyed, two probables and three damaged.

With the departure of the Japanese fleet, life almost returned to normal for the military and civilian population of Ceylon but for the FAA fighter pilots further action beckoned. Lt-Cdr Jimmy Garnett arrived from Dekheila to resume command of 806 Squadron, but the unit now found itself divided into two, with A Flight pilots, under the command of Lt Johnston, embarking on the carrier *Indomitable,* minus their aircraft. En route to its new theatre of war—the Mediterranean—the carrier would call in at Bombay, where a dozen Martlets were embarked for 806/A Flight. The Martlets had been delivered direct from the United States to the Indian port.[3]

Meanwhile, 806/B Flight retained its Fulmars at Ceylon, for local defence, although two sections were flown aboard Illustrious, the carrier having returned following its repairs in the United States. Illustrious had her working-up time cut short on 19 March to prepare to join the Eastern Fleet in the Indian Ocean and participate in the attack. She sailed four days later, escorting a troop convoy carrying some of the men allocated for the assault. A hangar fire broke out on 2 April that destroyed 11 aircraft and killed one crewman but failed to cause any serious damage to the ship. Repairs were made in Freetown, Sierra Leone and the convoy reached Durban on 22 April where her destroyed aircraft were replaced.

VIII

Madagascar: Securing the Indian Ocean

Fearful of further Japanese forays into the Indian Ocean, the British now turned their thoughts towards the island of Madagascar, against which action had been planned before the Japanese attack on Ceylon had materialised. Situated off the south-east coast of Africa, Madagascar is an island of considerable size, measuring over 1,000 miles north to south and being nearly 400 miles wide at its widest point. It was also a French colony and in the hands of the Vichy administration. It had been the decision of the Vichy government to allow Japanese forces to occupy French Indo-China which had provided the bases from which they could attack southern China and from where in more recent months, the attacks on Thailand, Malaya and Borneo had been launched. Madagascar was well situated to provide a base from which an enemy might strike at the main Allied sea routes round the Cape of Good Hope to India and Ceylon and to the Middle East via the Red Sea. It was feared that the French might be persuaded to allow the Japanese to install facilities there for the servicing of submarines operating in the Indian Ocean, both their own and German, or for other more elaborate and even more dangerous purposes. Clearly it was desirable that the island be occupied to prevent such an eventuality but the forces then available to Britain would not allow this to be accomplished.

However, plans were formulated for the capture of the main port of Diego Suarez, its naval base of Antsirane and the surrounding territory. Operation *Ironclad* was therefore to be put into effect with this limited objective in mind. Diego Suarez is situated on the extreme northern tip of the island and has one of the largest anchorages in the world. It was also easily defensible in its own right and separately from the rest of the island. A strong invasion force was assembled and air support was to be provided by *Illustrious* and *Indomitable.*

The French garrison possessed only a motley collection of aircraft, mainly

Potez 63-11 twin-engined reconnaissance bombers and two *escadrilles* (squadrons) of Morane 406 fighters. On the ground the French were weak in real terms, although quite strong in numbers. Their forces lacked heavy equipment, adequate artillery support, armoured vehicles, etc. Indeed, the greater part of the army was composed of Senegalese and local Malagaches under French officers. This then was the strength and disposition of the French air arm facing the British at the beginning of May.

Thus, at noon on **4 May**, the British task force moved to a covering position to the west of Cape d'Amer on the northern tip of Madagascar. Secrecy had still been maintained and the French had no inkling of their presence. The prime objective at Diego Suarez was the Antsirane naval base and its airfield of Arrachart. The sea approach to the harbour was through a channel known as the Oronjia Pass, which was known to be strongly defended. It was vital therefore that troops should storm and capture this area in order that shipping might enter the base in safety. During the night of **4/5 May** the transports, led by a minesweeper, approached the western coastline and anchored before dawn. Assault craft carrying the invasion force headed inshore into Courier Bay. Although minesweepers inadvertently detonated two mines, complete surprise was achieved and the troops were able to head straight across the Andrakoka Peninsula. Other troops went ashore in Ambararata Bay without any opposition, although an additional landing which was then made at Basse Point did encounter some limited skirmishing. Just before dawn the carriers launched their initial strikes, while a cruiser created a diversion off the east coast, to which position she had sailed during the night.

Illustrious launched three strikes, each of six Swordfish, to attack shipping in the bay just before 04:00, while Albacores from *Indomitable* set course to bomb Arrachart airfield. The first flight of six Swordfish, carrying torpedoes, sank the armed merchant cruiser *Bougainville*. The second flight, carrying depth charges, sank a Vichy submarine while the third flight dropped leaflets over the defenders before attacking an artillery battery. One aircraft of the third flight was forced to make an emergency landing and its crew was captured by the French. Later in the day, the sloop *D'Entrecasteaux* attempted to put to sea but she was successfully bombed by a Swordfish and deliberately run aground to avoid sinking. Three other Swordfish completed her destruction.

Fighters followed from both carriers to patrol over airfield and beaches and to attack French artillery batteries. The Albacores, escorted by Martlets, attacked Arrachart airfield at low level, setting the hangars on fire. Five Ms406s were destroyed and two more damaged, while two Potez were also hit. Immediately the news of the British landings had been digested, more aircraft were flown up to Anivorano, 50 miles south of Diego Suarez. From there over the next few days many sorties were to be flown, the Potez bombing vehicles, while Moranes gave top cover and made occasional strafing attacks. The French defence was highly effective in the beginning and the main Allied force was brought to a halt by the morning of **6 May**. The deadlock was broken when the old destroyer *Anthony* dashed straight past the harbour defences of Diego Suarez and landed 50 Royal Marines amidst the Vichy rear area. The Marines created 'disturbance in the town out of all proportion to their numbers' and the Vichy defence was soon broken. Martlets from 881 Squadron intercepted three of the Potez, shooting down two and forcing the other to retreat, while Swordfish dropped dummy parachutists as a diversion. One patrolling Swordfish sank the submarine *Le Héros* and another spotted for ships bombarding French defences.

On the morning of 7 **May**, Martlets from 881 Squadron intercepted three Ms406s on a reconnaissance mission. All three were shot down for the loss of one Martlet. In addition, 882 Squadron's Fulmar was shot down while providing ground support. Diego Suarez was surrendered, although substantial Vichy forces withdrew to the south. Next day the Vichy French submarine *Monge* attempted to torpedo *Indomitable* but was sunk by depth charges launched by two destroyers. It seems that the Fulmars of 806/B Flight saw very little, if any, action during the brief campaign and were probably more involved in providing CAP for *Illustrious.*

The carrier was now formally assigned to the Eastern Fleet and, after a short refit in Durban, sailed to Colombo and became the flagship of the Rear Admiral Aircraft Carriers, Eastern Fleet, Denis Boyd, her former captain. While plans were being formulated for the invasion of the remainder of Madagascar, *Illustrious* remained on patrol, thereby allowing many of the Martlet and Fulmar pilots to practice deck landings and take-offs. During one sortie, Lt Sidney Hall seriously damaged his Fulmar (X8531) when landing on *Illustrious.* A few weeks later a second Fulmar was damaged whilst landing-on, Sub-Lt Alan Donaghy colliding with the round-down in X8534. Yet another was damaged when Sub-Lt Roger Peacock landed X8564 to port, one wheel going over the side. The same pilot later damaged another Fulmar (DR648) when he crashed on landing and hit the gun turret, although he again escaped personal injury.

At the beginning of August, *Illustrious* participated in Operation *Stab*, a decoy invasion of the Andaman Islands to distract the Japanese when the Americans were invading Guadalcanal. During the operation a Japanese flying boat was shot down by Martlets from *Indomitable.* By early September, the campaign to secure the remainder of Madagascar, Operation *Streamline Jane,* was opened on **10 September**, following which 806/B Flight landed at Port Reitz's Arrachart airfield. However, six of her aircraft were assigned to *Illustrious* but as the landings eight days later resulted in no significant resistance, the carrier aircraft were not required. *Illustrious* called in at Durban on **21 September** and while there experienced another hangar fire that destroyed three Swordfish and two Walrus and damaged two more aircraft including a Martlet. Fortunately, 806/B Flight's six Fulmars had already disembarked and were re-embarked three weeks later. 806/B Flight continued to operate from Arrachart, until January 1943, when the Fulmars flew to RNAS Tanga airfield (at Tanga Bay, Tanganyika), where it subsequently disbanded. The remaining Fulmars were handed over to 795 Squadron, which had recently formed at Tanga. After a farewell visit from the Eastern Fleet commander on 12 January 1943, *Illustrious* sailed for home the next day. She flew off her aircraft to Gibraltar on 31 January and continued on to the Clyde where she arrived five days later.

Although 806/B Flight quietly disappeared into obscurity and its personnel despatched far and wide, 806/A Flight, re-equipped with Martlets and under the command of Lt Robert Johnston, had seen much action in the Mediterranean during the month of August.

IX

Operation Pedestal—August 1942

The ending of the second Italian offensive against Malta coincided with preparations to run a further convoy through the Western Mediterranean. The arrival of only two damaged freighters in June had done little to alleviate the ultimate problem facing the defenders—starvation, both in terms of food and fuel. By now, the overall military situation had changed greatly and not entirely to the disadvantage of the British.

The largest naval/air operation yet attempted by the Royal Navy was thus in immediate contemplation. As July drew to a close the nucleus of this new convoy, to be codenamed Operation *Pedestal*, was forming on the Clyde where 13 fast, modern freighters and a tanker were being loaded with mixed cargoes of urgently required supplies, totalling in excess of 85,000 tons. The bulk was flour but each ship also carried petrol and aviation spirit, shells and other explosives. This was an essential prerequisite, for to concentrate all stores of one kind in single ships courted disaster, should they then be sunk. Also included was *Ohio,* an American tanker which had been loaned by Texaco to the Ministry of War Transport on her arrival in Britain. She was manned by a British crew and loaded with 11,500 tons of kerosene, fuel oils and aviation spirit. Two other freighters were also US-owned but retained their American crews.

For air cover the faithful *Eagle* and *Argus* were again available but now they were to be joined by two of the newer armoured Fleet carriers—*Victorious* from the Home Fleet and *Indomitable,* which returned from the Indian Ocean specially for the operation. Support would be provided by the battleships *Nelson* and *Rodney*, supported by seven light cruisers and 26 destroyers. Late in the day it was decided to add the older carrier *Furious*—not as part of the escort proper since she was preparing to carry to Malta a further delivery of Spitfires—Operation *Bellows*. *Eagle's* complement comprised 16 Sea Hurricanes, six of which were stowed on outriggers, together with four additional spares each with one wing removed, stored in the forward hangar: *Victorious'* air group was still new and fairly inexperienced. She sailed from Scapa Flow for the Clyde, flying on six Sea Hurricanes. However, the main complement comprised 20 Fulmars plus 12 Albacores for anti-submarine work. To increase strength, six Sea Hurricanes flew onto *Argus*. On arrival in the Biscay area the Sea Hurricanes were transferred to the Spitfire-laden *Furious*, which had no fighter defence.

Indomitable's air group was a different story altogether. After several months of service in the Indian Ocean, this vessel and her escorts passed around the Cape and sailed up to Freetown, re-equipping two of her fighter units en route, 800 Squadron with a dozen Sea Hurricanes and 806/A Flight with its newly-acquired Martlets. The pilots were just getting familiar with these, although they had not had the time to practice operating together as a team; one of the new fighters was lost (on 12 June) when Lt Johnston, the CO, was forced to bale out of AJ133 when his seat collapsed and jammed the aileron controls, he was quickly plucked from the sea. Two more Martlets suffered landing accidents during this period, AJ132 on 26 June with Sub-Lt Lawley-Wakelin at the controls and Sub-Lt George Warren in AJ101 on 9 July. These two units were backed up by ten more Sea Hurricanes of 880 Squadron. The air group was completed by a squadron of Albacores. 806/A Flight's pilot roster now comprised:

Lt R. L. Johnston
Lt N. E. Bartlett
Sub-Lt(A) B. H. C. Nation
Sub-Lt(A) P. D. C. Street
Sub-Lt(A) J. A. Cotching
Sub-Lt(A) J. B. Madden
Sub-Lt(A) G. M. Warren
Sub-Lt(A) J. Lawley-Wakelin
Sub-Lt(A) T. G. Hartshorn

Never having sought to operate so many air groups together in a single operation, the Navy wisely arranged an exercise prior to the start of the convoy, *Indomitable, Eagle, Victorious, Argus* and their escorts rendezvousing to the west of Gibraltar during the morning of **5 August** for Operation *Berserk*, which lasted for three days. The codename proved appropriate, for much confusion reigned as each group sought to orbit and receive direction from their individual carriers. Four Fulmars were written off during the exercise and one pilot killed. Another of 806/A Flight's Martlets was also removed from the serviceability roster due to a landing accident but much of value was learned and 68 fighters remained ready for action with four more available as spares. From the experience gathered during *Berserk*, it was decided to allot the low cover role to *Victorious* due to the slow-climbing performance of her Fulmars, while the other carriers undertook to provide high cover; each vessel would remain responsible for provision of its own protective combat air patrol however. For identification purposes, the wing leading edges and tail fins of all aircraft were painted bright yellow—a choice of colour which in the event was to provide some identification problems.

Thus, as the mighty armada of vessels turned east and began to pass through the Gibraltar Strait at 02:00 on **10 August**, the scene was set for a great new adventure. But the assemblage of such a convoy could hardly be kept a secret and had already been observed and reported by an Italian agent based in the port of Ceuta, Spanish Morocco, just across the Strait. Had the full extent of the gauntlet the ships would have to run been known to those embarked, the air of confidence which exuded would have been somewhat diminished, for ahead of them, in Sardinia and Sicily, the Axis had amassed over 650 aircraft. The German contribution on Sicily stood at 255 operational machines.

The *Pedestal* convoy formed up into five columns, the central of which comprised the battleships and operational carriers; the others comprised the merchantmen, each column headed by a cruiser, with further such warships bringing up the rear. The whole convoy was covered by a screen of 21 destroyers. From the very start there were alarms but the cause of these proved to be patrolling anti-submarine aircraft from Gibraltar which had failed to show recognition signals, or to switch on their IFF devices. Four Sea Hurricanes were scrambled at 05:25 but found their bogey to be a Sunderland, which opened fire on them as they closed in to identify it! The gunners aboard the flying boat were no doubt aware of the fortunate escape of another patrolling Sunderland from Gibraltar two days earlier, when three Vichy D.520s from Port Lyautey, attacked and damaged it after it had strayed into French territorial waters.

Four more Sea Hurricanes which went off at 06:45 similarly intercepted a Hudson but identity was established in good time on this occasion. During the morning *Victorious* launched two surplus Albacores and an unserviceable Fulmar and these were flown back to Gibraltar. The first intrusion of note occurred at around 17:00 that afternoon, when a French civil LeO H-246.1 flying boat (F-AREJ) en route from the Vichy zone of France to Algeria, passed overhead. As a non-combatant, the aircraft was not intercepted but the crew, for reasons of their own, were not playing according to the rules; they radioed a sighting of the convoy, reporting two battleships, two aircraft carriers, two cruisers, 14 destroyers and 12 transports and this information was at once conveyed to the Italian Naval Headquarters. The Frenchmen later paid dearly for this unfortunate transgression.

Despite this unfriendly action, when two of 806/A Flight's Martlets were scrambled some two hours later and intercepted a Vichy Bloch 174 reconnaissance aircraft—out from North Africa to check on the convoy—the British pilots did not attack. Fully alerted by the report of the French flying boat, by nightfall the Axis had placed a forward screen of eight submarines, including three U-boats, in the area south of the Balearic Islands. The commanders had been urged to penetrate the destroyer screen and attempt to sink the carriers. The first sighting was made at 04:38, torpedoes being launched without effect.

With dawn on **11 August**, the snoopers were out seeking the convoy, one of which was intercepted and badly damaged by a patrol of Sea Hurricanes from *Indomitable*. During this period one of *Victorious'* fighters almost flew into the sea on take-off; the pilot succeeded in landing at once, at which point it was discovered that the engine had been incorrectly assembled! A second Fulmar ditched when the port wing suddenly caught fire. The crew were safely picked up by a destroyer. Around noon it was reported that a Spanish airliner had passed over the convoy and—although it was not harassed—it was assumed that the crew would have relayed their observations to the Axis. At this stage the convoy had closed to a point where Operation *Bellows* could be put into effect, which entailed *Furious* flying off her cargo of Spitfires. As these operations were underway, *U-73* came within range of the passing procession of major warships. Conforming with an order to leave the merchantmen and seek out the aircraft carriers, the commander of *U-73* put a salvo of four torpedoes in rapid succession into the port side of *Eagle*. She at once took on a list to port, which rapidly became more pronounced; with smoke and steam pouring from her, wracked by internal explosions, she capsized and sank within six minutes. Destroyers rushed to her aid and picked up 68 officers and 862 ratings from her company of 1,093, as they leapt into the swirling waters. All but four of *Eagle's* complement of aircraft went down with her. Thus, at a stroke, the fighter defences had been reduced by nearly 25 per cent of their strength. The four aircraft which escaped—Sea Hurricanes—were up searching for a snooper at the time, one section subsequently being instructed to land on *Victorious*, while the other section was ordered to land on *Indomitable*. Owing to a misunderstanding, one of the latter landed on *Victorious*.

At 13:47, *Furious* resumed despatch of her Spitfires, the final 22 aircraft going off by 15:12. As the final flight of Spitfires became airborne, one pilot discovered that his long-range tank was not feeding through. Initially, the pilots had been told that should they experience problems immediately following take-off, they were to bale out ahead of the nearest destroyer which would pick them up if not too busy. This was greeted with so much adverse comment that it was agreed that should problems arise, a landing could be attempted on the nearest carrier. The pilot in question favoured the latter option and having carried out a low pass over *Indomitable*, successfully landed at the second attempt. The naval pilots were reportedly delighted to receive a Spitfire and were keen to fly it into combat when the time came. Thus, *Indomitable* now possessed two 'foreigners', the Sea Hurricane from *Eagle* and a Spitfire. Unfortunately, a returning damaged Sea Hurricane collided with the Spitfire. Much to the disappointment of the naval fighter pilots, the Spitfire was considered too badly damaged to be of use and it, together with the damaged Sea Hurricane were both unceremoniously pushed over the side.

Even as the flying-off was still in progress radar again picked up an intruder. At 14:20 what was assumed to have been a specially converted Ju88 (or more probably a pressurised Ju86P from Crete) passed over at such high altitude that it was not spotted visually, the German crew apparently taking photographs of the convoy. Despite the lack of visual contact, the guns opened up a radar-predicted barrage and a section of 806/A Flight from *Indomitable* was despatched to investigate—without success. One of these fighters was forced to ditch 23 miles from the Fleet on return, the pilot being located by a Fulmar, which guided the destroyer *Westcott* to pick him up; ammunition had apparently exploded in one of his wing magazines, causing a fire—the second such occurrence that day.

With her task completed, *Furious*—with an escort of eight destroyers—back westwards and headed for Gibraltar to pick up further Spitfires for subsequent delivery. Three Sea Hurricanes were scrambled from *Indomitable* at 18:35 and succeeded in shooting down a reconnaissance Ju88. Gibraltar now signalled the Fleet that intercepted Axis wireless traffic indicated that a dusk air attack was in preparation. *Indomitable* and *Victorious* turned into wind and launched all available fighters, which climbed to the north, to 20,000 feet. The Luftwaffe had indeed despatched an attack and at 20:55 some 30 Ju88s, drawn from the Sicily-based units, dived from 8,000 feet, circling the vessels and seeking opportunities to attack. At the same time six He111 torpedo-bombers of 6./KG26 swept in at wave-top level. The patrolling fighters were unable to spot the attackers from above as the gathering gloom merged them with the darkening sea below but the guns put up a furious barrage and succeeded in preventing the torpedo-bombers pressing home their attacks, although a few torpedo tracks were spotted and easily avoided. The Ju88s then attacked; the leading bomber and one other selected *Victorious* as their target and dived from astern. The carrier swung away, all her guns engaging and her crews believing that they had shot down both the bombers.

As the Sea Hurricanes and Fulmars returned towards the Fleet between 21:45 and 22:00, several were by now very low on fuel and it was fast becoming extremely dark. Few of the crews were experienced in night landings and to add to their difficulties they were continually fired at by the escorting destroyers as they attempted to line up. When they realised the problem facing the fighters, *Indomitable* turned into wind and had taken the risk of turning on lights to allow the returning aircraft to get aboard. Unfortunately, during the attack on the carrier, a premature detonation in the after 4.5-inch gun turret had severely wounded the Deck Landing Officer and had smashed the illuminated night landing bats. However, by holding a torch in his mouth and others in each hand the deputy DLO, successfully landed-on seven of *Indomitable's* own Sea Hurricanes, four Fulmars and a stray Sea Hurricane from *Victorious.*

By dawn on **12 August,** reconnaissance aircraft from Sicily and Sardinia were on their way west and south again. The first patrol of four fighters—two Fulmars from *Victorious* and two Sea Hurricanes from *Indomitable*—had been launched at dawn. This was soon increased to three sections, totalling a dozen fighters, while all the others were brought to instant readiness; the ships' radars showed many 'blips' denoting searching or shadowing aircraft. Fourteen interceptions of various 'snoopers' were attempted but only two achieved actual engagements. With the arrival of daylight, the three Fulmars and single Sea Hurricane of *Victorious'* air group which had landed on *Indomitable* the night before, were flown off to return to their own carrier.

At 07:05, a Z.1007bis, the first of the Italians to find the convoy, was shot down by Fulmars and a second crash-landed in Sicily, badly damaged. At 09:00 a large group of aircraft was detected on the radar screens at a distance of 65 miles. This was a formation of 24 Ju88s from I. and II./LG1 on their way from Sicily. *Victorious* scrambled her Sea Hurricanes and these were joined by more Sea Hurricanes and Fulmars from *Indomitable.* In the ensuing series of combats at least eight Ju88s were claimed by the fighters and two by the ships, for the actual destruction of six or seven bombers—some 25 per cent of the raiding force.

It was now the turn of the *Regia Aeronautica* in Sardinia to try its hand and a very strong attack was in the making as midday approached. First off at 11:10 were ten SM84s of 38° *Gruppo BT*, each bomber armed with two 360 kg *Motobomba*—known as 'Mad bombs'—which were designed to be dropped vertically by parachute ahead of oncoming shipping. Impact with the water automatically released the parachute and a gyroscopically-controlled motor would start at a depth of ten feet, driving the bomb forward in a spinning motion which left no wake. If no impact with a target was made, it would subsequently self-destruct at the end of a pre-set time fuse.

Fifteen minutes behind this formation, came torpedo armed SM79sil escorted by CR42s, each fighter armed with a pair of underwing 100 kg bombs. Ten more torpedo-armed SM84s thundered into the air at 11:30, with an escort provided by 14 MC202s, followed by a further nine SM79sil. Finally, 16 Re2001s set off as escort. But before the first Italian aircraft had left Sardinia, a force of 37 Ju88s from KG54 and KG77 had started taking off from Sicily, the first departing at 09:55; all the bombers were in the air by 10:30. It would have been impractical to try and provide fighter escort over the distances involved, so early that morning

21 Bf109s of a reinforced I./JG77 arrived in Sardinia. These took-off from their temporary airfield at 11:45 to rendezvous with the approaching bombers and provide cover for them in the target area.

Meanwhile, the defenders had been gathering. At 10:55, two Fulmars had left *Victorious* to patrol at 10–15,000 feet and at 11:30 were ordered to look out for 'bandits'. Two sections of fighters from *Indomitable* were also in the air, including 806/A Flight's Orange Section of four Martlets—Lt Norman Bartlett (AJ102), Sub-Lt Pat Street (AM998) and Sub-Lt John Cotching (AM968/8M), with the CO Lt Johnston (AJ136) at their head. As the raid appeared on the radar screens, more Sea Hurricanes and Fulmars were scrambled from the two carriers. A pair of Fulmars spotted three large formations approaching of what they took to be Z.1007bis, about 40 miles out. Making an initial head-on attack, they noted that some of the bombers dropped what appeared to be 'parachute mines' when attacked—obviously 38° *Gruppo* releasing their *Motobomba*. The Fulmars' attacks developed into beam, quarter, then stern chases as the bombers turned for home. The pilots reported that three bombers fell in flames following their attacks. Three Sea Hurricanes meanwhile engaged a formation of SM84s and Z.1007s flying a few thousand feet below, as they closed to 20–30 miles from the leading vessels, which were now 60–80 miles south of Cape Spartivento and close to Galite Island. Their attack seems to have coincided with that of the Orange Section Martlets, which also dived in to the attack, the pilots believing their foes to be SM79s. Lt Bartlett saw white smoke stream from one, which then crashed into the sea; Sub-Lt Street made three attacks on one of five from which the crew baled out and Sub-Lt Cotching hit another in the port engine which caught fire. The bomber fell back from the formation but he had by then run out of ammunition.

Meanwhile, Lt Johnston had encountered some of the Ju88s and carried out a number of attacks on one—which was reported to have fallen—but his Martlet was hit by return fire. He radioed that he had been seriously wounded and as he attempted to land the damaged aircraft without the aid of flaps on *Indomitable,* 827 Squadron observer Sub-Lt Gordon Wallace witnessed the incident:

> A lone Martlet came in low and too fast; its hook caught a wire but that was torn out of the fuselage and the plane slewed out over the port catwalk a few feet in front of me. As though in slow motion I watched the pilot, Lt Johnston, try to climb out of the cockpit but the plane turned on its back and fell into the sea. He had been wounded in one of the many air battles. I felt numb.[1]

Thus, 806/A Flight had lost its gallant CO. His victim—and victor—may have been an 8./KG77 machine (3Z+ES), flown by Oblt Leopold Lagauer, which failed to return from this raid.

The air attacks continued throughout the early afternoon, the Sea Hurricanes and Fulmars gaining a number of successes against the Italian bombers and torpedo-bombers. There followed a lull of nearly three hours before hostile aircraft again appeared in force and at 16:52 the first signs were seen on the radars of two large groups of aircraft apparently heading from Sicily to Sardinia. This was the start of a co-ordinated assault planned by the Luftwaffe and *Regia Aeronautica*. Between 15:05 and 15:25, the Italians despatched from Sicily two Z.1007bis and two SM79s, to search for the convoy; this was spotted at around 17:00. Specially for this action, 13 Ju87s of 102° *Gruppo Tuff.* had moved from Castelvetrano to Pantelleria, led by *Capitano* Antonio Cumbat. The Stukas began taking off at 17:25, together with an escort of 28 MC202s. At virtually the same time, 20 Ju87s of I./StG3, led by Hptm Martin Mossdorf, also took-off, escorted by all available Bf109Fs of 8./JG53—also flying from Pantelleria; these headed south of the Italians, making for the island of Piana. The Italian Stukas soon found their quarry. *Capitano* Cumbat selected as his target 'an aircraft carrier located forward of the central line of ships in the convoy':

> During my short dive we were surrounded by the outlines of shells from the anti-aircraft guns of all the warships. I dropped my load of bombs and pulled out about 200m from sea level. During that critical phase Cavallo warned me, 'Fighter on your tail'. I had not yet reached my line of manoeuvre before two cannon blows ripped through both my wings and a machine-gun volley reduced my right fuel tank to the appearance of a soup strainer! We employed on our Ju87s a private camera operated by the gunners to try to get some pictures during our attacks but the results were very poor and not definite. From this attack I lost both my wingmen to the flak and myself did not obtain any witness of my results or documentation.[2]

At 17:05, it was realised that four potential waves of attackers were gathering, two to the south-east (the German and Italian aircraft from Pantelleria) and two from the north-west. The latter comprised two smaller formations from Sardinia; one made up of eight bomb-carrying CR42s of 24° *Gruppo*, which were being guided by two SM79s and escorted by nine Re2001s of 362ª *Squadriglia*; the second was formed by eight SM79sil and escorted by 14 MC202s of 153° *Gruppo*, all of which had departed their bases around 16:45. These latter formations appeared (to the British) to be awaiting the arrival of the forces from the south-east but they were, in fact, searching for the vessels.

Meanwhile, Orange Section of 806/A Flight Martlets had been sent off to the west from *Indomitable* to engage the Sardinia formations but found only a reported six bombers and 20 fighters—in fact the CR42s and Re2001s. Bouncing the formation, Sub-Lt John Cotching[3] (AM968/8-M) shot down the 362ª *Squadriglia* Reggiane of *Sottotenente* Michele Crimi, who was killed, while

Sub-Lt Joe Madden (AJ102) claimed a probable when smoke was seen and debris flew off the one he attacked. Apparently, the pilot, *Sottotenente* Antonio Bizio, baled out, was picked up and made a prisoner. In return, *Sergente Maggiore* Lucio Biagini claimed one of the attackers shot down—identified as a P-36 or Buffalo—but all the Martlets returned unscathed, although Lt Bartlett, landing into the sun, missed all the wires and damaged AJ137.

At 18:45, the last section of Sea Hurricanes was just getting airborne from *Indomitable* when I./StG3 Ju87s suddenly appeared out of the sun from a smoky blue sky, hazy with funnel fumes. Although Hptm Mossdorf had received clear and strict orders that only freighters and tankers were to be targeted, the carrier was considered a prize worth disobeying orders for and, before the guns could be brought to bear, the Stukas struck the carrier with two direct hits and three near-misses. Leading 1.*Staffel* was Oblt Heinz Migeod:

> We arrived from the east, and on the eastern rim of a huge convoy, which was covering the sea. We saw a huge aircraft carrier. We were 22 aircraft in three squadrons, with the new D-type aircraft. There was no question and the *Gruppenkommandeur* attacked the carrier and we all followed. And so, we forgot the strict order to concentrate on the freighters and tankers and saw this huge thing below us. The carrier must have been 35,000 tonnes and we went all onto this. We disregarded the order and we hurled all the bombs, the special bombs for the freighters and tankers, onto the carrier. We arrived in formation and followed each other into the dive. The flight lines on the deck fitted nicely into our sights. I saw the planes in front of me score damaging hits. I saw nothing in my vision, nothing else but a huge flash. Our bombs couldn't pierce the armoured deck but some of the bombs may have gone down the funnel. Then we circled and we saw planes sliding off from the deck [*sic*], and other planes taking off. They were very slow and disorganised, and we managed to shoot down one at low level [*sic*]. Then we went home.[4]

Sub-Lt Hugh Popham, a Sea Hurricane pilot of 880 Squadron had just taken off:

> The raid had reached its peak when, suddenly, a squadron of 12 Stukas appeared high in the sky over *Indomitable*. Fighters were after them and a hurricane of flak went up from all sides, as one after another they peeled off at 12,000 feet and dived on the ship. The 1,000-pounders rained down in a concentrated onslaught and in a moment, she had vanished behind a dense geyser of spray. Two, three, were hit and plunged across the sky into the sea but *Indomitable* was hit too. Smoke and steam billowed up above the wall of water and for a quarter of a minute it seemed as if she could never re-appear except as a smoking hulk. Then, slowly, as the mass of water heaved up by the near misses subsided, she emerged, listing, on fire fore and aft, nearly stopped but still afloat.

> From every ship, men watched her anxiously; isolated from the disaster, yet sharing in it, impotent to help yet suffering the wound as if it were to their own ship and their friends. The main hits had been forward of the forward lift and aft of the after-lift. The former had pierced the flight-deck and exploded in the mouth of the hangar, killing, or wounding with flash-burns, many of the ratings working on the aircraft. The force of the explosion raised the seventy-ton lift, which was up, two feet above flight-deck level, where it stuck jammed on its chains and started a fire in the torpedo store… The latter also pierced the flight deck, buckling the after-lift and laying waste the officers' cabin flats. A third thousand pounder had struck the side of the ship, just above the waterline, where it had burst on impact, wrecking the wardroom anteroom and killed the half-dozen officers—mostly off-duty pilots and observers from the Albacore squadrons—who were there at the time… [5]

Both aircraft lifts were damaged, one being forced above deck level and the flight deck was put out of action. Six officers and 44 men were killed and 59 more seriously wounded (see Appendix VI). On this occasion, 806/A Flight did not suffer any casualties but had lost its third floating 'home'—*Illustrious*, *Formidable* and now *Indomitable*! One of *Indomitable's* officers, on the receiving end of the attack, recalled:

> Looking like beer barrels, the 1,100 lb bombs seemed to float down towards us as though in some dimly remembered dream. The ship shuddered and the dream expanded into a huge sheet of flame which rose up ahead of the island and engulfed it. There was an enormous explosion ahead of me and then several behind me which seemed to lift the ship several feet. A wall of water rose alongside to some hundred feet then cascaded down on top of me, washing me into the catwalk. For a moment there was a strange silence as flames and smoke billowed near the forward lift and behind the after-lift. The ship began listing to port and was moving in a slow circle starboard.

Leading Telegraphist Arthur Lawson was aboard the cruiser *Charybdis* and also witnessed the attack on *Indomitable:*

> I saw the last fighter land on *Victorious*, then in the faint night sky I saw a group of black dots 1,500 feet overhead. They started to peel off, one after the other, in vertical dives, I realised they were Ju87s (Stukas) and they were diving on the carrier *Indomitable*. Though *Charybdis* was too far away from the *Indomitable* for our close-range fire to be effective, I opened fire with the single port pom-pom, hoping the tracer would warn *Indomitable* and her closer escorts. Heavy AA fire started at once. *Indomitable* received three direct hits and several near misses. *Charydbis* steamed over to her at high speed and as we approached, she appeared

> to be on fire from stem to stern. Smoke was billowing out of her hangar lifts and what I thought was the flight deck, dripping molten metal. This was actually blazing aviation fuel. *Indomitable* was temporarily out of control and *Charybdis* circled her ready to go alongside if need be. It appeared that the Fleet had been caught out by the Stukas' attack but what was really happening was that the enemy was throwing everything they had and could at the Fleet—high level bombers, dive bombers and torpedo planes made low level attacks. All ships were twisting and turning, whilst *Charybdis* blasted away at every radar contact approaching *Indomitable.*[6]

Another, on the receiving end of the assault, wrote:

> Round about 19:30 the attacks were being concentrated on the carriers and *Indomitable* was under continuous bombing, while fighting back tooth-and-nail. Suddenly the ship shuddered from stern to stern and one had the strangest feeling of great resistance being exerted by the whole vessel to stop herself being pressed underwater. A strange hush prevailed immediately following the hits, followed by the bedlam of the damage control parties going about their grisly work. My most vivid memory of that moment was seeing an officer finishing a drink he was having with half his head blown away![7]

One of the attacking Stukas was shot down by two Sea Hurricanes, although one of the latter was then hit by ships' gunfire and was forced to ditch, the pilot being picked up safely. While this was going on, one of 806/A Flight's patrolling Pink Section Martlets—AM998 flown by Sub-Lt Barry Nation—attacked a bomber identified as a Ju88 (possibly a reconnaissance machine) from out of the sun and claimed hits on its tail unit before it disappeared from sight. The aerial assault was virtually over however, at 18:50, minutes after *Indomitable* had been hit.

As soon as *Indomitable* had been hit, a cruiser and three destroyers had been despatched to her aid; by 19:30 she was able to steam at 17 knots, her fires under control. Within another hour her speed was up to 28 knots. Force 'F' now turned back for Gibraltar—it had come as far east as planned. Force 'X' and the convoy were now to proceed alone, heading south due east to pass the Cape Bon Peninsula through the Skerki Bank and then to swing westward, south of Pantelleria. As the ships took up their new course, those of *Indomitable's* fighters still in the air came in to land on *Victorious.* Due to the crowding caused by this influx, any seriously damaged aircraft which was not easily repairable was pushed over the side. One Martlet ran out of fuel while waiting to get aboard and ditched, the pilot (believed to have been Sub-Lt Hartshorn) being picked up by the destroyer *Zetland.* Overhead the remaining Fulmars patrolled until 30 minutes before sunset, the last landing at 20:15—watched, the crews reported, by Axis fighters up sun which made no attempt to attack.

Returning Luftwaffe crews reported that the carrier *Wasp* [*sic*] had been set on fire after six direct hits, a mistake of identity which is believed to have originated due to the lighter paint colours applied to *Indomitable* for her Indian Ocean service. An Italian submarine crew had also reported the presence of an 'American-looking' carrier. The Italian Stuka leader, *Capitano* Cumbat noted:

> That night, at 02:00 on the Catania Air Headquarters called me at base asking if I could confirm that my unit had scored hits on an aircraft carrier as the Germans were claiming it for their Stukas. I replied that I could not prove it either way but should they obtain better information then they should award credit to one of my two lost companions, who were seen to complete their dives. All I know is that I lost two very brave and enthusiastic young pilots that day.[8]

It was considered that the fighters had, during the two days of action, accounted for 39 Axis aircraft shot down and several more probables—about double actual losses. By the end of the day's fighting, *Indomitable* declared her score to be 26 plus six probables and ten damaged. From the British point of view, the *Pedestal* operation was considered a significant success, although the Axis command—who had greatly overestimated the number of vessels, both naval and merchant marine, which they had sunk—believed they had achieved a great victory. Tactically the attackers had enjoyed considerable success, inflicting grievous losses (nine merchant ships sunk with over 300 seamen lost) but strategically they had failed to prevent the re-provisioning of Malta. More than enough had been despatched in order to be relatively sure of getting something through and the gamble had paid off. The provisions aboard the four transports—some 32,000 tons—proved sufficient to keep the garrison fed and armed into the autumn, while the arrival of the tanker *Ohio*, with her precious life blood for the aircraft and submarines was a major Allied victory. Malta now had food, ammunition, fuel and more Spitfires—she could fight on!

Meanwhile, *Indomitable* steadily made her way home, battered but proud. Sea Hurricane pilot Sub-Lt Hugh Popham continued:

> Despite the thirty-foot hole ripped out of her hull below the waterline which had been discovered in dock, *Indomitable* was still capable of twenty-six knots… The after-lift was still working and such Fulmars and Albacores [and Martlets] as were still on board were ranged. The carpenters set to and built a ramp up to the rostrum of the forward lift and as we steamed up the Irish Channel the aircraft were flown off.[9]

806/A Flight had done its bit to ensure success but its reward was not forthcoming. On the return of Indomitable to Britain, the leaderless unit was disbanded and its pilots dispersed to pastures anew.

X

Post-war 1945–1960

806 Squadron was briefly re-formed with Seafire IIIs in August 1945 but the Far East war ended before it became operational. Nonetheless, fate intervened and took the lives of two young pilots, Canadians Sub-Lt(A) John Johnston and Sub-Lt(A) Peter Norton, when their aircraft (NN132 and NN600) collided during a beat-up of a trawler near Pladds Point on the south-west coast of Scotland on 8 October 1945. Re-equipped with Seafire XVs, the Squadron embarked on HMS *Glory* in September 1946 as part of the 16th Air Carrier Group stationed in the Far East, before being disbanded once again.

806 Squadron reformed briefly at RNAS Eglinton in May 1948, as an aerobatic display team comprising Sea Furies, Sea Hornets and a single Sea Vampire, VF315, the prototype, which had been under evaluation by the A&AEE at Boscombe Down. 806's sole purpose to give aerobatic performances in North America, were the opening of New York's Idlewild Airport in summer 1948 was the big attraction. For fully nine days, the International Air Exposition showcased the best of US military and civil aviation, symbolising American post-war might. Yet, even in front of patriotic crowds naturally impressed by their country's latest fighters, bombers and transports the British pilots performed superbly.

Lt-Cdr Dick Law DSO, who had commanded 804 Squadron flying Hellcats against the Japanese, was placed in command. The Senior Pilot was Lt Bruce Clark, who had flown Seafires with 894 Squadron. The other pilots were Lt Ian Martin DSC, Lt Nigel Fisher and Lt Dick Reynolds DSC, the latter an ace from the Pacific War. Training got under way upon arrival at Eglinton of two Sea Fury FB.11s (VR932 and VR944) and two Sea Hornet F.20s (VF457 and VF845). The Squadron diary for 10 May:

> Aviation took place—mostly inverted! The Martin/Law combine have been doing formation aerobatics [and later that day] Martin did his first roll on take-off in a Hornet and his second of all time [next day] ... the chaps have been brushing up their individual aerobatics—Ian and Dick in Hornets and Nigel and Dick R in Furies. Martin is sure to have a nightmare tonight on account of the fact that with full starboard aileron and starboard rudder he only just completed a hesitation roll, thus avoiding arriving in a heap.

All five aircraft were loaded aboard the aircraft carrier HMCS *Magnificent* for passage to Halifax, Canada, which sailed on 25 May. The voyage passed without incident. Upon arrival in Halifax, the Sea Hornets were disembarked by crane on 2 June. The Sea Vampire and Sea Furies came ashore the next day, during which process Sea Fury VR944 sustained slight damage to the rudder on the flight deck. They didn't have far to go, their initial destination being Royal Canadian Navy Air Station Shearwater, right on the eastern shore of Halifax harbour. 4 June saw 806's first flights from North American soil:

> At long last and after a hard morning's work, most characters climbed into the not so blue skies. A few vertical climbs from the Hornets and an inverted climb from the Fury cost the Royal Canadian Government a few 'bucks' in working hours. Biggest disappointment of the day was the Vampire, which would only 'wet start' until too late to take off.

Tragedy struck on 11 June, when Sea Hornet VR845, flown by Lt Nigel Fisher, crashed:

> Nigel took-off early in the afternoon for a local trip and aerobatics; cloud at 2,000 feet. He carried out a normal take-off and had turned onto the downwind leg prior to leaving the circuit when he suddenly zoomed into cloud. Minutes later he re-appeared, diving steeply and plunged into the sea.

Despite the unexplained loss, there remained a job to do. Gradually 806's team worked up, Lt Clark's logbook showing the progression from solo to formation and synchronised aerobatics. On 12 June, more Sea Vampire start problems reared their head but duly repaired, the aircraft left for New York on 18 June, so Lt-Cdr Law could give previews of his display for the Idlewild show. He returned nine days later. The jet was now much more reliable and all of 806's pilots soloed in it.

An early chance for the FAA pilots to show their prowess came on 23 June, when mayors from across Canada met in Halifax. For their benefit, 806 put on a two-aircraft Sea Fury formation aerobatic show and a solo Sea Hornet demonstration over Bedford Basin. Onlookers were suitably impressed. Otherwise, the work-ups continued unabated. 806 performed for the first time in public at Shearwater on 21 July, during what a local paper called 'the first naval air display ever held in Canada'. During a 90-minute flying programme, featuring all RCN aircraft types, the reporter said that the FAA team 'stole the show'. Even so, the diary states:

> It was not a good day for 806. Dickie Reynolds' engine [in a Sea Fury] badly over sped after executing some vertical rolls and Dick Law's ailerons jammed when he was on his back in the Vampire. The Sea Fury [VR944] was a write-off. With a tip speed of over 1,000mph, the noise given off by the propeller was akin to a [squadron] of Harvards diving flat out in fine pitch!

Idlewild's International Air Exposition was now looming large on the horizon. From Shearwater, 806 Squadron's pilots ferried their aircraft to Naval Air Station New York at Floyd Bennett Field on 25 July. The airfield in Brooklyn was to be their temporary home, looked after by the US Navy:

> Furies [including TG124, an RCN replacement for the damaged machine] have an uneventful trip to the Big Smoke. Things in the Vampire and Hornet flight were more exciting, however. Flying at 30,000 feet over the Bay of Fundy, Dick Law's [Vampire] canopy cracked, necessitating a forced landing in Portland, Maine. In so doing, it became the first jet to land there.

31 July was the big day—the opening of the International Air Exposition. Already tens of thousands had gathered by the time President Harry S. Truman arrived from Washington aboard his personal transport. Truman was on hand to conduct the official dedication ceremony of Idlewild Airport and watch a series of flypasts and demonstrations staged in his honour. Lt-Cdr Law wrote:

> Come 4pm, some thousand aircraft had flown over in impressive modern array. Among them were no fewer than 200 USAF B-29 Superfortresses, three Convair B-36s making the type's public debut and fully 150 jet fighters—P-80s and F-84 Thunderjets—as part of what Truman reminded the crowd was 'the first review since the Air Force became an independent arm of our national military establishment'.

The US Navy's displays began upon a signal from the President. Soon it was the Fleet Air Arm's turn, as Lt-Cdr Law recorded:

> There were five aircraft to demonstrate and four pilots available, so it was necessary for one to land half-way through the 15-minute demonstration and change

> machines on the runway. To start with, two Sea Furies performed an opposition take-off, passing in centre of runway and both executing a roll-off-the-top from take-off. Two Sea Hornets [including VR851, a replacement for the crashed aircraft] conducted a formation roll, each with one engine stopped. Line-astern and individual Sea Fury aerobatics presaged a Sea Hornet party piece, a loop with both engines stopped. To finish, the Sea Vampire, with a double roll-off-the-top and rolls.

The display was repeated daily for the next week. The last day of the exposition was designated as Navy Day. Although the Sea Vampire was grounded due to a burned-out turbine, the two Sea Furies and two Sea Hornets drew round after round of applause from the 215,000 spectators. The diary continued:

> One of the crowd favourites was Lt Ian Martin's loop in the Sea Hornet with both engines dead. The ground-scraping of the 806 boys was a sight to see. The crowd shuddered in unison when they were told that Lt Dick Reynolds had taken three inches off his [Sea Fury's] prop blades on a practice run along one of the runways. Lt-Cdr Dick Law, flying a Hornet, brought the craft zooming in low in front of the crowd and suddenly shut off one engine, feathered the prop and did a roll on one engine. Lt Bruce Clark, the fourth member of the squadron flew his Fury at grass-blade level, did a slow roll onto his back and streaked inverted past the gaping crowd.
>
> A break in the planned routine came when the Royal Navy pilots teamed up with the Blue Angels to do a formation fly-by. Despite the fact that these boys had never flown together before and had thought up the demonstration on the spur of the moment, the formation was tight and clean and very impressive, demonstrating the solidarity and co-operation of the two strongest navies in the world.

806's stay in the US had been a whirlwind of activity. Back at Shearwater, a short period of rest and practice flying ensued before focus turned to the Canadian National Exhibition. 806 transited via Dorval airport in Montreal to Toronto's Malton airport on 23 August, ready to begin displays a couple of days later:

> A different technique was required here, as the display area was not an aerodrome but along the water front of Lake Ontario. A 15-minute aerobatic show was given every evening at 5.30pm with the following innovations: a 'vie' of Sea Furies performed loops and rolls [two loaned aircraft were flown by RCN pilots]; two Sea Hornets looped in formation, each with one engine stopped and the Sea Vampire and a Hornet did formation loops.

An interested observer was Admiral Lord Mountbatten, then commander of a Royal Navy cruiser squadron. In a message to 806 Squadron he wrote:

> I cannot tell you how proud I felt of the Service when I saw the magnificent performance of your squadron at the Canadian National Exhibition. Please accept my heartfelt congratulations.

The Toronto event complete, on 11 September the team transited to Ottawa for a display there. It was the last performance of a highly successful tour. The next day, the FAA aircraft flew back to Shearwater, where they were readied for the long voyage home. Upon arrival back in the UK, 806 Squadron was quickly disbanded once again. An official FAA document summed up well its aerobatic exploits:

> The mission of this squadron was an outstanding success and has brought many messages of congratulations from the American and Canadian authorities. The spontaneous acclamation of the hundreds of thousands who witnessed the demonstrations by the Royal Naval aircraft clearly show that the pilots are to be commended on their maintenance of the Navy's tradition for daring, enterprise and efficiency.

806 Squadron's fourth resurrection occurred on 2 March 1953, when the squadron was recommissioned at HMS *Goldcrest* (RNAS Brawdy) with the Hawker Sea Hawk F.1 jet fighter, gaining the distinction of being the first front-line squadron in the Fleet Air Arm to use the type. The 'Ace of Diamonds' was emblazoned on all aircraft and the commander was Lt-Cdr P. C. S. Chilton.

Transition did not progress without the inevitable accident, the first occurring on 7 February 1954, when Lt Derek Monsell was obliged to eject from WF171 whilst flying from the new HMS *Eagle*. He was rescued safely from the Mediterranean. The Sea Hawks participated in the Malta air display in August 1954, where they delighted the crowds with their precision formation flying. On returning to home waters, the Squadron re-equipped with FB.3s and transferred to HMS *Centaur* and a return to the Mediterranean. A second ejection was successfully achieved by Sub-Lt M. Cahill on 13 March 1955, when WV866 was lost. He was quickly rescued by the carrier's Whirlwind helicopter. Its task of Sea Hawk trials completed, the Squadron was again disbanded, on 4 November 1955 but not before a fatal accident a few days previous had taken the life of Lt Martin Winfield, on 28 October, while flying WV848:

> Operating from the RN Air Station at Ford, near Arundel, 24-year-old Lieutenant Winfield was piloting a Seahawk [*sic*] aircraft in a test flight when his engine failed at 8,600 feet. Realising that he would be unable to make an emergency landing at Ford, he directed his aircraft to the coast with the intention of baling out over the sea. He lost height rapidly, passed over a built-up area on the coast and crashed

> into the sea five hundred yards from shore at Kingston Gorse, Rustington. He operated his ejector seat at one hundred feet when he had cleared the built-up area and holiday makers on the beach and subsequently died from his injuries.
>
> It is considered that Lieutenant Winfield, whose home was at Beckington, near Bath, remained in his aircraft and delayed his ejection until he was certain that heavy loss of life and damage to property had been avoided and in so doing sacrificed his life.
>
> It is relevant to recall the statement of the Coroner at the inquest on Lieutenant Winfield: 'I am certain that had he chosen to operate the ejector seat earlier, he could have saved himself. That might have meant a calamity in the Kingston Gorse neighbourhood. To avoid the possibility of it, he sacrificed himself for those people and died gallantly and in the best and highest traditions of the Service to which he belonged.'

Lt Winfield was posthumously awarded the Queen's Commendation. During this interim period, one of 806 Squadron's former COs, the charismatic Lt-Cdr Dennis *John* Kelly, was killed while flying a flame-red aerobatic Sea Hawk in preparation for the annual Farnborough Air Display. His aircraft (XE381) crashed into a railway embankment near Arundel Sussex.

But still the ghost of 806 Squadron would not quietly disappear into the past, for it was reformed for the fifth time, on 14 January 1957, under the command of Lt-Cdr W. D. D. MacDonald. At first equipped with the Sea Hawk FB.5, these were exchanged for FGA.6s in April 1958 and received a new CO, Lt-Cdr Peter Carmichael, a Korean War veteran. Whilst flying WV840 and operating from HMS *Eagle* in the Mediterranean, Senior Pilot Lt-Cdr G. A. Rowan-Tomson was obliged to eject from WV840 on 7 November 1958. He was soon rescued.

In February 1960, now commanded by Lt-Cdr W. W. Illingworth, the Squadron transferred to HMS *Albion*, destined for a tour in Far Eastern waters, here losing two aircraft within a few weeks of each other. First to eject was Lt M. T. H. Styles (XE449) on 6 September, followed by Lt Brian Marindin (WV915) on 28 November; both pilots were saved.

Disbandment for the fifth and final time occurred on 15 December 1960.

Endnotes

Chapter I

1 These were: Skuas L2935, L2965, L3004, L3013, L3014, L3106, L3018, L3023; and Rocs L3101, L3102, L3103, L3105, L3153 and L3156. Later, to replace attrition, Skuas L2878, L2902, L2989, L3011 arrived.

The code letter/digit combination L6 was allotted to the Squadron, and actually denoted that the Squadron had been allocated to the new aircraft carrier *Illustrious*, which was still engaged in sea trials. The code appeared painted on the fin, followed by the individual aircraft letter—hence L6A, L6B etc.

2 Only two pre-war incidents involving Charles Evans have been located. Having qualified in 1931 after attending No.19 Naval Pilots Course, he was posted to 402 Flight aboard HMS *Courageous*. On 29 January 1932, while flying a Fairey Flycatcher (S1409), he was involved in a mid-air collision at 400 feet with another aircraft of his formation. Unable to keep the port wing up, Evans nursed the machine down in a spiral and struck the ground nose first. He was only slightly injured—and hence earned the soubriquet of *Crash*. A second incident occurred on 22 May 1936 when flying a Hawker Osprey (K3641) of 447 Flight. Following a fast deck landing aboard HMS *Glorious*, the aircraft bounced, missed the wires and swung into the island. On this occasion he was unhurt, apart from his pride.

3 Albert *Lew* Ayres was nicknamed *Lew* after the famous American film actor of the time Lew Ayres.

4 Arthur *Daisy* Day was born in Bury St Edmunds (his family then lived about a mile from the author's house).

5 Captain T. W. Harrington DSO, former 801 Squadron Skua pilot.

6 *Bremse* was a small artillery training ship, but she was not present during the attack. She was sunk in September 1941.

7 The Bergen bomb story not substantiated.
8 *Ibid.*
9 see *Spitfire Ace: My Life as a Battle of Britain Fighter Pilot* by Gordon Olive.
10 Gus Hogg's adventures:

> Strapping my revolver round my waist and carrying my maps and parachute, I took the train to London in order to return to Worthy Down. I was hatless, my cap having been in the back seat and soaked in blood. Arriving at Victoria, I whistled a taxi to take me to Waterloo. 'I'm afraid you'll have to come along with me.' I turned around to see a London constable; I guessed that I must look rather suspicious. 'Do you think I'm a German parachutist?' 'No, of course not but you might be, so if I take you to the Railway Transport Office, you can identify yourself there.
>
> I had no identification papers on my person and it took half-an-hour's telephoning to prove my bona-fides. I missed the connection to Worthy Down. Eventually the police gave me an identification slip with the parting words—'You must remember, there's a war on!'
>
> I caught a later train and shared a compartment with a dear old couple who wanted to know if I was returning from leave. I arrived at the aerodrome without any more trouble and, having told my story at least fifty times, retired thankfully to bed.

Chapter II

1 See *War in a Stringbag* by Charles Lamb.
2 Fulmars included N1857/6C, N1864, N1865/6Q, N1866/6Y, N1867, N1871, N1874, N1876, N1877/6H, N1879/6B, N1880, N1881/6F, N1884/6K, N1885, N1886/6R, N1887, N1893/6G; replacements would include N1935, N1940/6B, N1943/6Z.

By the time *Illustrious* was declared operational (July 1940), 806 Squadron had received Fulmar Is (also a new reconnaissance-fighter), and these were allocated the single digit code 6 (instead of L6)—hence they would be referred to as N1940/6A, 6B etc. However, to confuse the issue, the aircraft did not actually carry the complete code, but only the individual aircraft letter, which was painted aft of the roundel. The digit/letter code was used in official reports only.

3 No complete list is available of the of the TAGs who were now with 806 Squadron but they are known to have included the following, although a number may have been posted in later in 1940 from RNAS Dekheila: PO(A) Sam Gould (killed accident 24/8/40), PO(A) George Muskett, PO(A) P. Hyde (replacement for PO(A) Gould), N/Air Colin Hearnshaw, N/Air Bob Kensett, L/Air Harry Newton (killed accident 24/8/40), L/Air Cliff Thompson, L/Air Norman Tallack, L/Air Denis Tribe, L/Air

Paul Douet, L/Air Harry Phillips, L/Air Les Stevens, L/Air Arthur Oakes, L/Air Jimmy Beach, L/Air Bob Roberts, L/Air Harry Fitzherbert.

Chapter III

1 See *Illustrious* by Kenneth Poolman.
2 They would remain prisoners of the Vichy until the Anglo-American landings in November 1942.
3 *Tenente* Nicola Dall'Olio's crew comprised *Sottotenente Pil.* Giuseppe Gaggi, *1°Av. Mot.* Giovanni Gambin, *1°Av.Arm.* Giuseppe Ranucci, *1°Av.Marc.* Giuseppe Agnelli, *Av.Sc.Fot.* Adelmo Vaccondio. All were killed.
4 An aircraft of 200ª *Squadriglia* returned with pilot *Sergente Maggiore* Umberto Massari dead; another, from 67ª *Squadriglia* (34° *Gruppo*), came back with *1°Av. Marc.* Guido Rebonato dead. Various aircraft of 201ª Squadriglia returned with wounded on board: *Capitano Pil.* Costante Lazzarini (*Squadriglia* commander), *Sergente Maggiore Pil.* Antonio De Rosa, *Sergente Maggiore Arm.* Dario Pioli, 1°Av. Marc. Edoardo La Pietra, *1°Av.Mot.* Carlo Casarini, while *1°Av.Fot.* Tolmino Latini was wounded aboard a 67ª *Squadriglia* machine.
5 Apparently L2164 of 228 Squadron flown by Flt Lt I. F. McCall
6 Those rescued were the observer, *Sottenente* Paolo Bacchione, the co-pilot *Sergente* Edmondo Bianco and *1°Aviere* R/T Raffaele Grazioso. The pilot, *Tenente* Primatesta and engineer *Av.Mot.* Salvatore Calafiore were lost.
7 Lt Rupert Brabner was Member of Parliament for Hythe in Kent. Following his stint with 805 he was posted to command 801 Squadron and participated in the two major Malta convoys in 1942, being awarded the DSO and DSC. He was lost shortly before the end of the war when the Liberator transporting him and others to Canada crashed into the sea.
8 L/Air Bailey's annotation was supposed to imply 'one shot down and two probables' for the action, and not by his own aircraft.
9 *Muscle*, as Sub-Lt Arthur Stephen Griffith was known, 'was a pysical fitness freak, playing every game better than the average, was a weight-lifter, and for encores would walk on his hands.' So, wrote observer Sub-Lt Gerard Woods in *Wings at Sea*.

Chapter IV

1 'The Duke of Plaza-Toro', a character in the Gilbert & Sullivan opera *The Gondaliers*:

In enterprise of martial kind,
When there was any fighting,
He led his regiment from behind –

He found it less exciting.
But when away his regiment ran,
His place was at the fore, O –
That celebrated,
Cultivated,
Underrated
Nobleman,
The Duke of Plaza-Toro!

2 This aircraft was believed to have been the 30° *Stormo* SM79 that had crash-landed on 28 November 1940 following combat with a Hurricane, rather than one of the torpedo-carrying aircraft from 279ª *Squadriglia.* However, it was credited to the Fulmar pilots.

3 Ivan Lowe was taken to Mtarfa Hospital, and then transferred to the 64th General Hospital, Alexandria. From there he returned to the UK, and on recovery was initially posted to non-operational flying duties, having been awarded the DSC. In September 1942 he took command of 882 Squadron for 'Torch' operations, during which he shared in destroying two Vichy aircraft on the ground. The following year to was promoted to Lt-Cdr and posted to lead 898 Squadron.

4 See *Illustrious* by Kenneth Poolman.

5 See *War in a Stringbag* by Charles Lamb.

6 *Ibid.*

7 See *Fighters over Malta* by Brian Cull and Frederick Galea.

8 806 Squadron's RAF maintenance NCO fatalities aboard *Illustrious*: Flt Sgt Harold Tyson, Flt Sgt Vincent Vignaux, Sgt Cyril Hyslop, Sgt Arthur Leach, Cpl Frederick Robson, LAC Clifford Goddard.

9 See *War in a Stringbag* by Charles Lamb.

10 Despite losing his leg, George *Grubby* Going refused to be invalided out of the service. He was awarded the DSO for his efforts. Later, he survived the crash in which Gus Hogg was killed (see Endnote 4/Chapter VI).

11 The surviving Fulmars were believed to have been N1940/6A (N1940), 6C (N1857), 6F (N1881), 6H (N1877), 6K (N1884), 6Q (N1865), and 6Y (N1866)

12 See *When Malta Stood Alone* by Joseph Micallef.

13 See *Memoirs of a Stuka Pilot* by Paul-Werner Hozzel.

14 Lt W. S. Bracegirdle RN.

15 II. and III./LG1's casualties included the following aircraft:

II./LG1 Ju88 (4245) crash-landed Catania, 70 per cent damaged: Observer Uffz Hubert Birklback wounded.

5./LG1 Ju88 (6187) crash-landed Catania, 70 per cent damaged: no crew casualties listed.

5./LG1 Ju88 (7157) crashed Catania, 100 per cent destroyed: no crew casualties listed.

8./LG1 Ju88 (8046) L1+CD crash-landed Pozallo, 80 per cent damaged. Oblt Theodor Hagen, Fw Knödler, Uffz Karl Cohnen survived.

9./LG1 Ju88 (2275) L1+CT FTR: Oblt Kurt Pichler, Fw Willi Strauchfuss, Fw Heinz Kopecz, Fw Hermann Busch—all lost.

16 Philip Vella, later founding member of the Malta War Museum Association and author of *Malta: Blitzed But Not Beaten*. A good friend to both authors, Philip died in 1989.

17 See *The Battle of Malta* by Joseph Attard.

18 As reported by the Luqa detachment of 2/West Kents.

19 See *Fortress Malta* by James Holland.

20 See *Fighters over Malta* by Brian Cull and Frederick Galea.

21 See *Memoirs of a Stuka Pilot* by Paul-Werner Hozzel.

22 Having safely reached Alexandria, *Illustrious* underwent temporary repairs that lasted until 10 March, when *Illustrious* sailed for Port Said to begin her transit of the Suez Canal. The Germans had laid mines in the canal earlier and clearing the mines and the ships sunk by them was a slow process and *Illustrious* did not reach Suez Bay until 20 March. She then sailed for Durban (South Africa) to have the extent of her underwater damage assessed in the drydock there. She reached Durban on 4 April and remained there for two weeks before sailing for the USA, ultimately arriving at the Norfolk Navy Yard at Portsmouth, Virginia, on 12 May for permanent repairs.

23 See *Fighters over Malta* by Brian Cull and Frederick Galea.

24 Replacement Fulmars included N1870, N1936. N1947, N1957, N1985, N1988, N1990, N1997, N2012.

Chapter V

1 Lt Alec Ramsay had actually shot down two Bf109s (from 8./JG77) in one sortie over Crete whilst flying a Hurricane.

2 Obfw Josef Prötsch's crew of IH+BM: Oblt Ehrenfried Bischoff, Uffz Kurt Noack, Gfr Hermann Treder, Uffz Josef Kain; all lost.

3 Ju52 (7057) of I./KGzbV.9: Obfw Josef Kastl (pilot), Fw Kurt Bemms, Uffz Rudolf Crein, Gfr Alfons Krampe, plus passengers Gfr Gerhard Enax and Obfw Adolf Niemann (all killed); Ju52 (6926) of I./KGzbV.9: Fw Walter Heyer (pilot), Ltn Harald Fischer, Fw Hans Tietze, Obfw Heinz Blaskow (all killed).

4 8./LG1 Uffz Gerhard Pfeil (pilot); Uffz Willi Wanner, Uffz Willi Reinhold; Uffz Karl Franz.

5 6./KG26 1H+AP Obfw Willi Kleinknecht (pilot), Oblt Alois Sporkmann, Gfr Hugo Kappes, Uffz Rolf Wienecke.

6./KG26 1H+FP Oblt Hermann Pfeil (pilot), Obfw Konrad Meyer, Uffz Kurt Hünecke, Fw Erich Borgmann.

4./KG26 1H+BC Oblt Eberhardt Stüwe (pilot), Obfw Heinz Trippner, Obfw Bruno Habert, Fw Heinz Amhof.

5./KG26 1H+FN Oblt Max Voigt (pilot), Ltn Bernhard Wintel, Uffz Raffael Reis, Obfw Albert Dürr.

6 7./LG1 Obfw Otto Engel (pilot); Uffz Johann Schiffers, Uffz Friedrich Zehrer, Fw Karl Muller

7 While recuperating in Egypt in 1942, Lt-Cdr Charles Evans, having been awarded the DSO for his leadership, married Miss Kyriakoula Doulcaris, third daughter of Greek General Doulcaris. She worked in the Greek Embassy, Cairo. Promoted to Commander, he then departed for USA to oversee repairs to *Illustrious,* followed by taking command of FAA fighter training in USA. Back in the UK he was appointed Commander Flying on HMS *Formdable* in the Pacific in 1945. Post-war he was Naval Air Attaché USA 1946-47, before taking command of the aircraft carrier HMS *Ocean* during the Korean War (1951-52). His final appointment before retiring was as NATO Deputy Supreme Commander, Atlantic 1960-62. Knighted in 1962, he passed away aged 73 in Athens on 27 December 1981 following a long illness.

8 5./KG26 IH+CN Uffz Oskar Klapproth (pilot), Gfr Karl Albrecht, Gfr Gunther Klaumunzer, Gfr Werner Ortel.

9 2.(Erg.)/LG1 L1+CV Uffz Heinrich Geisenhoff; Fw Herbert Mobius, Uffz Peter Diebold, Obgfr Gunther Peschke.

10 2.(Erg.)/LG1 L1+QV Ltn Wolfgang Meissner; Fw Anton Deissner; Fw Wilhelm Hausner, Fw Erwin Bock.

11 Following her arrival at Alexandria, *Formidable* received emergency repairs before departing on 24 July for permanent repairs at the Norfolk Naval Shipyard in the United States. 829 Squadron embarked with its Albacores to provide anti-submarine patrols during the voyage. She arrived on 25 August, and the repairs were completed in early December. After several days of sea trials, she sailed for Britain in company with *Illustrious* on 12 December. During the night of 15/16 December, *Illustrious* collided with *Formidable's* stern, but neither ship was seriously damaged. She was repaired at Belfast and was ready for sea once again by 3 February 1942.

Chapter VI

1 See *Haul Taut and Belay* by Vice-Admiral Sir Donald Gibson

2 *Ibid.*

3 Since 806 Squadron was now flying Hurricanes, Lt Desmond Vincent-Jones soon found himself redundant. Flying with Lt-Cdr Evans it is believed that he shared in ten successful combats, and later in three more, making his possibly the 'top-scoring' Observer of the war. By 1942 he was Operations Officer aboard HMS *Archer*, and the following year was appointed Air Staff Officer at HQ Western Approaches until

1944. Appointed Air Advisor HMS *Vindex* on Russian convoy. Various appointments post-war and retired 1964 as Captain. Died 1992.

4 Three of the more successful pilots, Lt Jackie Sewell, Sub-Lt Stan Orr, and Sub-Lt Gus Hogg, were now rested from operations.

Jackie Sewell, having been awarded the DSC, was posted to command 804 Squadron aboard HMS *Dasher* in 1942, participating in the North Africa landings. Subsequently in September 1943, having been posted to the USA, he formed 1837 Squadron on Corsairs, but whilst practising formation flying on 4 October 1943, his wingman (Lt D. J. F. Watson) collided with his aircraft (JT190) and both were killed.

Stan Orr, promoted and recipient of the DSC and Bar, returned to the UK for instructor duties before being sent to the USA to take command of 896 Squadron on Wildcats. Later, in 1943, he was given command of 804 Squadron flying Hellcats, and participated in raids on the Norwegian coast, when he shared the destruction of a He115 in the air, plus two more on the sea. He was awarded a second Bar to his DSC. With peace there followed a number of appointments including Lt-Cdr (Flying) aboard HMS *Ocean* during the Korean War with Captain Evans as ship's Captain. He retired in 1966, having been an RN test pilot and awarded the AFC. He died in August 2003.

Sadly, in the meantime, the youngest of the trio, **Gus Hogg** had lost his life in a preventable air accident. Also, having been awarded the DSC and Bar, he returned to the UK. In early 1942 he applied to undertake night flying training with the intention of joining the Navy's embryonic and largely experimental RNNFU. But fate would intervene on 17 March 1942. He was one of four passengers aboard Anson AX230 of No.3 Radio School, borrowed on the authority of the Deputy Station CO. Piloted by former 805 Squadron's Capt Skeets Harris RM (although inexperienced on twin-engined aircraft). The other passengers were former *Illustrious* Swordfish pilot, amputee Lt *Grubby* Going (see Chapter IV Endnote 10), Sub-Lt Duncan Richards (ex-803 Squadron) and RAF instructor Sgt Rich. The mischievous pilots planned to 'shoot-up' *Illustrious*, which was in harbour following its refit and was due to sail on 23 March; an unofficial report revealed:

> Gus Hogg sat in co-pilot's seat until Lt *Grubby* Going suggested that as he was senior, he should be in that seat. It seems that in the changeover one or the other may have accidentally closed the fuel cock to one engine. The Anson was forced down on one engine near Monkton railway station Ayreshire, losing both wings as it crashed under the railway bridge arch. Gus had apparently failed to fix his harness following the changeover and was thrown forward in the crash. He sustained severe head injuries and died in hospital that night. No one else was injured.

5 Lt Derek Percy Zachariah *Zac* Cox was the son of a WWI RFC pilot who was killed in 1917. On recovery of his injuries he was posted to the new aircraft carrier HMS *Avenger*, though not in a flying capacity with either of the two Sea Hurricane squadrons. He was lost together with almost the whole ship's complement when *Avenger* was torpedoed and sunk in November 1942 (see also Endnote 7).

6 Although the RNAS had disbanded, 805 Squadron's Martlets continued to operate in the defensive role and made claims for three aircraft destroyed and three more damaged up to July 1942. The Squadron disbanded in January 1943.

7 Lt(A) Pat Massy was originally a Swordfish pilot with 813 Squadron aboard HMS *Eagle* in 1940 and retrained to fly Sea Gladiators when three of the fighters were attached to the carrier for defensive purposes. He claimed an SM79 shot down on 29 July 1940, not long after the outbreak of war in the Mediterranean. By mid-1942 he had taken command of 883 Squadron (Sea Hurricanes) and embarked aboard the escort carrier HMS *Avenger* for the epic PQ18 convoy to Russia. He was credited with shooting down a He111 on 14 September 1942 but was lost with most of *Avenger's* complement on 15 November 1942, when the carrier was torpedoed in the Mediterranean. His DSO was announced two weeks later (see also Endnote 5 and the forthcoming *Air War over the Arctic: Murmansk and the Allied Convoys 1941-42* by the author)

8 On returning to Dekheila, Lt Robert Henley entered hospital for treatment for an eye injury sustained in August 1940. He was hospitalised for three months and did not subsequently return to operational flying. He was posted to Ceylon in 1943 and was appointed Lt-Cdr (Air) aboard HMS *Stalker* until the end of the war. He remained in the Navy and held a number of appointments, and in 1969, shortly before his retirement, he was Naval Air Attaché at the British Embassy in Spain. He died in November 1991.

9 Lt *Sam* MacDonald-Hall, following a spell with the RNAS, returned to the UK in 1942 for instructor duties. In September 1942, he was appointed commander of 807 Squadron, the first operational Seafire unit, embarked on HMS *Furious* for the 'Torch' landings (claiming a Ju88 damaged). There followed a posting to Ceylon as an instructor on Corsairs until the end of the war. Post-war he became a successful businessman in the aviation world, but sadly lost his life on 31 August 1990, when piloting his personal helicopter (a Hughes 500C), which crashed en route to Heathrow. He was the oldest helicopter pilot in the UK at the time (75 years-old).

10 PO(A) Colin Hearnshaw DSM did not return to operational flying during the war but did remain in the Fleet Air Arm post-war. By 1952 he was again operational, flying in the back seat of a Firefly of 825 Squadron aboard HMS *Ocean* (Captain Charles Evans), and participating in the Korean War. During one particular sortie his aircraft (flown by Lt W. L. Jacob) was hit by small arms fire when rocketing a radar station located in the Changyon/Sinchon area. Hit in the radiator, a wheels-up

landing was made in shallow water off Cho-Do, from where they rescued. Shortly before his retirement in 1972, now commissioned and holding the rank of Lt-Cdr, he was a passenger on board a Sea Heron (XR444) which ditched in the Irish Sea, 15 miles north-west of Wallasey on 26 June 1972. All three crew and eight passengers survived, with Lt-Cdr Hearnshaw requiring five stitches in a head wound. Following retirement, he emigrated to Canada, where he passed away in 1996.

Chapter VII

1 The Fulmar IIs included X8525, X8528, X8531, X8534, X8546, X8555, X8564, X8569/F, X8640, X8690. BP776 and BP782 would be later arrivals.
2 The experienced and successful Lt Henry Allingham RNR missed the action, currently hospitalised with a broken ankle. On his return to the UK he was posted to instructor duties before being promoted to command of 1831 Squadron forming in the USA with Corsairs. He did not return to operational flying. He was Mentioned in Despatches in 1946 when serving on HMS *Hunter.*
3 The Martlets included AJ100-102, AJ108, AJ132-137; AM968, AM997 and AM998 were replacements for early losses. 806 Squadron's single code digit was now '8', hence 8A, 8B etc.

Chapter IX

1 See *Carrier Observer* by Graham Wallace.
2 See *Impact!* by Peter C. Smith.
3 Lt(A) John Cotching was posted to 882 Squadron (HMS *Victorious*) following the disbandment of 806 Squadron and participated in the 'Torch' landings. He later flew from HMS *Searcher* during operations against shipping off Norway, claiming a share in the destruction of two Bv.138s, but was shot down by flak on 8 May 1944 and killed. He was awarded a DSC.
4 Heinz Migeod added: 'Our *Kommandeur* [Oblt Mossdorf] later had to go to Rome to report to Kesselring [for disobeying orders]. We all thought that he would not return to our unit.' Instead he was promoted and awarded the Knights Cross. Information extracted from interview conducted by Tinus le Roux, with permission.
5 See *Sea Flight* by Hugh Popham.
6 See *www.armouredcarriers.com.*
7 *Ibid.*
8 See *Impact!*
9 See Sea Flight.

Appendix I

Roll of Honour

Date	Name	Aircraft / Notes	Serial	Fate
28/5/40	N/Air J. B. Burton (TAG)	Skua	L2896	KiA
17/7/40	Lt P. D. Dean N/Air K. L. Jones	Skua	L2941	KAcc
11/8/40	Sub-Lt(A) H. W. Isherwood	Fulmar	N1880	KAcc
24/8/40	Sub-Lt(A) A. G. Day N/Air H. Newton	Fulmar	N1887	collision
	Sub-Lt(A) A. Ayres PO(A) S. H. Gould	Fulmar	N1885	collision
10/1/41	N/Air R. D. Kensett (TAG)	Fulmar	N1935	KiA
	Sub-Lt(A) J. Marshall	aboard *Illustrious*		KiA
	PO(A) N. E. Tallack			KiA
	Sub-Lt(A) H. Louden			KiA
	PO(A) J. D. Bushell			KiA
	L/Air H. Fitzherbert (TAG)			KiA
	Flt Sgt H. Tyson	Maintenance		KiA
	Flt Sgt V. Vignaux	Personnel		KiA
	Sgt C. Hyslop	aboard *Illustrious*		KiA
	Sgt A. Leach			KiA
	Cpl F. Robson			KiA
	LAC C. Goddard			KiA

Date	Name		Aircraft	Serial	Fate
18/1/41	Sub-Lt(A) A. S. Griffith		Fulmar	N1881	KiA
2/3/41	Lt W. L. LeC. Barnes		shot accidentally on ground		KoAS
19/4/41	Lt J. H. Shears	]	Fulmar	N1985	KiA
	Sub-Lt(A) E. J. Dixon				KiA
9/5/41	Lt P. Touchbourne	]	Fulmar	N1865	KAcc
	L/Air C. Thompson				KAcc
11/5/41	Lt P. D. J. Sparke	]	Fulmar	N1990	KiA
	N/Air A. S. Rush				KiA
9/6/41	Sub-Lt(A) N. Cullen (Ob)		Fulmar/803 Sqn	N1950	KiA
26/8/41	Sub-Lt(A) G. B. Pudney		Hurricane	Z4052	KiA
20/11/41	Lt(A) W. J. Pangbourne		Hurricane	V7858	KiA
23/11/41	Sub-Lt(A) A. J. C. Willis		Hurricane	V7308	KiA
5/4/42	Sub-Lt(A) K. J. M. Pettitt		Fulmar II	X8569	KiA
	Sub-Lt(A) H. S. Diggens		Fulmar II		KiA
9/4/42	Sub-Lt(A) A. Peace (Ob)		Blenheim/11 Sqn	Z7896	KiA
9/4/42	Sub-Lt(A) F. W. Bonnell (Ob)		Blenheim/11 Sqn	V5592	KiA
12/8/42	Lt R. L. Johnston		Martlet	AJ136	KiA

Squadron disbanded

Post-war

Date	Name	Aircraft	Serial	Fate
8/10/45	Sub-Lt(A) J. Johnston	Seafire III	NN132	collision
	Sub-Lt(A) P. Norton	Seafire III	NN600	collision
11/6/48	Lt(A) N. D. Fisher	Sea Hornet F.20	VR845	accident
28/10/55	Lt M. W. Winfield	Sea Hawk	WV848	accident

Appendix II

Combat Claims

NB: There may be discrepancies regarding aircraft code letters relating to specific serial numbers.

RAF Detling

29/5/40	Mid(A) A. G. Day and N/Air H. Newton	Roc L6M	He111 (claimed as Ju88
	Lt W. L. LeC. Barnes	Skua L6B	
	Sub-Lt(A) A. Ayres	Skua L6?	
2/6/40	Lt-Cdr C. L. G. Evans	Skua L2989	He111 probable (claimed as Ju88)

HMS *Illustrious* (Fulmar I)

1/9/40	Cdr R. A. Kilroy	N1940/6A	Hudson in error (believed Ju88)
	Sub-Lt(A) G. A. Hogg	N1866/6Y	
2/9/40			
11:20	Lt-Cdr C. L. G. Evans	N1940/6A	Z.501
	Cdr R.A. Kilroy		
	Sub-Lt(A) I. L. F. Lowe	N1886/6R	
14:50	Lt W. L. LeC. Barnes	N1879/6B	SM79
	Lt(A) A. J. Sewell	N1865/6Q	SM79

	Lt W. L. LeC. Barnes	N1879/6B	] SM79
	Lt (A) A. J. Sewell	N1865/6Q	
19:15	Lt W. L. LeC. Barnes	N1879/6B	SM79
	Sub-Lt(A) G. R. Golden	N1857/6C	SM79
	Lt W. L. LeC. Barnes	N1879/6B	] SM79
	Illustrious AA		
4/9/40			
10:05	Cdr R. A. Kilroy	N1940/6A	] SM81 (believed Ca.133)
	Sub-Lt(A) S. G. Orr	N1884/6K	
11:05	Lt W. L. LeC. Barnes	N1879/6B	] SM79
	Lt(A) A. J. Sewell	N1865/6Q	
13:45	Lt O. J. R. Nicolls	N1879/6B	] SM79 probable
	Sub-Lt(A) E. Buttle	N1876	
17/9/40			
11:00	Lt W. L. LeC. Barnes	N1940/6A	] Z.501
	Sub-Lt (A) S. G. Orr	N1879/6B	
	Sub-Lt(A) G. A. Hogg	N1874/6Y	
29/9/40			
11:24	Lt-Cdr C. L. G. Evans	N1940/6A	] Z.501
	Sub-Lt(A) I. L. F. Lowe	N1877/6H	
14:22	Sub-Lt(A) S. G. Orr	N1879/6B	Z501
	Sub-Lt(A) I. P. Godfrey	N1886/6R	] SM79 probable
	Sub-Lt(A) J. Marshall	N1893/6G	
1/10/40			
11:15	Lt-Cdr C. L. G. Evans	N1940/6A	] Z.506B
	Sub-Lt(A) G. A. Hogg	N1866/6Y	
	Sub-Lt(A) J. M. L. Roberts	N1857/6C	
12/10/40			
11:45	Lt W. L. LeC. Barnes	N1940/6A	] Z.501
	Lt(A) A. J. Sewell	N1865/6Q	
13:50	Lt-Cdr C. L. G. Evans	N1940/6A	SM79
	Lt-Cdr C. L. G. Evans	N1940/6A	] SM79
	Sub-Lt(A) I. L. F. Lowe	N1877/6H	
	Sub-Lt(A) J. M. L. Roberts	N1857/6C	

	Lt O. J. R. Nicolls	N1879/6B	SM79 probable
1/11/40	Lt(A) A. J. Sewell	N1866/6Y	Z.506B
8/11/40			
12:30	Lt O. J. R. Nicolls	Glad N5549	]
	Lt(A) A. J. Sewell	Glad N5513	SM79
16:20	Lt-Cdr C. L. G. Evans	N1940/6A	SM79
	Sub-Lt(A) I. L. F. Lowe	N1871	]
	Sub-Lt(A) J. L. M. Roberts	N1857/6C	SM79
9/11/40			
16:40	Sub-Lt(A) S. G. Orr	N1881/6F	Z.506B
10/11/40			
12:20	Lt W. L. LeC. Barnes	N1940/6B	]
	Lt(A) A. J. Sewell	N1865/6Q	Z.501
13:10	Lt W. L. LeC. Barnes	N1940/6B	]
	Lt(A) A. J. Sewell	N1865/6Q	SM79
12/11/40			
11:55	Sub-Lt(A) S. G. Orr	N1940/6B	]
	Sub-Lt(A) W. H. Clisby	N1881/6F	Z.506B
	Lt-Cdr C. L. G. Evans	N1940/6A	]
	Sub-Lt(A) I. L. F. Lowe	N1871	Z.506B, Z.501
	Lt-Cdr C. L. G. Evans	N1940/6A	Z.506B
13/11/40			
15:30	Sub-Lt(A) S. G. Orr	N1940/6B	]
	Sub-Lt(A) W. H. Clisby	N1935	Z.506B
28/11/40			
09:05	Sub-Lt(A) S. G. Orr	N1884/6K	CR42
	Sub-Lt(A) G. A. Hogg	N1866/6Y	CR42 probable
	Sub-Lt(A) W. H. Clisby	N1935	CR42 probable
10/1/41			
11:20	Lt R. S. Henley	N1881/6F	]
	Sub-Lt(A) J. Marshall	N1893/6G	SM79
	Sub-Lt(A) A. S. Griffith	N1877/6H	]

	Sub-Lt(A) S. G. Orr	N1884/6K	] SM79
	Sub-Lt(A) G. A. Hogg	N1866/6Y	on ground
	Sub-Lt(A) G. A. Hogg	N1866/6Y	Ju87
12:35	Lt W. L. LeC. Barnes	N1940/6A	Ju87
	Sub-Lt(A) I. L. F. Lowe	N1943/6Z	Ju87
	Lt(A) A. J. Sewell	N1865/6Q	Ju87
16:50	Lt W. L. LeC. Barnes	N1881/6F	Ju87 probable
	Sub-Lt(A) S. G. Orr	N1884/6k	Ju87
			Ju87 probable

Malta

16/1/41	Lt W. L. LeC. Barnes	N1940/6A	Ju88
			Ju88 probable
	Sub-Lt(A) G. A. Hogg	N1866/6Y	2 Ju88
	Sub-Lt(A) S. G. Orr	N1884/6K	Ju88
18/1/41	Lt R. S. Henley	N1940/6A	Ju88,
			Ju87 probable
	Sub-Lt(A) G. A. Hogg	N1866/6Y	2 Ju87
	Sub-Lt(A) S. G. Orr	N1884/6K	Ju87
			2 Ju87 probable
	Lt(A) A. J. Sewell	N1865/6Q	Ju87
	Sub-Lt(A) A. S. Griffith	N1881/6F	MC200 possible
19/1/41			
Morning	Lt W. L. LeC. Barnes	N1866/6Y	2 Ju87
13:15	Sub-Lt(A) G. A. Hogg	N1866/6Y	2 Ju88
			Ju88 probable
24/1/41	Lt(A) A. J. Sewell	Gladiator	Ju88
4/2/41	Sub-Lt(A) S. G. Orr	N1884/6K	] Ju88
	Sub-Lt(A) J. M. L. Roberts	N1857/6C	(claimed as Do17)

HMS *Eagle*

21/2/41	Lt R. MacDonald-Hall	Fulmar	]
	Lt P. S. Touchbourne	Fulmar	He111

HMS *Formidable*

Date	Pilot	Aircraft		Claim
19/4/41	Lt-Cdr C. L. G. Evans	Fulmar	]	
	Lt(A) A. J. Sewell	Fulmar		Z.1007
	Lt P. J. D. Sparke	N2012		2 Ju52/3m
	Lt R. S. Henley	Fulmar		Ju52/3m
	Lt J. H. Shears	N1985/6R		Ju52/3m
21/4/41	Sub-Lt(A) S. G. Orr	N1988	]	21/4/41
	Sub-Lt(A) G. A. Hogg	Fulmar		Do24N
22/4/41	Lt P. J. D. Sparke	N1870	]	
	Lt-Cdr C. L. G. Evans	Fulmar		Ju88
	Lt(A) A. J. Sewell	Fulmar	]	
	Sub-Lt(A) S. G. Orr	N1988		Ju88 probable
8/5/41	Lt R. MacDonald-Hall	N1990		He111
	Lt R. MacDonald-Hall	N1990	]	
	Lt P. S. Touchbourne	N1865		He111
	Lt L. S. Hill	Fulmar	]	
	Lt(A) G. B. Davie	N1870		He111
	Lt R. MacDonald-Hall	N1990	]	
	Lt P. S. Touchbourne	N1865		Ju88
	Lt R. S. Henley	Fulmar	]	
	Lt P. D. J. Sparke	N1990		Ju88
9/5/41	Lt R. S. Henley	Fulmar	]	
	Lt P. D. J. Sparke	N1990		Ju88
11/5/41	Lt R. S. Henley	Fulmar		Ju88 probable
	Lt P. D. J. Sparke	N1990		Ju88 (collision)
26/5/41	Lt(A) A. J. Sewell	Fulmar		He111
	Lt-Cdr J. N. Garnett	Fulmar	]	
	Lt(A) A. J. Sewell	Fulmar		Ju88
	Lt R. MacDonald-Hall	N1957	]	
	Sub-Lt(A) G. A. Hogg	Fulmar		2 Ju88
	Lt P. H. V. Massy	Fulmar		Ju87
	Sub-Lt(A) K. L. Wood	Fulmar		Ju87

HMS *Grebe* (RNAS Dekheila)

28/5/41	Lt R. MacDonald-Hall	N1957	Ju87
1/6/41	Lt R. MacDonald-Hall	N1957	] Ju88
	Sub-Lt(A) G. A. Hogg	Fulmar	

RNFS Western Desert

21/8/41	Lt H. P. Allingham	Hurricane Z4245	Bf110
20/11/41	Lt R. L. Johnston	Hurricane Z4560	Ju87 probable
1/12/41	Lt H. P. Allingham	Hurricane Z4245	Ju88, G.50
	Sub-Lt(A) H. S. Diggens	Hurricane V7017	G.50
	Sub-Lt(A) G. Dennison	Hurricane OL-C	G.50
	Sub-Lt(A) K. L. Wood	Hurricane OL-E	Ju88 probable
			G.50 probable
	Sub-Lt(A) D. G. Dick	Hurricane OL-Y	Bf109 probable
28/12/41	Sub-Lt(A) P. Fell	Hurricane OL	He111 probable
30/12/41	Sub-Lt(A) D. W. Langdon	Hurricane OL	] Ju88
	Two pilots 4SAAF	Kittyhawks	

HMS *Lanka* (Ceylon)

5/4/42	Lt M. Hordern	Fulmar II X8555	D3A
9/4/42	Lt R. L. Johnston	Fulmar II	D3A
	Sub-Lt(A) B. H. Nation	Fulmar II	D3A

HMS *Indomitable*

12/8/42			
Morning	Lt R. L. Johnston	Martlet AJ136	Ju88
	Lt N. A. Bartlett	Martlet AJ102	SM79
	Sub-Lt(A) P. D. C. Street	Martlet AM998	SM79
	Sub-Lt(A) J. A. Cotching	Martlet AM968/8M	SM79
afternoon	Sub-Lt(A) J. A. Cotching	Martlet AM968/8M	Re2001
	Sub-Lt(A) J. Madden	Martlet AJ102	Re2001

Based on the above tabulation, 806 Squadron was credited with 87 enemy aircraft destroyed, plus 14 probables, 1 possible and 2 shared.

Lt(A) A. J. Sewell	6 individual plus 8 shared (14)
Lt W. L. LeC. Barnes	6 individual plus 8 shared (14)
Sub-Lt(A) G. A. Hogg	7 individual plus 6 shared (13)
Sub-Lt(A) S. G. Orr	6 individual plus 6 shared (12)
Lt-Cdr C. L. G. Evans	3 individual plus 7 shared (10)
Lt R. MacDonald-Hall	2 individual plus 6 shared (8)
Sub-Lt(A) I.L.F. Lowe	1 individual plus 6 shared (7)
Lt P. D. J. Sparke	4 individual plus 2 shared (6)
Lt R. S. Henley	2 individual and 3 shared (5)

Appendix III

Commanding Officers

Squadron formed February 1940

Lt-Cdr C. L. G. Evans	February 1940–June 1941 (officially)
Lt D. Vincent-Jones	December 1940–June 1941
Lt-Cdr J. N. Garnett	June 1941–January 1943 CO 806/B
Lt R. L. Johnston	August 1941–12 August 1942 (KiA) CO 806/A

Squadron disbanded January 1943

Squadron reformed August 1945

Lt-Cdr A. C. Lindsey	August 1945–January 1946
Lt-Cdr A. W. Bloomer	January 1946–October 1946
Lt-Cdr R. P. Thurston	October 1946–June 1947
Lt-Cdr W. N. Waller	June 1947–October 1947

Squadron disbanded October 1947

Squadron reformed May 1948

Lt-Cdr D. B. Law	May 1948–September 1948

Squadron disbanded September 1948

Squadron reformed March 1953

Lt-Cdr P. C. S. Chilton	March 1953–February 1955
Lt-Cdr D. P. W. Kelly	February 1955–November 1955

Squadron disbanded November 1955

Squadron reformed January 1957

Lt-Cdr W. D. D. MacDonald	January 1957–April 1958
Lt-Cdr P. Carmichael	April 1958–October 1959
Lt-Cdr W. W. Illingworth	October 1959–December 1960

Squadron disbanded December 1960

Appendix IV

Extracts from Captain Denis Boyd's report on the bombing of HMS *Illustrious* 10 January 1941

When this very severe and brilliantly executed dive-bombing attack was over, the ship was on fire fore and aft, the flight deck was wrecked, and I decided to make for Malta at once, informing the Commander-in-Chief who detached *Jaguar* and *Hasty* (destroyers) as screen.

It was immediately clear that the steering gear had been affected as difficulty was experienced in checking the ship swinging, but at this time the electric steering gear was not entirely out of action. At about 12:55 the electric steering gear failed completely as did the rudder indicator from the rudder head; the 'not under control' signal was hoisted and the ship's swing checked with the engines. By 13:03 the ship was again under control from the steam steering gear in the Centre Engine Room and a course of 100° was set, speed being worked up to 26 knots by 13:13.

3rd attack—high level bombing

At 13:29, seven aircraft approached at 14,000 feet and were reported by *Valiant* (*Illustrious*' RD/F was put out of action in the previous attack). This formation was sighted and engaged well before bomb release; aim was inaccurate and the bombs fell scattered, the whole attack being similar to those carried out by the Italians recently. There were no hits but the steam steering gear failed at this time and the ship was out of control and turning in circles. A and B groups only fired, S and Y being out of action.

Speed was reduced to 21 knots by 13:38 and to 15 knots by 13:45 and at 13:48 the ship was again under control from the Steam Steering engine. Course was set for Malta (now 74 miles distant) and speed increased to 20 knots, but at 13:50 she was again out of control and began to swing rapidly to port. Speed was reduced accordingly. Further efforts were made to continue using the rudder but they were unsuccessful and orders were given to put the rudder amidships which was accomplished. By 14:35 the ship was under control steering by the engines and was heading for Malta, speed being gradually increased. The ship was steered by the engines from this time onwards.

4th attack—dive bombing

At 16:04 another group of aircraft was reported by *Valiant* to be closing; it was sighted at long range at 16:09 and consisted of about 15 Ju87s escorted by five fighters. They were engaged by the forward 4.5 guns with controlled and barrage fire and later by five pom-poms. This attack was neither so well synchronised or so determined as that at 12:40. The first wave of about six aircraft attacked from astern and both quarters and were well engaged, fire being continuous in spite of difficulty of seeing targets to port owing to the smoke and haze from the fire in the hangar. Only two bombs fell near the ship. Three aircraft carried out an attack from the starboard beam at least a minute after the first wave; the last aircraft pressed his attack well home and scored a near miss abreast the funnel. The remaining six aircraft were seen retiring to the north-east at a considerable height, and two attempted an attack through clouds on the port beam, but on being engaged made off without dropping their bombs.

Nine bombs were dropped, one (size not known) hit the after-lift causing casualties among those tending wounded and putting out fires. There were two very near misses, one starboard side abreast the island and one close to the quarter deck which caused damage aft and killed a number of wounded and those tending them on the quarter deck. Avoiding action was taken by altering course. There were no Fulmars present during this attack but there may have been some Hurricanes. The early sighting of this and subsequent formations was due to the prompt receipt of *Valiant's* RD/F reports. At 16:43 the ship was making good 17 to 18 knots. A list of about 5° to the starboard had developed, chiefly due to the amount of water in the hangar and in the wardroom flat. This water came from the hangar sprays and hoses and could not run away as the scuppers were blocked with debris.

5th attack—High level and dive bombing

At 16:56 *Valiant* reported enemy aircraft at 52 miles, closing. Seventeen aircraft were sighted at 17:10 outside gun range. They circled astern of *Illustrious* and worked up into the sun from her but then attacked the battle fleet with high level and dive bombing.

At 18:03 *Illustrious* reached the entrance to the Swept Channel. Tugs had been asked for to meet the ship there but as there were only two anti-submarine vessels to be seen I continued up the channel still steering by main engines and gradually reducing speed. Sunset was at 18:08.

6th attack—Torpedo aircraft

Malta reported by W/T that enemy aircraft were approaching and at 19:22, two aircraft were heard and sighted on the starboard bow. A blind barrage from 4.5' guns and pom-poms was fired. No torpedo tracks were seen and nothing more was seen or heard of the aircraft. At 19:30 *Hasty* on the starboard beam reported that she was investigating a contact and shortly afterwards fired depth charges. At 19:35 the ship was turned to port for the harbour entrance which was closed at slow speed waiting for tugs. At 20:25, a tug was secured aft and then two tugs were secured forward, the ship being about ¾ mile from the Grand Harbour entrance. *Illustrious* passed St. Elmo Breakwater Light at 21:04 and berthed starboard side to at Parlatorio Wharf at 22:15. The work of landing the wounded and dead was begun. All wounded men were got away at 02:00 and the dead by 03:00. The fires aft were finally extinguished by 03:00.

Bomb damage to *Illustrious.* The official report revealed:

No.1 Hit: Probably 500kg. Went through loading platform of P1 pom-pom and struck the top of the side armour. May not have burst.

No.2 Hit: Probably 500kg. Went through the flight deck right forward on the port side, through the Recn. Space and burst below the flare causing a large number of fragment holes and two tears on the ship's side. Caused a fire in the lamp room and decontamination store and flooded the paint store and the spare anchor gear store to a depth of 3 feet.

No.3 Hit: Probably a smaller GP [General Purpose] bomb. Burst on S.2 pom-pom killing the crew and most of the crew of S.1 but caused no casualties on the bridge.

No.4 Hit: About 250kg. Hit the after-lift and burst on the port side of the lift well, wrecking the lift and Y Group pump motors.

No.5 Hit: 250kg. or 500kg. Hit the starboard forward corner of the lift well and may have exploded on the flight deck or been deflected and burst at the after end of the lift well.

No.6 Hit: 500kg. Pierced the flight deck and burst on the hangar deck in which it made a large hole and caused violent explosion in the ward room flat. This bomb blew up the foremost lift, bulged the hangar deck forward and the combined effect of this and No.4 wrecked the hangar fire screens and set fire to C Hangar. Many casualties were caused in the hangar and the ward room flat; all leads and piping through ward room flat destroyed. Fires were started in the cabin flats on the upper deck abaft bulkhead.

In addition to these six hits there were at least three very near misses, splinters from which caused damage and casualties.

Appendix V

Extracts from Captain Arthur Bisset's report on the bombing of HMS *Formidable* 26 May 1941

The attack on Scarpanto aerodrome at daylight on the 26th May achieved surprise and it is hoped that a number of enemy aircraft were destroyed or damaged.

From daylight onwards, there were frequent calls for fighters to drive off enemy reconnaissance aircraft. Three of these were shot down. The small number of fighters available on board made it impossible to answer the above calls and maintain an adequate number in reserve to deal with bombing attacks. As a result, when the main attack developed on the Fleet, only two fighters were in the air and no more were available until after the attack was over.

The Fleet was attacked soon after 13:00 by a large formation of Ju88s and 87s, accompanied by Messerschmitt fighters. In the course of the attack, about eight aircraft definitely attacked *Formidable* and the ship was hit twice within a short space of time by large armour-piercing bombs, once forward on the starboard side and once aft on the starboard side of X.1 turret. The hit forward caused a large fire in the Fleet Air Arm workshop and severe structural damage from the main deck to Upper Gallery deck between 6 and 24 bulkheads. The fire was got under control in about 5 to 10 minutes and the ship was unable to maintain her position in the Fleet at 19 knots. The hit aft put X.1 turret out of action and shook the ship very badly. We were extremely fortunate, however, as the bomb was deflected clear of the ship and exploded in the water under the starboard quarter. The damage control organisation worked well, and it is satisfactory to note that all the armament except for X.1 turret, which was jammed, was in action very shortly after the ship was hit. A group did particularly well under very trying conditions from the heat and smoke of the fire.

It is much regretted that there were nine ratings killed and eight wounded as a result of the bombing. Of the latter two subsequently died from wounds received.

MAIN ITEMS OF DAMAGE

By bomb hit forward

All compartments above the main deck and below the Upper Gallery deck between 6 and 24 bulkheads seriously damaged and the contents destroyed. These compartments include the larger proportion of the Ship's Heads. 24 bulkhead itself is damaged and 37 is the foremost bulkhead which is at present watertight. All Cable and Capstan machinery out of action. Structural damage makes it inadvisable to fire A and B groups of 4.5-inch guns. A large amount of electric wiring damaged in the forward compartments. Foremost ammunition conveyor strained. Foremost aircraft lift balance weight out of line (repairs should not be difficult to effect). Assisted Take-off Gear requires re-alignment.

By bomb hit aft and underwater explosion

X.1 turret out of action. It is hoped to get the turret working shortly by ship's staff. From 144–171 bulkheads below the waterline, there are many plates on the ship's side buckled, rivets started and internal frames and stiffeners distorted. The full extent of the damage cannot be ascertained until the ship is dry-docked. It is considered however that the ship is 'seaworthy' aft.

Appendix VI

Extracts from Vice-Admiral Edward Syfret's report on the bombing of HMS *Indomitable* 12 August 1942

Two bomb hits—one forward, one aft—put HMS *Indomitable* out of action, but not in danger of sinking.

Seven aircraft, of which at least five were Stukas approached from astern at 15,000 feet. Each aircraft released a 500 kg SAP [Semi-Armour Piercing] bomb in a 70-degree dive—the first aircraft at 1,500 feet, the others at lower heights—and then passed over the ship at heights of 50 to 1,000 feet without firing machine-guns. The ship was damaged by two hits and three near-misses. No identifiable fragments were recovered. Detonation of each bomb was judged complete.

Hit No.1 struck the flight deck at 30 station six feet to starboard of the forward edge of the forward lift made a hole 14-inch diameter in the 60lbs flight deck, perforated the 10lbs upper gallery deck and detonated just above the upper hangar deck after a travel of 16 feet from the point of first impact. Fire broke out, including a petrol fire at the forward end of the hangar, but was under control after 40 minutes. The fire was below and slightly forward of A.1 turret and no great heat reached A.2. Clearing charges in A2 were undamaged, being in a closed locker. In A.1, the cordite exploded and split the cylinders. Some shell then fell through the damaged deck into the fire and eventually exploded. A number of large shell fragments were found in the wreckage and landed at Gibraltar. Bomb is judged to be 250 kg SC [General Purpose] type.

Hit No.2 struck the flight deck on the middle line at 164 station abaft the after-hangar lift, perforated the 14 lbs flight deck and the 10 lbs upper gallery deck and detonated just above the upper hangar deck after a travel of 16 feet from the point of first impact, in the cabins adjacent to the No.2 torpedo body room. Fire broke out without igniting the torpedo warheads in their mantlet stowage. Bomb is judged to be 250 kg SC type.

Near-miss No.1 carved a groove in the lower edge of the pom-pom director bulwark at 63 station, port side, and detonated in air five feet from the ship's side at the level of the upper hangar deck after a travel of 16 feet from the point of impact. Bomb is judged to be 250 kg SC type.

Near-miss No.2 struck the sea about 25 feet from the ship's side abreast 125 station, port, and detonated at an estimated depth of 25 feet, flooding all wing compartments between 113 and 139 stations, a length of 104 feet. Approximately 760 tons of water entered the ship causing a heel of 8 degrees.

Bomb is judged to be 1,000 kg or larger SC type. A fragment of bomb has been recovered in No.2 Naval Store which, on examination, shows that it was probably from a 250 kg SC type although it might have been from a 500 kg SC type bomb. The damage caused would indicate that it fell closer to ship's side than the 25 feet mentioned by observers.

Near-miss No.3 struck the sea off the port quarter and detonated under water with no serious effect on the ship. About a dozen splinters entered the Captain's apartments.

Select Bibliography

Attard, Joseph: *The Battle of Malta* (Progress 1988)

Cull, Brian & Galea, Frederick: *Fighters over Malta* (Fonthill 2018)

Galea, Frederick: *Call-Out* (Bieb Bieb 2002)

Gibson, Donald: *Haul Taut & Belay* (Spellmount 1992)

Hogg, Graham: *Unpublished Journal* (1941)

Holland, James: *Fortress Malta* (Phoenix 2004)

Lamb, Charles: *War in a Stringbag* (Bantam 1980)

Micallef, Joseph: *When Malta Stood Alone* (J. Micallef 1981)

Poolman, Kenneth: *llustrious* (Cerebus 2005)

Popham, Hugh: *Sea Flight* (Seaforth 2010)

Shores, Christopher, Cull, Brian & Malizia, Nicola: *Air War over Yugoslavia, Greece & Crete* (Grub Street 1987)

Shores, Christopher, Cull, Brian & Malizia, Nicola: *Malta: The Hurricane Years* (Grub Street 1987)

Shores, Christopher, Cull, Brian & Malizia, Nicola: *Malta: The Spitfire Years* (Grub Street 1991)

Shores, Christopher, Cull, Brian & Izawa, Yasuho: *Bloody Shambles Volume 2* (Grub Street 1993)

Smith, *Peter C: Impact! (Kimber 1981)*

Wallace, Gordon: *Carrier Observer* (Airlife 1983)

Website

www.armouredcarriers.com

Index of Personnel

806 Squadron Aircrew 1940-1945

RAF Maintenance Personnel attached 806 Squadron

806 Squadron Aircrew Post-War

RN Others

Regia Aeronautica

Japanese